The Homo Spiritus Sessions

Volume 1

The Homo Spiritus Sessions

Volume 1

✦✦✦

Eloheim and The Council

Channeled by
Veronica Torres

First edition January 2012
ISBN: 978-1-936969-14-2

Copyright 2011 Veronica Torres
Eloheim.com

Published by Rontor Presents

Cover Art by Holly's Creative Design
Hollyscreative.com

Interior Design by Mary T. George
Epubpub.com

Velcro® is a registered trademark of Velcro Industries B.V.

Contents

Introduction

The Homo Spiritus Sessions is a series of books created to share channeled messages from Eloheim and The Council.

The Council is comprised of seven different groups: The Guardians, The Girls, The Visionaries, The Matriarch, The Eloheim, The Warrior, and Fred. During a channeling session, each of The Council members take a turn sharing their teachings. For more information about The Council, please visit Who are Eloheim and The Council? at the end of this book.

The Council is best known for their multitude of practical tools, which support our journey out of the fear-based operating system into the consciousness-based operating system. These tools are developed during private sessions and public gatherings. It has long been my desire to offer these tools in written form. This series, along with the companion series, The Choice for Consciousness, allows me to do so.

Each book in the Homo Spiritus Sessions series consists of the transcript of one of our public sessions, enriched with supporting material. The supporting material includes information about Eloheim and The Council, descriptions of tools referenced in the session, and over 126 definitions of terms and concepts.

Each of the Homo Spiritus Sessions books can stand alone, but taken together will allow the reader to follow along with the progression of the teachings including the introduction, in-depth explanation, and evolution of The Council's tools.

July 7, 2010

Summary

Guardians: Did energetic work with the group.

Visionaries: Described how to deal with the awareness and responsibility of being a creator, no matter what your creation is. They explain, "When you can't point fingers anymore, instead of asking 'Why did I create this?' you say, 'Wow. This is my fascinating creation.' You have to shift out of the idea that you have to understand why it's there and instead say: 'It is here.'"

Eloheim: "Despite feeling very different as you change, you'll eventually catch up to it and feel better. When in doubt, tell your truth. Truth is unassailable."

The Girls: "When you allow yourself to feel the 'wow' and be open to it, what you're actually doing is opening to your soul's insight."

Warrior: "You can't hide from the truth of your creation anymore. Say yes to whatever the truth of your creation is; open to it, experience it deeply, and embrace it. Because the truth of your creation is the doorway into the big picture of Homo spiritus living."

Fred: "You have reached a place where you can experience your physicality from your soul's perspective, even if only in short bursts."

Matriarch: "You have arrived at a remarkable simpatico. 'I love myself enough to love my creation because it's part of me and I love my creation enough to recognize how wonderful I am and thus that makes me love me.'"

Guardians

Bring it in. Bring it to the center. Let's all be here together now. Let's all bring it here, right now. We just felt a deep shift in the energy in the room. Very, very deep shift, so just hold that shift. Remember, you don't have to understand it. You don't have to explain it. You don't even have to repeat it. Just be in it, whatever it is. There you are. OK, we'll be back.

Visionaries

We spoke to you over the last few weeks about the idea that you've gone up the stairs, you're on the landing, and you're getting ready to go up to the next set of stairs. We talked last week about the idea that you can't point fingers anymore, meaning you can no longer say: "That person did it to me. That person did it for me. That person did it, period." You no longer have the option of saying that someone else creates in your life or something else creates in your life. Nothing can create in your life anymore, and every time you point your finger and decide you know, and decide how it's going to be, and decide and decide and decide, you're turning over the only power you have in this life, which is the power to create your reality using your free will to actually create in this life. And [to] create in this life is an opportunity for you to actually experience something magnificent. You can go right along living the victim mentality quite nicely, but if you actually want to experience the magnificence that's possible with the Homo sapiens moving into Homo spiritus paradigm you have to stop looking at other people and other things as creators and start to recognize and acknowledge that you are the one. You are the one who put it there.

Now: very, very, very important. You didn't put it there to cause you pain. You didn't put it there to confuse you. You didn't put it there to make it hard. So you end up recognizing, "OK, I created it. However, it sucks. So, what the fuck." It's something like that. You might not use that language but it's basically that language. It's basically that attitude. It's basically, "Damn it!

Why, why, why, why is it here?" And it's not why, why, why, the tool that Eloheim taught you. It's: "Why, why, why, shit." That's not the tool. And that's what you guys do. And it's worse now, because now we say you can't point fingers, so you can't escape any of it. You can't escape any of it. And all of it is presenting itself and you're having the opportunity to say, "Oh my God, it's here. Why?" And what we'd like to talk with you primarily about tonight is that that is not the question to ask. That is not the question to ask. It is not: "Why is this here?" It's: "Wow, this is here. Wow, I am an amazing creator. Wow, I have generated something really, really complex, complicated, fascinating," whatever word you like, whatever word applies. But it's not: "Why?" It's: "Wow." That's the difference between pointing fingers and not. Because you have to shift out of the idea that you have to understand why it's there and instead say: "It is here."

An example that might work is this: When you go to Disneyland and you ride around on the rides, you don't sit around going, "Why are there pirates in the Pirates of the Caribbean?" You say, "Wow, I am transported into a completely new world here. What does this give me? What does this generate in me? What feelings am I having? Am I a little scared? Is it a little shocking? Is it a little surprising? Is it a little funny? Am I getting wet? Am I cold? What am I doing here? What is the experience I'm having in this wow?" You might get a brainiac and say, "Why did they choose that color paint?" or something like that, but don't take the example so far that it ruins it. Stay with the truth of it, which is when you find yourself in an experience it's not: "Why is this here?" It's: "Wow, look at my creation. And I'm going to acknowledge my creation." And last week, we talked about the idea that if you wanted any of your creations repeated and if you actually hired a theater and hired extras and hired props and hired all these people to try to re-create an experience that you had, it would be a very large undertaking. Yet you can have a variety of experiences that are incredibly detailed, incredibly complex, incredibly full of stimulus and interest and coincidental sort of things—not that they are coincidental—but these synchronicities, you can have these fabulously detailed experiences and you don't have to do anything other than breathe. Breathe into them and they are there for you.

You know you'll go to a movie theater and watch a very complex movie that's been created for you for your entertainment but you don't take your own creations out of that perspective. Like, "Wow, look at this fabulously detailed creation I have presented for myself, that I can explore, that I can roll around in, that I can feel wow about." So we'd like you to start experiencing your creations from that perspective where instead of a "why" you let yourself have a "wow." And that doesn't mean that it's not painful, but what it means is that when you're in it, you're not feeling pain because you feel like you're a victim, you're not feeling pain because you feel like you have no choices, you're not feeling pain because you feel stepped on. What you're feeling is: "Wow, this is just mind-blowing. This is just mind-blowing how detailed and in-depth and powerful it is that I've created this environment to explore. This is here for me to grow from. This is here for me to have an experience with and it's amazing."

We've talked to you in the past about how you have the right amount of oxygen, you have the right amount of water, the temperature is correct, to be here on the planet—and even this is amazing, of course—but that you can be walking down the street in a town that you didn't expect to be in that day but for some reason you had to drive up there and take care of something and then you decided, "Oh, I'm a little thirsty." So you walk down the street and you're looking for a place to have coffee and you run into someone and, "Oh my God," as it turns out you went to grammar school together. And that person says, "Have you heard about so-and-so?" and you say, "What's going on with so-and-so?" Then so-and-so is having some kind of an adventure and then you get caught up in their adventure and the next thing you know, you've had an opportunity to transform some triggers and grow and compare you to you. And the next thing you know, you've had this marvelous journey. That's the wow. Wow. Like, "Dang, I did that." And this is a point where you can start having that sense, not necessarily of pride, but: "Wow, I did that. I did that for me. I did that for me. I created all of these complex interactions in order to have that for me." And that's the beauty that we would love for you to start living.

So, the no more finger-pointing thing, we know it can be kind of hard because you realize, "Oh my God, I point fingers every second of every day," but what you're pointing fingers at you can start having the wow of responsibility, the wow of creatorship, the wow of: "Yes, I did that. Yes, I did that. I did it for me. I did it for me so that I could have the experience that that scenario offers me." And a lot of times—we are going to add and then we're going to go—a lot of times you can't actually realize your growth unless you're triggered again. So you get triggered, you get triggered, you get triggered, you do a lot of work on it, you get a little blank space where you're in the post-work period, and then you get triggered again and that gives you the chance to do compare me to me. So, sometimes triggers, even though they're difficult, they come along perfectly timed to give you the opportunity to say, "Wow!" And so "wow" is sort of the buzzword for tonight.

Eloheim

Wow! The Visionaries kind of took our topic again. That's OK because they did a good job. We were surprised even when they said the wow thing. It caught us by surprise. That was a good one. But our topic was going to be this idea that when you encounter your life you are not—how should we say it—we just keep hearing you guys say: "Why would I create this? Why would I do that? What am I supposed to be getting out of it because you want it to go away. What? What?" And we're just changing to a new W word. So, even though they stole our topic they did such a damn good job about it we don't really have anything to add. That's all right.

Comment: Wow is hard to top.

Eloheim: Does anybody have anything they want to ask or talk about before we do whatever we're going to do next?

Comment: Please explain the Fred hangover. [Fred was the last Council member to join our group. Read more about Fred in Who are Eloheim and The Council? section at the end of this book.]

Eloheim: A lot of people are reporting physical reactions after the meeting last week, and that has now been nicknamed the Fred hangover, and they vary from headaches, not sleeping, not not sleeping, sleeping all the time, neck stiffness, general just kind of not feeling good. There also seem to be having to run-to-the-bathroom kind of symptoms going around. Part of what's going on with that, you have to recognize, is the idea that you are detoxing big-time. You're letting go of stuff. Because they opened up a bridge, we believe they called it, a bridge between you and your soul that was unimpeded. It may not have stayed open for a long time, and it may not have been felt very strongly by everyone, but we know plenty of people felt a lot. And that unimpeded bridge also takes you into a vibratory rate that you're not accustomed to. That's why we had to wait and wait and wait before Fred could come along. One of the reasons. You had to be ready to occupy a vibratory rate that was that high. When you occupy a vibratory rate that is that high, it shakes things loose. For lack of a better way to explain it, it shakes things loose. And as you go through that detoxing, you have a variety of ascension-type symptoms that can come up. Oftentimes, it can just feel like when you feel like you've got a little bit of a bug, sometimes you get a runny nose, runny eyes, the runs, whatever you get, it's a little bit like a bug because you're letting stuff out of your cells.

Question: I also experienced feeling like I wasn't completely here and it was a little disconcerting when I was driving or taking care of business with someone. I felt kind of dizzy and not grounded but just walking away from whatever I had to do and gain some sort of familiar feeling back. What would you suggest?

Eloheim: One of the symptoms that Veronica had very strongly was she felt like she was dying and part of that felt like she was dying thing was that she was dying to her old way of being. And in a sense that's what you're describing, is like, "I'm not who I used to be. I'm not who I used to be." And that "I'm not who I used to be" can show up in lots of different ways. It sounds like for you it just felt like a general not connected to what's going on around you in the same way you were before. And the way through that, of course, is to just, like you did, just sit with it and say, "OK, something new is here, something new is here." And it will probably get a little more comfortable. Although it's highly likely that Fred will come in again tonight, and you'll get another dose and who knows. You guys might be in for a little bit of a shakeout period.

Being in the moment and not trying to use your brain to understand it but simply say "wow" is going to be very helpful, too. It's one of those things—it's kind of the proof is in the pudding thing. You're going to find your way through it. But you had access to such a high vibratory rate and such high energy that we have a strong suspicion that it's going to facilitate things changing more quickly that you're wanting to change. You will get a little more comfortable with it. It's like you're in the ocean and then you get the surfboard and when you get up on the surfboard you finally get your balance and, whoosh! you go surfing instead of just letting the waves pass by all the time. That's probably a good accurate assessment of it.

Right now, you're used to the waves just kind of passing you by, passing you by, and you go up and you go down and you go up and you go down. And now you have a surf board and you're like, "How do I work the surfboard?" Well, you can imagine once you figure out how to work the surfboard, things are very different. We know you like that one. Energetically, that's a very clear assessment. But let's just look at that. You stand up on the surfboard. You fall down because almost nobody gets it the first try. And you stand up and you don't stand up at the right moment and the wave passes you by again. And you're like, "Hang on, I was supposed to be on that wave." So there's that adaptive period where you get a sense of this tool, this new project, this new way of being. And the stopping pointing fingers thing, awareness of the pointing fingers, is what brings the surfboard into the picture. Because instead of being washed by the waves, "Oh, I'm in the waves, here comes another one, oh, that one's a big one," that sort of thing, all of a sudden it's: "Wow, I have a way to get above that and to ride on top of it instead of being knocked around by it. But what do I have to do? I have to stand up and I have to balance and I have to try. I have to try something very radically new."

"The idea that I can't point fingers at anybody anymore is a radical concept. Everybody in my life, everything in my life, is my creation and as my creation I take 100 percent responsibility for it being there and I take 100 percent responsibility for how I choose to interact with it." That's the key part, the second part. You guys have been practicing taking 100 percent responsibility for things being in your life but you've always also had that "Why is it here, what is it teaching me, what the hell?" And now it's not so much, like the Visionaries pointed out, it's not: "What the hell?" It's: "Wow." And that's a big shift. That's a big shift. It was a big shift to get into 100 percent responsibility, even if taking 100 percent responsibility meant "I'm taking responsibility even though I don't like it." Now it's: "I'm taking responsibility, I know there's something here for me, I don't have to figure it out as much as I have to allow myself to experience it without throwing barrier after barrier after barrier up between me and the experience," which is the pointing fingers thing. So, you have this beautiful creation there for you and you spend a lot of time in it going, "Why, why, why," or "God, and he did and she did and it did." Which is all that static we've talked about between you and the creation, you and magnetizing needs met. It's a big deal. It's a really big deal but we gave you the visual of the staircase for a reason because we wanted when we started up the next set of stairs for you to recognize we're making a big change. We went up the stairs, we were on the landing, we rested, and now up we go again. And stuff got left behind on the landing, which is stuff that should have been left behind. Anybody else? Questions?

Question: Is there a way to light up the energy better as a new tool being able to communicate how rapidly things are changing for us?

Eloheim: Communicate to other people, you mean?

Response: Yes. Communicating to ourselves but we are in communication with other people and I'm losing them.

Eloheim: Yeah. That's a big challenge. That's sort of: "Nobody gets me." Veronica is remembering that song: "Nobody likes me, everybody hates me, I'm going to eat some worms." And it's not that nobody likes you, everybody hates you, and you have to eat some worms. But it certainly is: "Nobody gets me, I can't figure myself out either, oh shit, I hope Wednesday comes soon." We think it's more that. It doesn't fit with the rhyme of the song but it feels a little more accurate. Yeah, there's this sense, especially right now—we hate to say this because we don't normally say things like this—but you're just going to have to ride it out for a bit longer because between last week and this week and probably next week, with Fred coming in and rocking the situation with everyone so drastically, you don't have your feet under your shoulders as it is, so nobody else is likely to get that, either. We shouldn't say "nobody," but it would not shock us if people had difficulty understanding that. And sometimes the best thing to do is take refuge in the truth and say, "Yeah, I know, I'm confusing myself." Because you are. "Everything is really new for me right now, too. I'm in a new period." And for you, because you just left your job, you could, if you needed to, fall back on that and say, "Yeah, everything is just new with me leaving my job. I'm just sorting some things out." And not expecting people to get it is probably a safe refuge because it needs to shake out within you first. We wish we had something far more fascinating for you than that, but really, that's the truth of it. The truth of it is you probably would like to have some more time with it before you had to explain it to people, anyway. So, now you have more time to have more time with it, which is simply to not try to explain it. And it's OK to say, "Yeah, I'm really changing," or "Yeah, things are really up in the air for me. I don't quite understand it, either. Yeah, I said six but I ended up with ten. I'm sorry, I'm confused, too." The nice thing about the truth is it's unassailable, so if someone says, "You said six and it's ten," you say, "Yeah, you're right." What can they do with that? "I'm mad at you?" "I'd probably be mad at me, too." You just keep telling the truth. You don't have Velcro for their trigger about your changing. Because part of what happens is like... with Veronica, she thought she was dying; and in a sense, if you feel like nobody gets you, you might kick in the: "Oh my God, I'm alone forever," and we don't suspect that will be true. Your wavelength is just real different than everybody else's right now. That doesn't mean alone forever. It just means the wavelengths are different. And it's an interpretation thing. You can think, "Oh my God, this means alone forever," but you can also just say, "I think I'm just a little different," right? More different than normal. Maybe by next week we'll have something more to say on that, but this week, that's all we've got for you.

Comment: I'm seeing my daughter as my creation, and myself is my mother's creation. I was able to experience and transform all of my finger-pointing in a week with my daughter by loving myself and loving her. It was like a repeat creation of my teen-age years. It feels as if all of this information has all been for me.

Eloheim: And the beauty is it is all for you. And it's all for you and you and you, too. You're having simultaneous, individual experiences of pretending you're individual while in truth all being one. That's a pretty cool and interesting and fascinating creation. You don't have to wear 3-D glasses but it is in Technicolor.

The Girls

When you have "wow," when you're in "wow" as previously explained—we don't have to go into detail—when you're in "wow" the thing about wow is it's a place of that four-year-old, that ah! excitement, that place. So let yourself have that ah! about your wows. It's not "wow" and then think. It's "ah!" and then open. It's this. That feeling. It's the opening, the opening, that we're looking to have you get into. Because when you allow yourself to feel the wow what you're actually doing is opening to insight. You're opening to your soul's perspective. You're opening to the bigger picture. And when you open to wow and then you think… it's like what the Guardians have been teaching you not to do, at the beginning of every meeting when they say, "Be here, be here, don't think," and all that stuff they say, that's the tool, that's the energy that you want to put into play when you start into the wow. Because you want to go "wow" and then allow, "wow" and then allow, "wow" and allow. It's not "wow" and then think and get depressed. "Wow" and then: "Oh, I still don't understand." That's not going to work. It's just not going to work.

When you start taking 100 percent responsibility for the experience you're having, then when you don't point fingers anymore and you revel in your creation, that's the moment when you've got all of the pieces in place to then—boom—be in your soul's perspective and insight from your soul and a high-vibrational conscious experience. It's not the place to then go back to thinking. That will be very hard on your body. It will be very hard on your body if then you go back to thinking. The vibratory disconnect is going to be very harsh on you and of course we never want you to be harsh on yourselves. So you go into wow and then you allow the soul's insight to come in. "Wow" and then you allow all the color crayons to be present. "Wow" and then you allow the bigger picture. That's the point of this is: "Wow, look at this creation," and then open again. Wow is an opening to your creation and then open again by bringing in even more of your soul's perspective, even more of the moment, even more crayons to color with, even more of what is true now, even more. Wow will take you into even more. And that's really the beauty of this. And when you're tempted to go into thinking: "And why did this happen to me?" or "Why did I create this?" or "Why would I ever create this?" that's going to take you drastically and perhaps painfully out of that "wow and allow" place. So that's not going to be easy on your body. It's not going to be easy on you.

So, allowing yourself to do what the Guardians have been teaching you week after week, which is to go into that space of: "I'll release anything I don't need, and I don't need to think about it," and all of those things that the Guardians have been teaching you, that pattern they've been teaching you has been taught to you so that you have the opportunity when you are ready to open to wow to go into that allowing place to further deepen your experience.

Letting yourself love yourself well involves wow and allow. And we made a rhyme, so we are totally cool. Eloheim thought the pinnacle of the meeting had been reached at the beginning but, well, not a chance. Let's just see if there's anything else floating around here...

You know, when you are in community and sometimes that community isn't conscious... you know, you're out at the grocery store or something and you're in this wow and allow place, it is a very open place and sometimes you can interface with people who are just going, "Huh?" Or they just feel like they don't quite fit into your creation, and what we'd like you to do with that is to look at them as comparing you to you. Because they are there showing you the truth of you and it can also be there showing you the truth of the ghost of Christmas past. Your creation shows you the truth of you, of course, but it doesn't always show you just what's going on. It oftentimes will show you the opportunity to compare you to you. So when you're in an environment where you see people doing odd things, say, "How is this me comparing me to me?" And don't get into a hoity-toity "I'm better than them" kind of thing. The compassion you can have for the fact that you were in that kind of pain, you were in that kind of anguish, you were in that kind of judgment, you were in that kind of barriers rather than boundaries, and now you're not. So don't make it about them because that would get into a judgment space, but keep bringing it back to you. "Wow, I see that behavior and I'm so glad that's not true right now." That's all you can say. "That's not true right now." You don't have to go, "Oh, that used to be true. It's not true anymore." Just: "It's not true right now. It's not true for me right now and it's nice to see how I've grown. It's nice to have a compare you to you thing here now." So that's the compassion. And be careful that you don't think you have to fix them because they don't need you to fix them unless they ask. They're just giving you an opportunity to compare you to you and to learn more about who you are.

We've said it before but we're going to say it again. You push so hard and at such a constant pace that you very, very rarely give yourself the opportunity to pat yourself on the back. You don't ever stop and say, "Wow, check me out." So we want you to compare you to you on a regular basis because that's the only way we really sense you'll feel progress. Otherwise it's just: "Yeah, I grew, but boy, I got some more to grow about right now." But what you're growing about now is different than what you grew about before. And that's what we want you to know. And that's kindness to yourself, to recognize that what you're growing about now is different than what you were growing about before. Comparing you to you, you are making progress and things are changing. That's important stuff. That's probably all we get tonight but we got a rhyme, so our contribution fit nicely. It's always a pleasure. It's fun. And now that the whole Council is here, we'll just give you a little preview, now that the whole Council is here we're going to have opportunities to do some interesting things so… don't think about it!

Comment: Wow.

The Girls: "Wow" is right. Look at your creation. Excellent. So we'll have some fun with new things coming up in the next few months, new things that are going to be activated. Because you have to remember that Fred—and yes, his name is Fred, don't ask why, mostly because it's entertaining. Weren't you ready for some lightness? The Matriarch, the Visionaries, the Guardians, Fred. It's been a while since we've had a funny one. Ours is the last funny one you've had and that was a while ago. Not that Fred's necessarily all that funny. He's not, let's be sure. This is not the comedy part of the show. But what we're saying is that his, their, it's vibration even takes our vibration up. This isn't just somebody that was hanging out on a street corner and we said, "Do you want to come play with us?" No. It's not like that.

He—we'll just call him he because it's easier in your language—he comes from a level, vibratory rate, whatever you want to call it, a plateau, we don't even know what the right word is, he comes out of a very primordial kind of a place and because of that primordial, in-the-beginning-there-was-all-potentials kind of an energy it makes many, many, many things possible now that weren't possible before by having him on the team. That's the best way we can describe it. There will be more about that. You don't need to think about it because wow, there's plenty more for you to do, be, it.

Warrior

Yeah. So the Visionaries got their wow and the Girls got their rhyme and Eloheim gets to answer your questions and the Guardians shift your energy so we'll just rock your world. How about that? Not to be one-upped or anything like that.

Last we left you we were sitting on the side of an opening, a meadow maybe. And we looked around and we talked about quite a few things we were seeing there, and now we want to talk about what it's like when you're... just after the battle—not the meadow, not the meadow in knee-high grass, we've covered that. But you could say as we sit here and look out at this field we remember the last time we were here, let's just use that as our picture. We remember the last time we were here and the last time we were here there was a battle and instead of going straight into the battle let's go into just when it's done. And as we all stand around breathing hard and wondering just exactly how many of our parts are still attached and that sort of feeling and we look around. You know what there is to be seen. Bodies. The horses. The wagons, whatever else is around. There's always something else around. The weapons. The blood. Let's be honest. You still hear the cries. Maybe not the screams we heard last time but the cries. The whimpers. That last exhale as someone ends their incarnation. And most of this is difficult to hear just in this moment we are describing, it's difficult to hear, because all you can hear is the pounding of your heart and the breath coming in and out in such a ragged way. And your adrenaline is coursing through your body at such a rate that you feel hyper-aware but your body processes are so loud that that's taking up all your ability to perceive things.

So it's a sense of inhale, exhale, inhale, exhale, this deep breathing. It's the deep breathing. And as you breathe this deeply, the smells and the sounds start to become more aware, you start to become more aware of your surroundings and you are still looking for danger, you're still looking for foe, you're still looking for what's coming at you. And slowly but surely you recognize there is no more to look for. There is no more to deal with. And—boom—everything is different from that point on. Because for all the time before, it was about the fighting and from all this time after, it's about the aftermath. And in this case you have been doing a similar thing. You've been fighting and fighting and fighting within you. You've been fighting your habits. You've been fighting victimhood. You've been fighting just what it's like to be Homo sapiens. And now just as radically as the change we described we experience on the field of battle, you have this change. It's that drastic. And you change into, you change into, something else. All of your attention changes into an attention on something else.

That's why we tell you this story because we want you to know how drastic this change that everyone has been talking to you about tonight is. Moving out of victimhood, moving out of, oh, sort of taking responsibility and moving into not pointing fingers. Moving into this wow and allow thing that they are talking about. It's such a radical change. It's such a big shift. It is similar in degree to the change we have described. And you're asking yourself to use a new set of skills. Previous to this, your skills have been fighting and fighting and resisting, ducking, running, dodging, attacking, and now your skills are opening and allowing and seeing from a new perspective. It's a whole completely different paradigm you're entering into. And instead of resistance, you're moving. You're moving through your creation rather than resisting it. You are dancing with your creation rather than fighting it. You're saying yes to your creation rather than trying to find a way to blame it on somebody else. You are not able to hide from the truth of your creation anymore, and that's really the key point of this whole thing. You can't hide from the truth of your creation anymore.

Whatever the truth of your creation is we advise you to say yes to it, to open to it, to experience it deeply, to embrace it, because the truth of your creation is the doorway into the big picture of Homo spiritus living. We got you into the moment and now you need to say yes to the moment. "Where am I lying to myself? What is true now?" But it's a whole different level of it now. It's a whole different level of it now as you move into the truth of you being expressed without looking for someone else to take the blame. Without looking for someone else to be the fall guy. Without looking for somebody else to be the one that did it. There's no one else to take the blame for how you interact with your creation. There's only you choosing the "wow" or you choosing the "why?" That's your choice. "Am I going to choose wow or why?" Wow or why.

Now you say, "OK, I have this creation and I say 'wow, it's pretty fascinating' and I want to know why it's here." And we would say to you the Guardians would ask you not to do that. Why? Because they know how to shift your energy out of: "I have to think about it and understand it," into: "I'm experiencing it and allowing more." Allowing more. That's the whole point of this. You get more when you allow. When you wonder and think and have to have it explained, you get less. We have a strong suspicion you want the more. And if you want the more, you go to "wow" and if you want it to stay the way it's been, then you can stay in "why" all you want. "Why" is going to be limitation. "Wow" is going to be expansion. And when you go in, as the Girls said, and allow more wow, well, then you start the process of living from your soul's perspective, seeing the things the way your soul sees it. Your soul sees it all as fascinating, all as interesting, all is educational, all is helpful. Just exactly the beautiful creation, the detailed creation that you presented to yourself, all of it is ready for you to experience more of. You have to decide if you're going to be in the mode to experience more of it or to go and think about it. And part of that comes down to you having judgment about it, too.
We haven't talked about neutral observation in a very long time. It will help you. Observe it neutrally. Believe it's going to teach you something. Go into wow. Same thing. Different level of it. You have the opportunity right now to experience

yourself on such a deeper level when you let go of the addiction to finger-pointing and embrace the reality, which is that you have created an incredibly complex and beautiful script with deeply, deeply, deeply imagined sets and co-stars and props, and you've laid it all out so that you can wander through it and experience, experience, experience. It's like the greatest ride at Disneyland you could imagine. You created every single bit of it and it's time to revel in it and enjoy the complexity and fascination of it. And if it's difficult and painful and hard to deal with, that's interesting, too. That's fascinating, too. And when you're not trying to blame it on someone else and instead take responsibility for it, it will pass very quickly and give you its gift. When you're trying to get rid of it, it's harder for the gift to be given to you.

We walk right now through this field of people. What we see is parts of the journey that are no longer with us. Parts that were left behind that have been dropped away. And you're doing this, too. You walk through the battlefield of the journey you've had on your internal battle and parts and pieces of you are scattered all over the place. Why? Because those are the parts and pieces of you that you no longer need. Mostly what they are are combatants that were always busy with the fists and the sword ready to find somebody to fight with about what was being created, rather than say, "Yes, yes, yes, I created this. Even this I created." Those parts of you that are defensive, just imagine that's a whole battalion. "I got defensive about x, y, z. There's a whole battalion going out onto the field of battle to fight what I think I need to be defensive about. Oh, I was jealous. There goes another battalion. The sniper squad is up there just looking for that one to be jealous about, too." All those low-vibrational states, it's like you're sending out your army. You're sending out your army to go do battle with what? To do battle with your own creation.

You're fighting yourself. This is why our energy is on the Council, because you fight your own creation constantly and we have to come in and give you all these battle metaphors. Why? To wake you up to the truth that you fight your creation. It's like going to the movies and arguing with what's on the screen. Well, going to the movies is about seeing what's on the screen and interacting with it. And you can disagree with it, but standing up in the middle of the movie theater and saying, "Hang on, you're making me defensive," isn't exactly the point. But that's in essence what you're doing all the time. Your creation is being pushed across your screen and you're arguing and defensive and triggered and angry and jealous and you name it about it 24/7, and what we'd like you to say is: "Wow, wow, wow," and the wow and the allow opens you to see what's on the screen. Because really, what you see now is a bunch of people fighting. You fighting yourself is all the static. It's just like a melee on a battlefield with all the things going on and you can't see the other king. You can't see the other troops. You can't see shit because you're so focused with your eyes up close to it with the shit of your static interacting rather than allowing yourself to say yes to it, manage your triggers, handle your habits, and let it show you its truth. The movie you never see is the beautiful creation you've made, because what you're always seeing is the static going on in front of the screen, the battles going on in front of the screen. You've yet to see the movie but it keeps playing. And the movie, we could say, is your soul's perspective on how Homo sapiens transform into Homo spiritus. That's what you have the opportunity to experience. That's the gift you're being offered. And every time you don't point your finger that's one little battle that can poof away and instead be replaced by a glimpse of the movie going by. You got it? That's all we've got then.

Fred

You've reached the time now when you can have the opportunity to experience your physicality in a way that has never been experienced before. And part of what they've been talking about tonight when they talk about the idea of saying "yes" and "wow and allow" is the idea that physicality has been burdensome. Yes, you have fun sometimes with your bodies, and yes, you sometimes have fun with your environment, but most of the time you find reasons for your physicality to be considered burdensome, painful, difficult, obnoxious, uncomfortable, you name it. You have many words for it. We don't need to list them anymore. What you're having the opportunity to do is to reorient your perspective on the physicality and give the opportunity for you to experience it in a brand-new way. And this brand-new way is experienced through the openness, the openness, to the truth. And the truth is that the physicality is your creation. The physicality is your opportunity. The physicality is your avenue to experience the completeness of you, all of you. All of you is enwrapped into the physicality. All of you is encapsulated in physicality and offered to the experiment that you're part of.

Physicality is required to be part of this experiment. Physicality is required to have this opportunity to experience free will. Physicality is really required so that you are fooled into believing you're not all one. Physicality is the unique expression that this planet offers and the way that you experience physicality here is quite different than the way you have opportunities to experience it elsewhere. So, letting go of your physicality and your enjoyment of physicality is something we would recommend against. You have an opportunity now to pull your physicality into the experience of "wow and allow," so opening up to the idea that physicality is part of the journey, part of the experience. It's one of these things that seems so obvious when said out loud but you actually overlook it constantly because it's constantly there. It's one of those things like knowing how to spell certain words you don't have to think about or knowing the easy sums, you know what the mathematical answers are and so it's not something you ever think about but that does not take away the truth of those mathematical sums. Yet you overlook the necessity, the validity, the remarkableness of the physicality on a regular basis. You overlook it because it's always there.

We will say to you now that if you did not have physicality, one, you would not be here and, two, you would miss it. You are quite the envy of many, many souls that don't have the opportunity to experience physicality and to enjoy free will and to have this experience. They are quite compelled to observe your environment and compelled to encounter you as they can by watching and by wondering and tracking, let's say, your progress. Because you have something very, very unusual and you forget this. You forget this all the time.

As you start to work this bridge that we have opened between you and the authentic expression of your soul, one of the things that you're going to realize is how just incredibly valuable it is to be in physicality. Your soul's perspective doesn't include the perspective you have on physicality. This is one of the reasons why this whole thing was done is so that your soul could experience physicality. But not just physicality from a gross, low-vibrational way but so that your soul could experience a vibrational rate that actually could house it so that it could experience physicality from a soul's perspective. It's quite easy for a soul to experience physicality from a physicality perspective but for a soul to experience physicality from a soul's perspective is something that has not been done. This is why you're here. This is why we are working with you. This is why the whole thing has been set up, is so your soul can experience physicality and keep its perspective. This is not something that's been done. This is not something that any of you know exactly how to do. This is brand-new. The opportunity that's being presented to you now is to bridge that gap. You have done much, much work on bringing your physical bodies into a vibratory rate that could support you doing this and you've gotten to a place where most of you can have your soul's perspective downloaded into you at least in short bursts if not for long periods of time, but it requires constant attention because there's so much habit and ingrained pathways that say that you must have it be the way it always has been. And it requires an incredible amount of attention from you to move it into another paradigm. This other paradigm, though, offers you the doorway to your soul's perspective and allows you to experience physicality from a brand-new perspective. We suspect that this will be quite worth your time. We continue to hold this bridge open so that you have the opportunity to download your uninfiltrated soul's perspective, but you have to continue to make the choice over and over again to experience that perspective and to allow yourself to experience it. If you don't allow yourself to experience it, if you don't open the doorway, it cannot be forced on you and that allowing, that willingness, is what raises your vibration high enough for you to actually experience it. That is all we have for you tonight.

Matriarch

As we come in, we're just opening the heart chakra energy in all of you. We're allowing you to access the open heart chakra energy that we can offer, is perhaps a better way to say it. Part of what gets opened up in you when you access the higher-vibrational connections is the ability to appreciate. And when you appreciate on the level that you're capable of appreciating, you end up with the heart chakra opening up so wide that it starts to remind you of the truth that you're all one. It's one of the closest places you get to experiencing that truth before you actually start living from your soul's perspective is when your heart chakra opens and you can actually embrace what is from a place of loving yourself. You love yourself so deeply that you can embrace all that is as your creation. It's beautiful. Loving yourself deeply because you're embracing what is as your creation. You love yourself so much that you can love your creation and you love your creation so much that you can love yourself. It's a remarkable simpatico. It's a remarkable exchange. It's a remarkable gift you give and you're giving it to yourself and then you're reflecting that gift back to yourself.

"I love myself enough to love my creation because it's part of me and I love my creation enough to recognize how wonderful I am and thus that makes me love me." Let's just sit for a moment in this energy.

"I love my creation. I love my creation as myself. I am my creation. My creation is me. And there is love." And when we say love we mean that deep appreciation, the appreciation that goes so deeply in. The details, the attention, the willingness, the commitment you've made to your beautiful creation. Remember, if you had to re-create any five-minute period of your day, if you had to rent a theater and re-create it yourself, can you imagine the work you would have to go to. Even just sitting on the couch, can you imagine the work you'd have to go to to re-create the couch, to re-create the table, the carpet, the very dirt in the carpet, the smell in the air, the light coming in from the window, the breeze blowing through, the sounds in the yard. Can you imagine? It's literally impossible, yet you create and create again every moment of every day, and your deep appreciation for that is the love you have for you and the love you have for the created and that reflects back and forth, back and forth, in this nice infinity pattern. We invite you to explore that.

And now, unbelievably, it seems we've only been together for a moment, but it seems that we've also come to the end of our evening together, as well. We deeply appreciate the jump you've made because you have made a distinct jump into a new way of being and we feel it profoundly and we are grateful to have the experience of sharing it with you in this way. And for now we will say goodnight.

July 14, 2010

Summary

Guardians: Remarked on a strong connection with us through our power chakras. We are constantly in a state of renewal, bringing in new energy and growing. As we do so, it is necessary to release. They advise us to allow for things that no longer serve us to be available to be released.

Visionaries: As we expand and become more conscious, we naturally take time to contract (go inward) to experience the change. The Visionaries advise us to be generous to ourselves in allowing for an expansion-and-contraction way of interacting with the world, rather than demanding that it has to be a certain way.

Eloheim: On being in the world: Allow for your vulnerability, and know that your truth is unassailable. Answered questions on fear of putting oneself out there on the Internet, and also on what would be a good spiritual topic to teach to eight-year-olds.

The Girls: When we go out into the world with our power chakras and our heart chakras, our second chakras are also affected. The third chakra contains: "This is me taking me into the world," and the second chakra contains: "This is me allowing the world into me."

Warrior: Continues their story of going to see the king. They advise: Don't let fears and habits tell you who you are.

Fred: Be open with willingness to experience more of the truth of you.

Matriarch: The truth of you can open into much, much more. The truth is a starting place to expand from.

Guardians

Tonight we feel a very strong connection to you through your power chakras. So we would ask you to just allow release. Remember, you don't have to say what it is or even know what it is, but just allow release. Allow for openness. Allow those things that no longer serve you to be released; to be available to be released is maybe a way to say it. Remembering, of course, that as you use the restroom and as you sweat and cry and breathe, just to name a few things, you're constantly letting go.

You're constantly releasing, you're constantly in a state of renewal. And as you bring new energy in and as you grow, that renewal not only makes a necessity of release but it offers such a changed perspective that we invite you to allow that to happen. And when you look at your power chakra and you look at how you connect with others in the world, more how you walk in the world, how you go out into the world, how you present yourself, how you express yourself, how you emanate your truth, more of that is what we're looking at, and as you enter into that aspect of yourself right now, as you put your attention into your power chakra, as you attend to the energy there, we would invite you just to open up and be willing for that which does not serve you to be released. It's always that line, "That which does not serve me may be released now." And our ability to help move that energy out of your space is, of course, why we're here.

There is a lot of energy coming out of your power chakras now. There's a lot of... well, we'll let the Visionaries talk about it. They're so much better at putting it into words but we'll keep moving the energy and we'll let them come in and explain what we were just going to say.

Visionaries

As you walk in the world and as you present yourself to the world and as you emanate in the world and as you are you in the world and as you move with what is, IS and you tell the truth and you acknowledge where you lie, et cetera, as you do all those things, what happens with your power chakra is that it sort of pulses. The pulse that you experience is this sort of emanation and then contemplation, emanation, reflection, emanation, acknowledgment. There's this pulsation or breathing—pulse feels like the nice word for it—so there's pulsation, in and out, in and out, that goes on in you when you take on the ability to move into the world from your conscious power chakra. And that pulse, what can often happen is that as you expand out into and then your natural contraction, just like your breath, expands and contracts, as you expand into the world the natural contraction can sometimes feel like, "Oh, I'm being a hermit. Oh, I'm resisting or rejecting the world. Oh, I'm afraid. Oh, I'm in denial. Oh, I'm not on the bus. Oh, I'm not growing anymore." And what we want to say to you—especially at the levels that you're growing, the speed at which you're growing, and the attention you're putting on living consciously—as you expand into the world it's a big deal, and as you contract for contemplation it's equally valid, equally valuable. It is not a mistake of some kind that you go into that period of contemplation or contraction.

So let yourself have the balance of expanding and expressing the truth of you and then if you need some contemplation time, take it and allow yourself to have it. Not beating yourself up, of course. Not abusing yourself for taking the time to handle that which you are doing. See it's a natural thing. It's natural that when you open up that there will be some sort of contraction. You've seen this in your life so many times. You go out, maybe you're out with a bunch of people, and then the next day you want to be a little more quiet. It's not something that's strange or unusual. There is a natural expansion and contraction. And then maybe the next time you can expand even more because you evaluated what you did in the first place and you see how it worked and what it meant to you, and then you open up in a new way. And that's really what's happening.

We see you opening up in a new way. As you emanate the truth of you, you're opening up in a new way, there's an opening up in a new way, opening up in a new way going on. And that opening up in a new way requires that you allow it to happen. Allowing that opening up. And again, we're going to remind you that sometimes you start to fear what you open up to. And you fear, "Oh, God, if I contemplate my shadow, I'm creating more shadow." And we'll remind you yet again, that when you can contemplate your shadow you're creating more contemplation, which of course is consciousness. When you're conscious about your shadow, when you're conscious about your expansion, when you're conscious about your habits, you're not creating shadow, you're not creating expansion in a negative way, and you're not creating more habit. What you're creating is consciousness, which fuels your ability to engage. Fuels your ability to expand. Fuels your ability to release. Fuels your ability to be in a position where you can be the truth of you in the world. And that truth of you in the world facilitates raising your vibration, which facilitates a deeper connection to your soul, which allows you, of course, eventually to live from your soul's perspective. And that's really the name of the game, is living from your soul's perspective.

So we invite you, especially tonight because the energy is so palpable with your power chakras, as you feel maybe the words that we're saying or the rest of the Council say expand, let that expansion happen and then maybe you need some contemplation. And see if you can feel that normal expansion and contraction that you feel in your power chakras, similar to the way you feel it when you breathe. Because this is the way that we see—you don't just open your power chakra and run out into the world and balls-to-the-wall and go crazy. Especially as light workers, you have too many alternate expressions where the first time you stuck your head out of the crowd, it got cut off. So you are not the kind of people who are going to stick your head out of the crowd and just keep sticking it out. You kind of do the little poke-up-the-head thing, and that's OK. Because every time you poke up you're seeing something new, the vista changes, because you're bringing a new set of eyes to it. So, allow yourself that generosity, we'll say, be generous to yourself in allowing for that expansion and contraction way of interacting with the world rather than demanding that it has to be in a certain fashion. All right? Give it a try.

Eloheim

Let's just take a quick look at the energies, have some eye contact with all of you, and see how you're doing. Let's see what's on the agenda tonight. It's interesting that the Visionaries and the Guardians started talking about the power chakra because it's been a while since we had a conversation about the power chakra. It's about darned time. Because really, when you start talking about moving into the world, emanating your truth, "where do I lie to myself," all that stuff, what happens is that you start bringing into the power chakra a new sense of knowing yourself. You start to know yourself on the inside.

We've talked a bazillion times about how your internal world creates your external journey and all that, and that's all well and good, but then there's that part where you make a decision and you start *being* some other way in the world. It's all well and good to know "Oh, I'm creating my reality, look at that parking space, it's mine." And then there's the time when you just say, "Oh, now it's time for me to be different. Now it's time for me to walk in this world in a new way. Now it's time for me to approach the world in a new way." And part of this going-up-the-staircase thing we've been talking about for a while now, is the idea that you guys are starting to be more and more comfortable with the concept, and even with the action of being different in the world, bringing who you are into the world in a new way. And you've had the thing where you've been conscious, you've had the thing where you've noticed other people being unconscious, you've played around the edges of it. But it's quite another subject when you say, "I am going to be the truth of me in this world. I am going to be the truth of me today. I am actually going to tell my truth in this environment, regardless." And that's a whole different thing. Because then all of a sudden you're taking your shiny new self out into the world, and that's where your power chakra starts to get involved. Because it starts to be like: "OK, the truth of me, the middle of me, the core of me, is going to interact with others now, and I'm not going to put a face on it and I'm not going to lie and I'm not going to hide and I'm not going to pretend."

So that your power chakras are stirred up tonight is not surprising to us. Because you've done a lot of work to bring yourself to a point where you can move into the world in this new way. So it's a collective kind of like [takes a deep breath] wow. It's a little bit like when you're on a journey and you have to drive to the airport and then you wait around at the airport and then you get on the flight and you fly to someplace, and then you wait around at that airport and you change planes and you fly some more. And it's three days later, practically, and you get off the plane and you're in the other airport and you're collecting your baggage and you're like, "Oh, we're here." You're not really there yet, because you're still at the airport, right? And you're still half asleep and you haven't eaten anything real for a really long time and you're dehydrated and the weather is different and you can't believe it's dark because it feels like morning to you, and you've got bags and you're trying to find a cab and you're not there, but you're there.

That's what you guys are doing tonight. You're not there, but you're there, in the sense that you have arrived at a place where life can start to really shift—but you're still in the airport of it. And you're going to get yourself, and you're going to kind of gather it all together and you're going to schlep it off to the car and you're going to get to the hotel and you're going to lay flat on your back and then you're going to wake up. Wake up to the truth that you're in a new place. That's how we see you guys. So, if you feel like you're not on solid ground, just remember that time you went to Australia or something. "Oh my God, I feel like I've been in an airplane for three days. I literally think it's been three days I've been in this plane." That kind of a feeling.

So, what do you do about that? It's all well and good to describe it, but what do you do? What the Visionaries were telling you about that expansion and contraction. And we can already hear what the Girls are going to say. You can probably say what they're going to say before they even have a chance—"Be nice to yourself during that expansion and contraction." But it's the acknowledgment that "I don't have to have all the answers, it doesn't have to be all laid out, I don't have to have it perfect. What I'm ready to do is to allow it now. Allow it to be true. Allow myself to have the truth of me in my life. To tell the truth about me." And again, we're going to remind you the difference between vulnerability and weakness because this one is one that we can always replay.

Weakness is when you're in a position where you don't feel secure, you don't feel strong, you don't have certainty, maybe you don't feel completely safe, and you hide or lie about it. Vulnerability is when you're in the exact same position and you tell your truth about it. When you're in a position of vulnerability it's actually the ultimate strength because there's nothing hidden, there's nothing pretend, there's nothing fake, there is no way to topple you. You may crumble but you can't be toppled. Do you understand? You may crumble because it's like, "Oh my God, this is the hardest thing I've ever had to deal with." Yeah, OK, and you kind of crumble and then you use some tools and you perk yourself back up. But it's not like you're going to get knocked off your center. It's not like anyone's going to come along and give you the big revelation about what an idiot you are. Because you told your truth.

Now we've said, maybe not to you guys but we've talked about it in a private session, that if you cannot stand the word vulnerability, which for some of you it's triggering, we understand,

you can use the word open or openness. But we would encourage you to stick with vulnerability because even though
it's triggering, there's a reason why we use that word. And we
use that word because it's been misused for so long we want to
reclaim it. Most of the misused words we give up on, but this
one we want to reclaim, because vulnerability is so much like
the rose opening. It's so much like the butterfly coming out of
the cocoon. It's so much that point of: Anything could happen.
And what you most often think is: Anything could happen *bad*.
But in vulnerability there's: Anything could happen, period. So
we like this word vulnerability, and we're trying to reclaim it.
So, we're going to ask you to see if you can make friends with
vulnerability. And again, vulnerability is the place where you
tell the truth about how you're feeling. You tell the truth about
what is going on with you. And by telling the truth about how
you're feeling and what's going on with you, it gives you an
unassailable foundation to stand on. And if the unassailable
foundation is: "I feel shame right now," well, that's a fascinating
thing to explore. If instead you pretend you don't feel shame,
you're weak. There is a weakness to you.

And we always remember, Veronica hasn't studied much mar-
tial arts but boy, has she seen a lot of movies. And there's always
that movie where they show you: If you're standing like that
they can just push you over, and if you're standing like this we
can't. You've seen this in movies. This is this weakness/vulner-
ability thing. The weakness thing—boof—a feather can knock
you down. Because you've built your foundation on lies, on
shame, on lack, on fear, whatever, whatever low-vibrational
state you find yourself in. But when you build your foundation
upon truth, you are strong and vulnerable. Vulnerable being
open to all possibilities. And this tool, of course, it's down the
road a little. You can't have this tool in the beginning. But it's so
important at this time because the tendency we see in you guys
is that you grow, grow, grow, and then you freak yourselves out
because you've grown so much, so fast, that you want to kind

of close in and go, "I'm afraid of what happened there." Or the survival instinct kicks in that says: "OK, it's all well and good to have grown as much as you did, but that's enough of that. Don't keep on with that. That's enough for now. We're going to just go back to the way we used to do it. Remember how good that used to feel?" And you're like, "Well, it sort of felt like suffering but it also felt like familiar suffering." Now, when you get to the point where you find yourself tempted to go back into habit, we're going to invite you to go into vulnerability. And you can say, "I'm tempted to go back into habit."

This is where short, factual statements are your best friend. The way that you be vulnerable is by using short, factual statements to clearly illuminate what you're feeling, what you're experiencing, what the reality is that you're interacting with. You tell your short, factual statements, you put a period at the end, and you see what happens. And we're telling you, it's going to rock your world. It's going to clarify so many things for you. And you want certainty, and what we can give you is moment-to-moment clarity. And the only place you get moment-to-moment clarity is, of course, in the moment. And the only way you get it is by giving up your addiction to certainty and allowing clarity to be, not a substitute, but show you that it's a different path in the forest and that there are more fascinating things on that path. You have to make the commitment that clarity is not only good enough but is good. Or that you're willing to try out what it feels like to live from clarity. It's like trying anything. "I'm going to be a vegetarian." OK, you have to learn new things. "I'm going to move to England." Well, you're going to have to learn to drive a different way. New stuff is normal. You guys do it all the time. It's just when it's about—really, when it involves your survival instincts, you freak out. It's completely understandable. And it's also a choice.

We've been talking for a while that we were evolving the survival instinct, evolving your relationship to the survival instinct, and this is just another place that we're involving it. The survival instinct says: "Don't tell the truth because then people will have ammunition against you." But the actual effect of not telling the truth is that you become weak. When you tell the truth, yes, they may have "ammunition" against you but you're unassailable. It doesn't matter what they have. Your unassailable position is the position whose foundation is in truth. And your reaction to truth is your choice. That's why it's unassailable because it continues to be your choice. You get to make choice after choice after choice to have a relationship to truth that allows you to be vulnerable rather than weak, and that's really the invitation that right now has for you, is making the choice between vulnerability and weakness and deciding to continue to choose your reaction to the situations that you find yourself in rather than habitually react to the situations you find yourself in. And if you find yourself going habitual, listen to the Girls and let them tell you, "That's OK. Be nice to yourself." We can almost do their voices. "That's OK!"

Question: On vulnerability: When we're designing things like websites, meaning we're now going to be out there, there's a lot of fear. What words, what energies, can help to deal with vulnerability of this type?

Eloheim: Yeah, that's a good one. First off, we'll just share, many of you know this but the idea of being a public figure is completely contrary to Veronica's core emotion. It's absolutely triggering. It completely triggers her core emotion to be a public figure. And when she created a Facebook account she cried through the entire process, she was so afraid to be public. So we have a database about this. So yeah, for her to be in the position she's in now took an incredible amount of work.

Now, when you think about taking that step and go from being, like you said, one of the masses to sticking your neck out, and it's interesting because there are how many millions and millions of websites? But yet, "That one's mine, I'm sticking my neck out." That's interesting, that dynamic, right? You're one of a sea of millions, yet you feel this. So you have to make friends with a few things. The first thing would be "Yes, I have alternative expressions where sticking my neck out got me whacked." And that's where you go into "and making a website is unlikely to get me whacked" so you have to remind yourself of that. "So far, making my website has not gotten me whacked, how about that?" So there is a sense of having a realistic perspective, giving it some perspective about what's really going on and recognizing that some of the feelings are habitual and a lot of the feelings are feelings that are coming from other [alternate] expressions. So, "Here I am, feeling more exposed in the world and these things come along with it." Because if you step back from it you recognize "OK, I've created a blog, I'm one of hundreds of millions of blogs, so my actual exposure at this moment is not that much. Yet I'm still feeling this threatened. I'm still feeling this is danger. This is creepy," whatever word you like. So, there is a perspective thing. "Yeah, that's all well and good until you get 5,000 Facebook friends and then what do you do, Eloheim?" Well, by then, you've learned a little. So there's the first, you have to make friends with the idea that: "Right just this second I am having an out of proportion fear for the amount of exposure I'm actually having." That's just a reality check in the sense of not letting the cart get before the horse. The next thing you have to make friends with is that not everyone's going to agree with you, and some people will disagree with you vehemently and nastily and say mean things that you would never imagine saying to another human being—and sometimes they'll do it over and over and over again. And there's a nickname for that on the Internet. It's called the haters. And the haters—that's just what they call them—the haters are going to be present. And part of what goes on with the haters is it's sandpaper. You have to put them in the sandpaper department. And you get to do the compare-you-to-you thing. And you'll see how your reaction to them can shift over time.

The fear that you're feeling is out of proportion to the amount of hater mail you're going to get, even in that regard. So it's also that feeling of: "Oh God, not everybody's going to take time out of their life to tell you they agree with you, nor that they disagree with you." In fact a very, very small percentage of people will ever bother to do that. And of that percentage a very, very much smaller percentage will be haters; and an interesting thing will be to see how you handle the haters as compared to the people who are appreciative of what you're doing. So, that's one thing to just be aware of, that that's coming, because it seems to come for everybody. We have not yet met anybody who is online in any public way that doesn't have to deal with that. Certainly Veronica does. So we imagine it's out there. There are a lot of people we've talked to that have had this experience.

And another thing to do is to say the pleasure, the joy, the growth, the expansion, that you get giving to yourself, and this is where your issue is, remembering, "I'm giving this to myself," so every post that you write, every picture that you place, everything you do, you're doing it for you. Not for anyone else. And if other people like it, great, and if other people hate on you, they're sandpaper and you do it for you, and you do it for you, and you do it for you. So what we would say is before you hit "go" on any of your posts, you say, "Is this post for me?" That would be your good gut-check, they call it sometimes. "Is this for me?" And if any of it's not for you, take it out. That would be the way to do it for you. But a lot of yours is carryover. A lot of yours is not just carryover like alternate expressions carry over, but "I'm a stranger in a strange land" vibe that you have. "I'm really, really, really not from here and now more people are going to know I'm really, really, really not from here." That's what's really going on for you more than it happens even for Veronica, is: "I'm really not from here and now a bunch more people are going to know I'm really not from here, and I'm kind of tired of dealing with the fact that I'm really not

from here." So there's a fatigue before you even get started. And
the way through that fatigue is to say, "This is for me. This is
for me. This is for me." Because sometimes it's wanting other
people's certain kind of reactions that creates the fatigue. It's
like: "I want them to know the truth of me and they have no
way of knowing the truth of me even if I do the best I can to
explain it." So you have to let go that it's for them or for their
reaction and say, "This is me creating me. This is me reflecting
me. This is me emanating me."

What's interesting to us is that you had this experience with
your aunt and your father and your job and then you just jump
right into another one. If you guys ever are confused about the
whole Mount Everest example, like, "Oh God, it was so hard,
it was so hard, it was so hard, and then I decided to climb
Mount Everest. Because why not? I'd already rafted down the
Amazon and that was over and I only got malaria three times,
so why not try something else? There's not really so much malaria on Mount Everest. I've heard about frostbite and sometimes people die, but that's alright I think I'll go try it anyway."
This is the poster child for this week of just that.

Veronica says, "If I just rested on my laurels." But sometimes
she does. That sometimes is her position. "God, Eloheim we
were doing fine. We could've just rested there. We didn't need
any of this other stuff. Webcast and the Council and my God,
Q&A webcast is on Sunday. We could have just not done any of
that. We were doing fine." That's only when she's really berserk
about something. She doesn't really get pissed at us as much
as she feels vulnerable and then the vulnerability of that: "Oh
my God, I'm a public figure and the haters can hate on me and
people can misinterpret things that are going on." Just today,
she had a thing on Facebook—here's an example. She had a
thing on Facebook where she posted "free transcript" and "join
us tonight for the webcast." So the guy clicked on the wrong
link and he put a message saying: "What do you mean by free?
PayPal came up when I tried to get to it."

Well, in the past, she would've been freaking out, but she just went, "I think you clicked the wrong spot." But in the past that would've really hurt her feelings. Like misinterpreting. Oh lord, you guys. She didn't always tell you guys about that stuff. There's been a lot of that kind of stuff. Today, she was tempted to have a judgment about him but instead she just said, "Well, that was his experience." So there was a big you-to-you thing that happened. But there is an example. She's trying to give something away and getting shit for it. Like, "It's free! It's free!" "What do you mean by free?" Wow, there's re-languaging going on all the time, but free means free. That's where she would have gone in the past, but today she just said, "I think you clicked on the wrong link." And he had and he said, "Cool," and it all worked out. But that's taken four years, literally.

Anybody else have a question?

Question: I have an opportunity to teach people my age [he is 15 years old] and younger—there will be eight-year-olds—pretty much anything in the metaphysical department. At first I thought I would teach them aura-reading, but now I realize it needs to be simpler and hands-on rather than a lecture. Can I get some suggestions?

Eloheim: How many hours do you have to teach these kids?

Response: One. Just a taste.

Eloheim: And you'd like to teach them aura-reading?

Response: Yes.

Eloheim: What would we teach a group of eight-year-olds if we if we had the chance? Wow. You only have an hour so you don't want to just talk to them because you'll lose them. It's not a question we've ever contemplated. What would we do if all of a sudden a bunch of 8- to 15-year-olds showed up? You know, we probably would want to talk to them about how they feel when other people are having strong emotions. Now, we don't know if that's what you want to talk to them about, but that's what we'd want to talk to them about. Like, "How do you feel when other people are having strong emotions?" Because you kind of want to start, if you get them young, you want to start teaching them where their emotions stop and other peoples start. And that's something you could probably use a review on yourself. So, you teach what you most need to learn until you've learned what you most need to teach. And for you especially, this might be helpful in the sense of when someone else is feeling a very strong emotion it's very easy to do mob-mentality and to feel that emotion with them. And if you're eight, you're starting to look at boundaries, you're starting to look at: "This is me, this is who I am, these are my preferences," and the idea that you have an idea of who you are.

Now, how could you go about teaching that? Well, you know laughter is really contagious and so people can probably buy into the idea that laughter is contagious and so you can tell them, when someone starts laughing you're going to tend to laugh, too, and if someone feels sad, you may start to feel sad, too. And it's OK to feel sad because someone else is sad—but knowing it's a choice. Knowing that you're doing it because you want to be friendly to them or you want to be a good classmate but it's not that you have to. And it's the same thing if someone's feeling angry. There's a temptation to feel angry, also. That one's a little more uncomfortable for people because they're a little bit more aware of when they're angry than when they're not. But that's what we would teach them. And we don't know if that sounds fun to you or interesting to you at all, but that's what we would start with. If we had a bunch of little kids that's what we would start with, is helping them know when it's their feeling and when it's not.

Knowing what's your feeling and what's not is such an important thing to figure out and have a read on and have a sense of the truth of. Or you could do aura-reading. But if you do aura-reading you're going to want to have some kinds of exercises for them to go through. It's the same kind of a sensitivity, really. It's knowing what is them and what's you. "This is where his aura stops" is another way of actually teaching the same concept, so maybe you can make a combination. But you better have some really wowie-zowie examples or games or toys or something, or else we're not sure you're going to hold their attention span. Good luck with that. We are so glad we get the forty-year-olds and the fifty-year-olds instead of the eight-year-olds. We're not sure that eight-year-olds are our department. But we think we told you a while back that the reason you're fifteen now is because we needed you for a whole other group of things. So, here you go. You and the eight-year-olds.

OK. The Girls have something they want to share. Are we surprised?

The Girls

One of the things that's really important here is that when you start talking about your power chakra and how you are in the world, going out into the world—boom—you hit your second chakra pretty darn fast. Eloheim has been teaching you that the heart chakra and the power chakra have been going together because you're moving your power chakra out into the world and then you're combining it with your heart energy. Well, there's also a combination of sorts that goes on between the third chakra and the second chakra. And the second chakra is all about how you actually interact with other people. The third chakra is about: "This is me taking me into the world," and the second chakra is kind of like: "This is me allowing the world into me." These are kind of simplifications and it's certainly not an exclusionary thing, like this is the only thing going on, but it is an important aspect of what's going on.

So as you take your power chakra out into the world and you expand and you do all of that stuff and all of a sudden you let the world in, by going out into the world you start to let the world in, too, is what we're trying to tell you. There is a little bit of a flow between the third and the second chakra. The third and the second chakra. It's the sense of: You put the third chakra out and more comes into the second chakra. Now each and every one of you probably has issues in your second chakra because of this exact reason. Because you're letting people in. Because you're interacting with people in new ways. Because you're having sex with them, et cetera. So, as you bring people in, one of the main things you have to do is that as you bring them into your life, as you allow people in, you don't go into judgment about yourself based on their reaction to you. The temptation is you go out into the world, you have this expansion, "Oh my God I'm being vulnerable, it feels kind of scary, oh no, there are all these people in my life now, what do they think of me? What do they think of me? How are they reacting to my expanded nature? What are their opinions about me?" That whole thing. You've been there, you've done it, you know what it feels like.

So again, it's: "I am going to open up and expand and experience the world in a new way, and I'm going to come from this expanded experience into the world and I'm going to tell my truth about the experience. And then as people come into my life and I start to interact with people more, I'm going to keep telling the truth. I'm going to keep telling the truth." And the truth continues to be: "Wow, I'm letting people into my life and I feel scared. I'm letting people into my life and I'm nervous. I'm letting people into my life and I don't know what they think of me. I'm letting people into my life and they're judging me. I'm sure of it. It's got to be. Why wouldn't they be? I feel crazy because I'm doing all this new stuff. I'm in this new way. I'm this new person." And the temptation is to fall back on habit, which says: "Get small, close down, stop doing that, they're not going to like you, they're threatening you, you're in danger," et cetera. It's none of those things.

The truth is: "I feel uncomfortable but I also want my life to be different." So you have to move through a bit of discomfort in order to have the experience of change—sometimes, not all the time, but often—and that discomfort will trigger you into habit and to judging and being mean to yourself because that is the default place you used to go to. And the interesting thing is all those things are lies, so they make you weak. The vulnerability place is to say, "I feel like judging myself," rather than actually judging yourself. "I feel afraid," rather than just going ahead and being afraid. Short, factual statements about the state you find yourself in. That is the freedom. The freedom is short, factual statements about the situation you find yourself in rather than habitually making yourself small through berating yourself. It's what you guys tend to do if you're not paying close attention. And it doesn't serve you. It doesn't help and it doesn't feel good. And it kind of shuts things down because if you get into that place where you expand, expand, expand and you start to have more things coming into your life and maybe you even go into that contraction phase the Visionaries told you about, that's fine. That's not shutting down. That's just contemplating. And in fact, in that contraction phase a lot of times is when you catch yourself trying to be habitual and re-evaluating things. But all that contraction phase is, is an opportunity to make sure you keep telling yourself the truth, keep using your short, factual statements, keep letting yourself be kind to yourself and keep realizing that change does not come without change, therefore: "I have to go through some transformation in order to have the transformed experience I desire." If you wish to have transformation, you must transform. If you need change, change must happen.

You know the funny example of this, of course, is the one that goes something like this. "Eloheim, I don't like my job. I don't like my boyfriend. I don't like my house. I don't like my car. I don't like my clothes. Sometimes I don't even like my dog." OK, get a new job, buy new clothes, get a new house, get a new boyfriend, take the dog into a different environment, play in the park instead of at the house. "Well, I can't do any of those things." Well, why not? "Well, they all sound hard and scary."

OK, stay home and do nothing then, will that change it? No. It won't. At a minimum, you have to change your energetic relationship to situations in order to get something transformed, but every once in a while, it feels good to move things around a bit, too. If you're not happy with your life, you have to make changes. And you'd be shocked how often we hear "Oh, really? It won't just change?" All right? So, of course, be nice to yourself but be nice to yourself in recognition of the fact that habits creep in and want you to be the way you've always been, and the way you've always been has bounced between suffering and fear. And some angst and anguish thrown in. And every once in a while, you have a little bit of fun.

Eloheim, part 2

OK, we have a little bit of time before we have to rush ahead here, we think. We seem to be having a challenge with math recently. So it says 47 minutes have elapsed and normally we go 80 minutes, so that means we have a lot of time left. But we still the need the Warrior and Fred and the Matriarch.

Question: [Reading a book on the chakras—asks about other chakras.]

Eloheim: Yeah, there's lots of different chakras in the body. We don't usually talk about the others than the seven main ones, and it's interesting you bring this up because we were actually going to talk about it earlier. When we talk about the chakras and how the different members of the Council resonate to the chakras and we go into chakras, mostly what we're doing is trying to give you a frame of reference for a specific energetic that we're referring to. It's not as much as it's about specifically this part of your body, as much as it is an energetic aspect of being human. And because most, if not all, of you are familiar with the idea that the seven chakras are placed in the body and they're energy centers and they tend to resonate to different types of activities and behaviors, that's why we use that example; but we certainly don't mean to say it has to be that.

Some people have asked us about this and it's like… don't get too caught up in the fact that we say chakras as much as recognize we're talking about aspects of human behavior and aspects of you and your growth system.

Somebody was trying to say, "Well, what about the chakra that's here by your thyroid?" and we don't want to get into all the different energy centers in the body because, of course, there are so many. That's why we talk about the seven main chakras and we just kind of be general about it. Just like the Council resonating to the different chakras is really just saying they're kind of responsible for different aspects of your life, but it's easy to kind of slot them into the chakra concept because you already know of it. So, yeah, there probably are chakras where you indicated there are, especially if you feel like that feels true. Then they are for sure. Because for you, it's true. So we're not trying to discount any extra chakras or new chakras or chakras we never talk about. We're not making any commentary on chakras. We're just saying that there are certain core, standard aspects of being human and it's easy to talk about them if we say chakras. So, thanks for bringing that up because that's something we actually wanted to clarify.

Question: The Girls just talked about, "You can't change without change, if you don't like something in your life do something about it." I live by the adage that if it's not easy I don't do it. So, if something is in my life that I don't like and I want to do something about it, it might not be easy.

Eloheim: There's a difference between "I don't do it in my life unless it's easy" in the sense of like business opportunities, a place to live, manifesting things flowing smoothly into your life, and dealing with habits and triggers and other lifetimes and all that stuff, because transforming a trigger is very rarely easy. But saying, "I only do things that are easy" takes away from the idea that you can transform triggers. So, the "do" that you're talking about is third chakra, being out in the world. "I'm not going to do this project unless this project falls together in a way that feels flowing." The "do" the Girls are talking about is: "Oh my God, every time I drive down this street I get triggered. So what am I going to do about the fact that I get triggered every time I drive down this street?" Well, that means you need to look at what you're doing. It's two different doings. There's two different departments here, and the language screws us up.

So, there's the sense of: "I want to be in the flow of grace, ease, and bliss around projects, around my job," around that kind of stuff, but there's also that sandpaper and growing and trans- forming triggers and breaking habits—and that's not necessar- ily easy but you can use ease, which means using your tools, to move through it in a different way. Confronting your core emotion is not going to be easy, necessarily, but it generates ease in your life by not constantly being triggered. You get trig- gered, you transform some of them. So it's not a mine field. There's a little path you can stay on. Does that make sense? And you have to be careful with the idea that "I don't do it unless it's easy" is a little bit of a lateral-pass-to-the-angels energy, just a little bit. Because it's a little bit like "I'm not going to do it unless it's easy, so somebody else better make it easy." Whereas "I'm not going to do it unless it's easy because I'm creating my reaction to the situations I find in my life," because somebody could say, "Oh my God, I have this big job to do and every- body isn't agreeing with me and it's so hard I'm not going to do it anymore." And another person could say, "Wow, this is a real opportunity for me to look at how I have to be in control." So the same exact circumstance could be seen as being easy, mean- ing: "It's easy for me to see how I can use this as sandpaper," rather than: "It just has to go smoothly or I'm not going to do it.Response: What comes to mind is when I do that and look at the triggers, then it flows. If things didn't line up, though, I would hesitate.

Eloheim: It may line itself up to where you go, "Wow, this was worth the investment," or it may line itself up to say, "God, I'm just done with this." Because sometimes, even though you're transforming your triggers and even though you're realizing, "this is sandpaper, this is sandpaper," you're like, "I want to do this a different way. I'm not interested. I don't have to stand here in all this sandpaper." Good example: Veronica likes this show called *Deadliest Catch* with the guys on the crab boats. So, you could say, "I'm going to go make my living as a crabber," and you're going to be out there in the deadliest job and it's hard and crazy. Yeah, OK, that would teach you a lot, but you also just might want to do it some other way. You could beat your head against the wall learning in any environment but you also have the right to say, "This is just a bit more than I am interested in." And it's not because it's too hard but maybe it's just too much. It's too many triggers coming at you.

Veronica had a job and she quit it, and she said, "It's not the job, but it's the people I work with, they are all pushing the same button on me. I can't have 30 people push the same button. I have to quit this job and let one person or maybe two push the button, that I can handle. I can't handle 30 people pushing the same button every day all day long." Maybe that's an easier to understand example.

Question: I have a friend who has been living with this guy for ten years and has been complaining about it for ten years. She wants to kick him out but he brings in some income and she's afraid of not having that income. I didn't know how to support her other than to say, "Let's look at the fear, you know it's about lack of money, you're in financial flow," et cetera.

Eloheim: And that's the journey of consciousness. The truth of the matter is she is in a relationship to his money, not to him. And money is common and she doesn't remember that.

Question: So to help her transform that fear?

Eloheim: Just say what we just said. "You're in relationship to his money. And there's lots of money you can be in relationship to."

And that's a good example where what is the truth here? The truth is a short, factual statement. "I am in relationship with your income." OK, maybe you get a roommate. Here's a great example. We tried to do it with the crabbing boat but we don't think that was a very good example. You need income. Who are you getting it from? You're getting it from a guy who you don't want to be in relationship with. OK, there's lots of money in this world. Other people need roommates. Other people need a place to live. How about: "I will learn this lesson, yes, but I want to learn it in a situation that's not so intense." We've told you guys before that you have a queue of things that are coming into your life, and when something comes up and if it's just too much, the how ridiculous does it have to get, that's where you can pull the ripcord.

You have a queue of things that come along. And you have the right to say, "This is too ridiculous to learn this with you. I will learn it. I'm not running away. Put it back in the hopper. I need somebody else to learn this with." So, she's learning about her relationship to money and she's wrapped it up in the relationship to this man's money instead of money. That's what we would say. And we know who you're talking about and we think she can hear it.

Warrior

Yes. So. We want to talk to you tonight about what it's like when you go to see the king. You know we don't particularly have a fondness for royalty. We're not especially fond of people who get to have authority simply by being born. We're sort of more into the idea that your authority comes from being surrounded by people who respect you and will follow you because they respect you. Someone who is simply born hasn't done much, as far as we're concerned. So, every once in a while, one of these types will call you—that's what you say, we don't have cell phones where we're at right now—so they tend to ride up on a horse. We've told you about them before. They wear ridiculously impractical clothing. And they try to make nice with us. The ironic part of being made nice with by someone sent by someone who is only important because of the way they were born is that by the time it gets to the messenger, it is so diluted in importance that it is almost not even worth getting up to piss on. But what else are we doing today?

So we think we told you that it is our pattern, you may call it a habit, we don't care, your judgments don't trouble us, to take these messenger types and throw them in the creek and roll them around in some dirt. We, of course, don't have to do this. We have many men who respect us who do it for fun. They roll them around in the dirt, they get rid of all their ridiculous things with flags hanging off of them—try moving through the forest silently with that shit. All that shit has to go. We roll them around in the mud. They hate it. It's entertaining, we'll admit it. Until you've rolled the representation of a person who has authority because of the order in which they were born to a specific person, until you've rolled that person in mud you don't know fun. So, once they've been rolled in mud—and we have to admit sometimes we don't feed them either, we tell them they can eat if they catch their own food; they don't know how—once we've got them appropriately dirtied, they'll say something that's supposed to flatter us. Trying to have one of these types flatter you is the most ridiculous thing. Eloheim likes to say: How ridiculous does it have to get? That's pretty fucking ridiculous. You're going to flatter us now, by what? Telling us how cool we are. This is when we typically sharpen things just to see if it'll make him piss. Every once in a while, it does. We consider it bonus points if it makes him piss while he's telling us how important we are. That's extra fun.

So, by this time he's dirty and hopefully he's pissed himself and everything's sort of sharp, it's time to go trudging off to the castle. Or whatever passes for a castle. Let's just use the word castle, why don't we? How often do you get to talk about castles, after all? The interesting bit is that as you're moving back to the castle this person thinks he's in charge. Ha! God, that's a riot. And this is what happens in your life, too. Someone who has some degree of authority, presumed, has the right to tell you how to be. That's what you do. Now, what we want to say here is this: This presumed authority is fear. In your world, it's fear. In your world, it's fear and habit that have presumed authority in your life. And they're just as ridiculous as the messenger of a being that came out of a womb at a specific time in a specific castle to a specific woman who slept with a specific man having any sort of actual authority in your life.

Habit and fear are the same ridiculous nature. They're only there because it's always been that pattern, you see. It's always been a pattern that the son of a king has authority over you and it's only been a pattern that fear and habit have authority over you. It's just a pattern. It's just a pattern. And in our example, you see what we do with him. We take him off his horse, we roll him around in the mud, we don't feed him, and we let him piss himself just for our entertainment. And this is the kind of behavior you should have with your fears and your habits. Let them piss themselves for your entertainment. It's not that they really have authority over you. If we weren't interested in tromping off to wherever it is Mr. King wants us to go this time, we'd send the man packing. "Piss off, we're not interested in you." We've done it many times.

You have the same kind of authority over the things that presume to tell you who you are, which are fears and habits, primarily. They presume to tell you who you are. Just like this guy coming on his horse in his silly white clothes wanting to tell us "Oh this, that," and scrape and bow and "You're so important," and this, that and the other crap. And we just say, "You're not telling us who we are. Are you kidding? You have no idea who we are. You may have seen some of our actions but that doesn't tell you who we are. You don't know my dreams and passions. You simply have seen actions I've done. Don't presume to know me." And you can say the same thing to fear and habit. "Don't presume to know me. Yes, you've been around for a long time. Yes, you've been part of my life. But don't presume to know me. Because I'm connecting to my soul's perspective and having an experience of the reality of me, and you, fears and habits, don't presume to know me. Don't presume to know me." Do you understand?

So, now that we've had a little bit of teaching, let's talk a bit more just for fun about what happens next. We're telling this long story, this tale we'll call it. And you know you want to get a little bit past the rolling the guy in the dirt and hoping he pisses himself because that's interesting but it's not all that much fun. The ridiculous nature of these beings is that they cannot stop being who they are—just like your patterns, right? They cannot stop being who they are. So even though we've rolled them in mud and made them piss themselves and haven't fed them, they still try to ride their horse with some kind of pride, which is even more ridiculous because the truth of them is not how they ride their horse. The truth of them is who they are inside. But instead of being true to that and saying, "I'm scared," or "Could you please feed me?" or "Jesus, I'm just a person. I've got this job but I'm a person, too, and I'd actually like to be able to shit outside of my drawers for once," instead of telling the truth about themselves, they try to pretend and they get to ride their horse in their own excrement. Sitting in your own shit. Sound familiar? And so they smell so bad that we throw them in the river again. Of course, we don't do that. This is what's good about having people who respect you. They'll throw shitty people in the river for you.

So, we get to the castle eventually. There's lots of things that happen on the way. Mostly it involves telling him to shut the fuck up—that's the English way of saying it—because habits and fears are noisy, right? These are all habits and fears, just pretend, but it's more fun if we tell it like it's a fairytale. Right? Much more fun. Plus, there's visuals. Well, you might not see them but they entertain Veronica. So, we ride up to the castle and you have the masses there and the expectation and the fear and the titillation and the envy and the anxiety and the you name it and it's there, because the king has sent for the warriors and they've come out of the forest. And this one turns up her nose and that one sees if he can imagine stealing our purse and this one over here, this one over here we wouldn't let come with us last time, and that one there is starting to look like he might be good size after another winter or two. We're keeping an eye on that one.

You are a public figure and all of them are trying to tell you who you are, all of them are giving their impressions of you and again, where are you going to go next? Where are you going to go with that? What are you going to do with that? What do you react? And for us it's just another opportunity to turn in, but we've had much practice at that. When you arrive at the castle gates after being summoned by the King, the towns-people gather to watch you ride through and all of their fears, their hopes, their passions, their desires, their angers, and their anxieties are projected onto you and it is your choice how to handle it. Your choice how to deal with it. And your choice because you go to see the King. And that will be the part of the story we'll tell next time. Going to see the King. That will make some of you come back. Because we're to see the King next time. And we'll tell you right now, the King, well, let's just say we've had some mixed experiences with him. Yet for some reason we're on speed-dial and that is going to be the lesson of next week's story. He is afraid of us and he respects us and he calls us and what do you do? And we will tell you then. So, there you go. You're going to see the King. Goodnight.

Fred

Open your eyes. Open your eyes to the truth of you. You must open your eyes and by this we mean open the perceptive ability that you possess. Open to the opportunity to see the truth of you. Open, open, open. You must constantly be opening to the more that exists. You have such an incredibly limited perspective of what is reality. You have such an incredibly limited perspective of what is possible. You have such an incredibly limited perspective and we understand this. We're not judging you but we want to help you to see that your soul's perspective is incredibly vast, and in the meantime, you're allowing yourself to live from such a narrow perspective. Do not succumb to the idea that there's only this or that. Do not succumb to the idea that duality is your only option. Do not succumb to that. It is not true. It's not even close to true. It's never even been near true. It simply was a way that you decided to experiment. It's an experiment that's seen its day. It is an opportunity now for you to open into the reality of you and have that expressed completely. It is an opportunity for you to open to the reality of you and have that expressed completely. You've never had this before. You've never lived this way. You've never ever tried it. It's never been possible. This is why you haven't tried it, and now it is possible. Now you have the opportunity. It's open for you. Just open your eyes to the truth of you. Open your eyes to what's really going on. Open your eyes to the possibilities that exist.

Do not succumb to limitation. Do not succumb to narrowness. Do not succumb to the idea that there are very few choices. There is so much available to you and so many opportunities presented to you in so many ways, so many ways you can be true, so many ways you can express you, so many ways you can offer the world your emanation. When you feel trapped, when you feel limited, when you feel like you're still in duality, just allow yourself to say, "I open to the idea that there is more here. I open to the idea that I can experience more here. I open to the idea that my soul's perspective is available to me. I open to it and I'm willing to experience it." No one can override your free will. No one can get in the way of your opportunity to say "No." And only you can say, "I am willing." And there is so much for you to experience and see and be, and every time you feel limited and every time you feel constricted and every time you feel duality coming on, we ask you to say, "I am open to more, I am open to more, I am open to more." Because you have so much there but you have to open to it, open, open, open to it. Allow yourself to see the truth of you. Allow yourself. It's not as though it's hiding. It's there. But you have to open your eyes to it. Open your eyes to it and become it and allow it to embrace you. Be the truth of you by this way. Be the truth of you. It's always there, the truth of you is right there waiting for you to embrace it. "How, how, how?" We hear you scream and we say to you: The how is by willingness. Open with willingness and don't demand the answer that you project is going to be coming. Allow it to be something even grander. That is all.

Matriarch

You've had a long talk tonight about your power chakra and a long interaction with your power chakra, and now we just want to remind you of the heart/power chakra combination. And as you go out into the world and you emanate the truth of you and you bring the truth of you into the world know that it goes not only with the truth of you expressing but it goes with the knowingness of yourself. Let us see if we can explain this.

It is true that the sky is blue, yes? But the knowingness that the sky is the air that you breathe. The sky is clouds to shade you on a warm day. The sky is a place for the birds to fly and all the other things you know. That's what we're talking about. It's one thing to know the truth of you. It's one thing to know your preference, but it's another thing to give it room to breathe. Now, some of you like to use the word love for this, and that's OK if you do. We like the word "expansion" quite a lot. Just let it expand into its completeness. "I know this truth of me and what does that truth expand into?" Remember, it's not a stopping place. "I know this truth of me" isn't then: "That's finished." It's: "I know this truth of me" and that can open into something more. That can open into something more.

The truth of you is the starting place. It's the starting place. And that starting place allows you to open and open and open again. Yes? OK. So, take that in and let it open again. That's all for tonight. Thank you for allowing us to be in your presence.

July 21, 2010

Summary

Guardians: Advised us to, "Bring your attention, focus your attention, align your intention to this moment, to the expansion of the experience of you."

Visionaries: This is a time full of triggers, some of them "old" triggers. These issues are difficult because we're taking them up by their roots, and the roots are in deep.

Eloheim: A detailed discussion of grace, ease, and bliss (serenity), with examples. Then, questions are answered from the group regarding the tool: Short, factual statements.

The Girls: You are allowed to say no, allowed to set boundaries, allowed to change just because you want to; all without needing to justify it to anyone.

Warrior: The story of "going to see the king" continues, and illustrates the point that you are your true self regardless of your circumstance, and you do not let others tell you who you are. Knowing who you are and emanating your complete self is the fabric of your being.

Fred: There was a time when you were formless. You were in a place where there was no change and you moved into a place where there is possibility.

Matriarch: The balance between possibility and perspective. All possibilities infuse you; keep challenges and triggers in the proper perspective. Every experience you have is another opportunity for you to explore the truth of you.

Guardians

Bring your attention, focus your attention, align your intention to this moment, to the expansion of the experience of you. The expansion of the experience of you, that's the invitation. We're getting an enormous opening in the crown chakra tonight. Enormous, enormous opening in the crown chakra, so allow yourselves, in essence, to bask in that. Because when you open your crown chakra in this fashion and in this environment, you're able to bring in your soul's perspective and connect yourself to almost a universal energy, is what we're feeling tonight. So again, as that appears, that opening, that invitation is being expressed and experienced right now, allow yourself to allow. Allow yourself to allow. And, of course, by that we mean allow yourself to allow the flow of energy through you. It's all well and good to have a big, open crown chakra, but if it doesn't actually connect to the physical form then.... So, let's see what it's like when we allow the open crown chakra to then funnel that energy through the body, down the spinal cord, and feel it all the way down through the chakras—if you like that term. Excellent. All right, perhaps we'll be back later.

Visionaries

When you bring yourself into the opportunity to experience the completeness of you many, many things happen. Part of what's going on is that as you experience the completeness of you it is colliding with your experience of real life. The completeness of you has never been expressed and experienced consistently through the physical form. You've never brought that level of awareness into the physical form. So when you do, there is this almost like the tectonic plates are scraping against each other and you all are in a position where you're being challenged quite deeply to find your balance, to find your footing, to find how to walk the road of the completeness of you expressing in the physical form. And most of the resistance to this is coming from the idea that the completeness of you is such a change. It puts your, the friction—how should we say… just a moment. The completeness of you coming into physical form creates friction within you primarily around the survival instinct. That's how we have all summarized it but we'd like to look at this more deeply with you tonight.

The idea is that as the completeness of you starts to express in the physical form, you are unable to continue with life as you have. You are unable to just let things keep going on. Then, when you start to confront the changes that are asking, knocking on the door, the changes that are being requested of you, that's when the survival instinct flares up, that's when the idea that change is hard flares up, that's when you start to feel like, "Oh God, how much more is this going to ask of me? How much more am I going to have to do? How much more do I going to have to respond to and be attentive to?" And what we're seeing in you is an avalanche of triggers that you're having to attend to—and you have tools and you know how to deal with them but it's the consistent, over and over again, having to constantly attend to the triggers, that we have noticed wearing down on the people we've been interacting with—and namely, Veronica.

So, as you are dealing with triggers after triggers after triggers it's a sense of drowning. "Help. Let me out. I know what to do but God, is there a breaking point? Is there a place where I get to have a rest?" And part of what's going on here is that as you leave the landing and you start to walk up the next staircase on this ongoing analogy we've been using for the transformational time you're in, you have to clear out, you have to let go, you have to finally break those neural pathways and those habitual responses within you. And one of the real good ways to do that is to just keep pounding, literally pounding the trigger, until you change it so frequently that it actually breaks within you. Its hold on you is broken. So part of the reason you guys are getting literally pounded is that that is helping to loosen the grip that these habits and these neural pathway responses have on you.

Now, that's all well and good, but it's hard and it's painful and it's challenging and it's frustrating and it's discouraging and it's draining and it's a lot of other things, too. We recognize that. What we want to help you with tonight is giving you some energetic support for that journey and also letting you know that it's not that you've somehow failed and gone back to the beginning and, "Oh God, it hasn't been this hard in a long time," as much as it's really just scraping the bottom of the barrel and getting the last little bits off. It's like you're washing the dishes and one of them sat out overnight and there's all those hard, crusty bits that are stuck on the side and you want the dish to be clean and so you have to do some elbow grease to get those hard, crusty bits off. In essence, these last patterns that we see you guys loosening now are very similar to that, and a lot of these patterns that you guys are dealing with are very core issues that you feel like you've dealt with five thousand times and here they are again and here they are again in rapid succession and you just want to say, "Have I done nothing? Am I a failure? Has all this work been for nothing that it's this challenging now?" And what we see is you're just really getting to the root of the issue. You're really getting to the root of the issue. And you couldn't have gotten to the root of the issue without the work you'd already done. By getting to the root of the issue you're freeing yourself from the "eventually" and "soon." But energetically, you just need a little bit of support and a little help with the elbow grease to dislodge the final aspects of these things that are holding onto you.

So, if we took the time to go around the circle and have you each list off the big challenges that you tend to experience—and it might be money, it might be health, it might be relationships, it might be authority figures, whatever yours is—we would imagine you'd also be able to talk about how it seems like it's really up right now and you're having more triggers for it and it's more intense. We are really just pushed up against a wall, so it's not a very good time to give up because you're giving up right at the end. But we understand the urge to give up because you're also in a very intense time. And it is like you've done the whole big sink full of dishes and you get to the last one and it's got all these crusty bits and you think, "I'm tired of doing dishes, thank you very much, I want to be done." Well, just like if you stop and you don't do that final dish you can feel kind of like, "Oh, the kitchen doesn't feel completely clean," you can also imagine that if you stopped right now it would be challenging to feel like you'd actually accomplished what you came here to accomplish. Now the kitchen idea kind of breaks down eventually, and so we don't want to take these examples too literally, but it's a pretty good one for the meantime.

So, the invitation here is to stay the course, but to stay the course with an awareness that the reason your core stuff is up is because you're really getting down to releasing those pathways and the habits that you've had around them. And that's why it comes up. It comes up because you're getting to the root of it. That's mostly what we wanted to share with you tonight. If you feel like it's up and up and up for you it's because you really getting down, down, down to the root of it now. And so the request that's being made of you is to stay the course, pay attention, and to recognize that you haven't gone back to square one, you're actually very, very close to starting a new path, starting a new time, starting a new adventure, but you have to finish up a few things before you are ready to make that new transition. OK?

Eloheim

Hello! Grace, ease, and bliss. Or grace, ease, and serenity, if you insist. We've talked about it many times and we want to talk about it on a different level tonight. First, let's do a little bit of defining. Grace. You know you've heard this term "the grace of God" or living in grace or being graceful; and we like this word for many reasons but one of the reasons we like it is because it has a connotation of beauty, of delicateness even, like when you see a ballerina, they're graceful. So that graceful is kind of moving in the world in a nice way. "Oh, she's graceful." It's not very triggering, one good word to grab ahold of that doesn't trigger you, which is nice after we talked about vulnerability last time. When we think about grace, most of you can buy into the idea of living in a state of grace is a cool thing. And the state of grace from our definition is that moment and that recurring moment when you realize that you are not a victim, that you are a creator, that line in the sand—that's such an important line that gets drawn on the spiritual journey. It's where the spiritual journey really starts, where you recognize "I am not a victim of my circumstance. I am not a victim of my world. I am not a victim of others. I am a creator and I am creating." That's the moment of grace. And you're all like: "Whew, I've done that one." And a lot of times you have to do it over and over again. You get into situations, somebody runs into the back of your car, you get a letter from some three-letter agency. You're like, "I'm a victim, I know it. Oh wait, wait, wait." Grace is a reoccurring encounter. But that's grace.

Ease is the idea that once you decide you're a creator, you are not alone in that. You're not alone in "Oh God, what now?" You're not alone in "oh my God, the whole world is set up as a victim and now I've decided I'm a creator and I am by myself," is really the tendency that you guys have had. So, ease is that place where you say, "It's not easy, this is a big step, it's not an easy thing I'm doing, but there is an ease, meaning there is movement here." And that movement we have defined as using a bunch of tools that we've been coming up with for years now. So that you're not alone in that place. You're not alone in the state of grace. And ease is kind of like a lubricant, in a sense. It lubricates your journey. And, of course, it requires an incredible amount of attention.

The resulting state from figuring out that you're living in grace and then using ease to deal with what living in grace brings up is what we've called bliss. Now, the feedback that we've gotten on the word bliss is that it feels unattainable. OK, we can understand that. And because bliss has this strange definition, what does it mean? Is it happy? People didn't really like [the word] bliss, so we decided that serenity was a good word. So, most people now, we're all on the same page. You have this idea of grace, ease, serenity. And you guys have been incredibly good at doing this around consciousness, around judgments and preferences, even around habitual responses. There are certain parts of your life where you're like: "Grace, ease, and bliss—I got it. I got it." Then the mortgage bill comes and grace, ease, and bliss just goes out the window and you're back in victim. So, what we wanted to talk about tonight is the idea of using grace, ease, and bliss around the first chakra—and by first chakra, we're just using that as a catchphrase to encompass the idea of survival. Survival stuff—security, stability, the idea that you're not going to get dead, in essence. The first chakra is where the rubber hits the road. "Am I dead or not? Am I going to get dead or not? Is this likely to get me dead or not?"

What we're recognizing is that you guys have some issue with the ability to be in grace, ease, and bliss around first-chakra issues. So what we want to talk to you guys about is what you can do about that, of course. And one of the things that you can do about it is be aware of it. That's why we're bringing it up, partially, is just to say: By the way, are you recognizing that grace, ease, and bliss is not an overall thing? It can be, but it is a moment-by-moment, stimulus-by-stimulus thing, as well. So when you're in grace, ease, and bliss or you're looking at grace, ease, and bliss around money, bills—survival in general—the first reminder, of course, is to go back to what grace is, which is: "I am not a victim." And that's thing that we've been talking about for the last few weeks, and that's why this comes up, is because we're taking this to a deeper level. At first, we were like: You're a creator. Great. Then we said: And you can't point fingers, too. And it's like: "I guess I really am a creator. If I can't even point fingers then I must've created it." So, the idea of reminding yourself about the state of grace. Reminding yourself about your desire to live gracefully and to be in grace.

So, the bill comes, whatever the bill is, and you're triggered by it and you say, "OK, I have a choice and my choice is to recognize that I am a creator." And as you experience living as a creator, you don't have to have the answer. You don't even have to have the money to pay the bill. You don't even have to have the idea about how to pay the bill. That is all not in this moment. The moment is recognizing your creator aspect in relationship to the bill or the guy runs into you with his car or the dog running through the road—whatever—you created it all. And you don't get to go forward unless you start from that state of grace. That's really the essence of what we're talking about. You don't get to go up the next set of staircases and you actually don't even get to feel good. Because if you feel like a victim you don't feel good anymore. When you guys feel like a victim now, it's like shit. So, grace. The first step is to say, "I created this. I created this. I created this."

Ease. "I'm not alone in interacting with my creation. I'm not alone in interacting with my creation." And this doesn't mean: "I'm not the only one who's stressed out about money." It means: "I have tools. I have insight from my soul. I have the ability to be in the moment. And I also have the wisdom that although right now this feels overwhelming, this is a miniscule part of the vastness of creation." You have perspective. And that's an aspect of ease we haven't really focused on before, but what we want to help you with is perspective. Because as you start to bring more of your soul's perspective in, your human perspective on things is going to be altered and as your human perspective is altered on things, you're going to start seeing how things that in the past felt like a nuclear bomb going off are actually just another piece of sandpaper, just another handhold on the climbing wall of ascension, just another opportunity for you to know yourself more deeply. It's not a disaster. It's an opportunity. And sometimes you have to sell yourself on this, we know. Sometimes you have to be like, "OK, I have to fake it 'til I make it on this one. But the alternative is suffering. And we know how we feel about suffering.

So when you are able to get into the state of grace, recognize "I created this," use your tools, you have a new way of interacting with the world, bliss, serenity—whatever you want to call it. And the main thing we just want to make sure you're conscious of is that this three-step process or this two-step-and-a-result are available to you on individual subjects. It's not just: "Am I in grace?" and then it's on, off. It's not like: "Oh, I realized I'm not a victim," click, never having to think about it again. So, catching yourself, recognizing when you're being a victim, and recognizing when you want to be a victim. Because there's that place in you that says, "I want to be a victim here because I can't figure out how not to be." In the sense of: "I want to be a victim of the fact I have this big bill come in because I can't figure out how to be a creator here." Well, you don't choose to have the answer. You choose to be with the trigger. It's the same thing as short, factual statements. You make a short, factual statement about the truth of now and you see where the truth takes you. The truth doesn't take you to the perceived answer that you thought would fix it and make it go away. The truth takes you to what you're actually learning. And we're not 100 percent sure that has sunk in and is being worked on all the time. So, that's another reminder we wanted to give you.

Grace. You reacquire the state of grace by recognizing that you are creating and the ease and the perspective shift in all of that, that's the work you guys do. And you guys know what that's about. You've done it lots and lots and lots of times. But the temptation is: "Oh God, I did it again," and you feel somehow like you went back to the beginning, like the Visionaries were talking about. If you think you're only supposed to do it once. Right? "I only have to do this once. Grace, ease, bliss—no problem." And then something from your childhood comes up and you're all the way back over here again and you think,

"Wait, I was over there just the other day." So we don't want you to think that it's like Monopoly where you only go around in one direction. Life is not that simple and souls are far more complex than that, too.

So, if you find yourself where you can be in bliss about one thing and you're in victimhood about another, that doesn't mean you're broken is what we really want to sink in. So that you can also not feel like a failure when you have to remind yourself: "I'm a creator." Because part of this thing about: "Oh my God, I'm pointing fingers again, that must mean that I don't realize I'm a creator." No. Just right now, you forgot. Because you have neural pathways telling you you're a victim. You have society telling you you're a victim. And you have habit telling you you're a victim. That's a lot to tend to. And as you're on the stuck-on crunchy bits, that's the place where the elbow grease of: "I am a creator, I have tools that will change my life on this little subject, even though that's the stuck-on crunchy bit." We just don't want you to feel like a failure if you have to go back. Because it's not technically going back. It's just catching more parts up. Like 95 percent of you is going in the direction you want to go and the stuck-on crunchy bits need a little extra spic and span-y stuff. OK? That's important. It's especially alive in you when it comes to first-chakra stuff but for some of you it's especially alive when it comes to heart-chakra stuff, power-chakra stuff. Have to set a boundary? "Oh, shit. I'm a victim." Have to tell someone you love them? "Oh, shit. I'm a victim." Right? It's not just survival issues. But everybody's got bills, so that's a good place to start, but it's in all areas and we really just want to help you to see that it's an unfolding. And when you see a rose open, all the petals are opening but some are on the outside and some are on the inside. Some of these issues are more readily seen and some of them take a little longer to be revealed. OK? Yes? Anybody have a question?

Question: When you said that in ease, when recognizing we're not alone, you're referring to whom?

Eloheim: You're not alone in like: "I am by myself with no help." So it's like the tools, your soul, the fact that you are all One—if you resonate with that. You're not alone in the sense of: "Oh my God, I've had this revelation and there is no support system. There's nothing for me here."

Response: Yeah, I'm not feeling that anymore. You're always saying that souls find everything interesting.

Eloheim: Yeah, they do.

Question: Do they prefer suffering over non-suffering, or as you say, we're all working through the suffering parts and recognizing things that trigger, trigger, trigger. Since everything is interesting, I guess I'm getting to: When is it going to be lying on the beach in Hawaii is interesting?

Eloheim: Well the thing is, is that all of it is interesting to souls, of course, and they're not addicted to watching you guys squirm, but you have to remember that not only is everything interesting to souls but they also have an agenda. You have an agenda. We've called it "checking things off your list" in the past. And you're not a victim of your soul, you're a collaborator, even though you're experiencing the intensity of density. So you get to have the intensity of density but you are part of your soul and you're collaborating, so you're not a victim of it and your souls don't want to just watch you squirm but your souls do want you to attend to the things that you collaboratively decided were good and helpful and fascinating and interesting and needed to be attended to. And a lot of this stuff, as we've talked about before, is carryover from alternative expressions where you didn't tend to it. So, there's a lot on your lists and you've done an amazing amount and you have more and you have the stuck-on crunchy bits where it's the last little roots of the issues that you've dealt with in other ways.

It's not so much as we want to see you squirm as how squirmy do you have to get before you decide you'd rather handle it in a different way? It's an offshoot of "how ridiculous does it have to get?" Are you really still squirming about the bills in the same way you've squirmed about the bills for the last 40 years? When are you going to say, "I'm not going to do it that way anymore," as an example. Some other people are really, really connected to the suffering around their jobs or the suffering around their relationships or the suffering around where they live, and the tension about changing those things is so unbearable to them that they stay in it. Even though they are suffering they stay in it because the idea of changing is so incredibly challenging to them. And that's pretty much what we see with you guys a lot, is the idea of changing is so challenging that you prefer to suffer.

Then you guys will say: "Does my soul want me to suffer?" Well, no, actually your soul would probably have more fun if you changed but your survival instinct, it always comes back to the survival instinct that says, "change is too dangerous." That's why we had to evolve the survival instinct and have tools, so you have options to the default that the survival instinct wants to generate in you. So, the survival instinct says: "Don't change," you say: "Hang on. This relationship is stifling me, this marriage, this job, this whatever, however I handle my bills,"—whatever it is you have going on—"this is stifling me." And the survival instinct says: "But don't change, because that's dangerous." And you say: "Yes, but feeling stifled has its own inherent danger." And then you weigh it out. How ridiculous does it have to get before you say it's worth the risk of change. That's why "how ridiculous does it have to get?" comes along.

Now, that said, it's very interesting if you can instead of having to get it ridiculous say, "I just want to try something else. I've been doing it this way for long enough" is an interesting statement to make. "I've been doing it this way for long enough. The results of doing it this way no longer enchant me." That's an option for you guys. And it doesn't even have to suck for you to make that choice. You can just say, "I've been doing this this long and I'm ready for a change," without having to be forced into changing. Because forcing light workers into changing lights up so many triggers because you get back into that mode of: "I am being persecuted," and then you're a victim again. You see? So, "how ridiculous does it have to get?" has a real hazard in it because how ridiculous does it have to get—you get all this crazy stuff happening then you guys feel forced, and when you feel forced you feel persecuted by authority, you feel in danger of having your head chopped off again, and you feel victimized. So if you let it get really ridiculous chances are you're going to react from a victim mentality instead of seeing that it's getting ridiculous and creating from that place.

That's another aspect of this that comes up. We don't want you all to be victims and we want to help you get out of the places where you're stimulated to be victims and that's one of them. "How ridiculous does it have to get?" pushes you into victim-hood if it goes too far. Or it pushes you into: "I have to get really, really pissed off and be a bitch and then I have to deal with the fact that I was a bitch and I fire-hosed on people."

Response: I've been putting it out there that I'm ready for a change in many areas of my life, and some things have changed and some things haven't. So those things that haven't changed, when I say I'm ready for a change it feels really clear, the feeling is of clarity. What is holding that change from not happening?

Eloheim: Around what subject?

Response: Well, let's use financial.

Eloheim: So, "I'm ready for it to change." That's great to set an intention and it's great to be clear that that's what you want and then you have to, of course, look at the things you have in the way of it changing. And you've done a lot of that work around this subject, of course. But then you also have to look at: "What do I get out of it staying the way it is?" Apparently, that hit a nerve! "What do I get out of it staying the way it is? What do I get out of it staying the way it is?" And it's beyond just comfortable, it's beyond: "This suffering is the suffering I know." It is: "Maybe people won't ask a lot of me if I stay in this position." Last week on the webcast, we talked about people having an equal sign between the idea that if they have a job people will get to tell them what to do. Again, you people do not like to be told what to do. How frequently do we say "we suggest"? We know this about you, right? We suggest you consider thinking about possibly contemplating maybe that this might sort of have something to do with something around the idea of what you think you might be kind of interested in every once in a while. That's the kind of stuff we have to do—and you guys come here willingly.

So, "What am I getting out of it staying the same and why do I believe it can't change? Why do I believe it can't change? What do I think it's going to take to make it change? What is it going to cost me? What is it going to require of me? What are people going to think if it changes?" It's all that static and baggage and preconceived notions. And this is where short, factual statements are going to be your lifeline. "I think x, y, z"—and then sit in it. Again, the short, factual statements don't work unless you sit in what you experience. What you say and then what you experience.

[To new attendees] We're not sure you guys were here for short, factual statements, so we'll just do a quick review. You make a short, factual statement about what is going on. "I don't like the way I'm relating to my money situation" and then you say, "period" because the period is like a little pneumonic thing to tell your brain: "and we're not just going to use the neural pathways we always use for this." It's like a stopping point to the whirling that your mind wants to do when it revisits problems that you've visited ten million times. And then you see what comes up. And the temptation is to want what comes up be the answer to the fact that you have a problem with your money situation, but that's not where we're going. "I have a problem with my money situation, period," and then you see what comes up. And it will be fascinating because chances are you'll get stuff from your childhood, from your partnerships, from your teachers telling you you suck, whatever. And then you attend to what comes up because that's the static between what you wish your life looked like and what your life looks like now. And when you tend to that static, then you magnetize. See, there is nothing keeping what you want from your life but the static that's between you and it. And short, factual statements are very good at helping clear out the static.

You make a short, factual statement and then say, "period" to tell yourself that you're looking for something else here, and then attend to what comes up, no matter what it is. This is kind of like when people flash a Rohrsarch picture and they say, "What's the first thing that comes to your mind?" Short, factual statements are a little bit like that. Because it's saying: "Here's a statement. What's the first thing that comes to your mind?" Because that first thing that comes to your mind is a clue to what is actually active in the dynamic of the thing you're desiring.

That tool is not being used enough. We can guarantee you that. Because it's good. And it's an advanced tool, so it's right at the right stage for you guys to be using it. And it's a tool that says: "I'm a creator," because it's a tool of responsibility. When you make a short, factual statement and you see the static and you attend to it, that's creator stuff there. So, you can sit back and say, "Oh God, my money situation," or you can say, "This is how I'm feeling," and then attend to what's in between. And that's really, really, really an underutilized tool. Guaranteed. You know how we know? Because you guys don't come and say: "I did short, factual statements and this is what happened," very often. So we know it's underutilized because we know how powerful it is energetically. If it were getting used a lot, you guys would be reporting it more. Right? Busted.

Hey, we've got checks and balances. We have our ways. We have our ways of knowing what you do. And it's easy to forget because it's an advanced tool and because it really is where the rubber meets the road about "I'm a creator." Because when you say, "I've got this problem and instead of re-thinking again about the solutions that haven't worked, I'm going to let myself see what's really going on," this is grown-up stuff. You can feel that. And you're big grown-ups now, so guess what? And you're getting the crunchy stuck-on bits—and the crunchy stuck-on bits, short, factual statements is a really good scouring pad. Honestly. So let's have, maybe, we won't call it homework because we don't want to trigger everybody, but let's have a collective consideration of potentially agreeing that next week we go around the circle and talk about maybe a short, factual statement experience you had.

Response: No. [group laughter]

Eloheim: That's very short and factual!

Response: I don't like it because it triggers my mental thinking. But can I say something else?

Eloheim: First, we have to attend to what you just said: You don't like it because it triggers your mental thinking—but see, that's the static. So the short, factual statement is x, y, z and then you think, "Oh my God, now I'm thinking about it." Well, there's your next short, factual statement. "I don't like that this triggers my thinking." So you just keep going and eventually you'll get to what's underneath that. It won't take that long.

Response: I have to think of the short, factual statement without all the other periphery that makes me think, and I'm not supposed to do that.

Eloheim: Well, you think of the short, factual statement and then you let go of the thinking. We know this is a place where you're working but still, you have to describe the state you're in and you have thoughts about the state you're in. Maybe it would be interesting for you to feel about the state you're in. So, making a short, factual statement about: "I feel" is OK, too. It doesn't just have to be "I think." "I feel." For you that's probably better because it's not as triggering of the place where you're doing a lot of work.

Response: I had an opportunity to do that when I was busted on Sunday. I know that in my history, if I get hurt the first place to go is to anger. I had an opportunity to be hurt on Sunday, so I watched myself go through the dance between wanting to be angry. First, it was: how do I feel about that? Well, I feel kind of vulnerable and hurt. Then I could feel it creeping up, my anger. I just kept watching the anger. I realized I just wanted to be angry because it was easier. It's just a habit. But it was pretty cool to just watch it.

Eloheim: That's great. And that's like what we used to say: That emotion is a jacket, don't put it on. You have a row of jackets hanging on pegs by the front door and [one of them] is anger. "Am I going to put it on or not?" And if you do, take it off. And yeah, OK, you're angry, but like you were realizing, what's really going on? Anger is happening but is that just a container for a whole bunch of feelings that you don't want to look at? Is it just a container, is it a habit, is it a default reaction, is it neural-pathway ingrained? And most of the time those strong kinds of emotional states can very well be these default places where you've always put it. Like you very eloquently explained. So, watching your emotional state. And of course, that's consciousness. Watching the emotional state is being conscious. So you're creating more consciousness, not creating more of the emotional state. Interesting. And you got angry because of what happened at the meeting or the temptation to anger was because of what happened at the meeting?

Response: I got my feelings hurt. But it really was nothing. It was just an opportunity to practice.

Comment: I think I'm a little bit where Mary is with the short, factual statements. It's a little bit difficult for me to put things into words, too. I'm more of a feeling person and instead of having words I have concepts and so to go for the words I'm

out of the concept and I oftentimes have a hard time expressing myself because I conceptualize more than I think in terms
of sentences. Feelings would be good. Up until fairly recently, I didn't have very many triggers, so when I did get them,
saying: "Yes, period." Saying yes to the concept and period just
stopped everything. Or if it was a little more complicated I
would say, "This really doesn't matter," and then that's kind of
a laughing thing because none of it really matters. So it lightens
everything up.

Eloheim: So, instead of having a short, factual statement that
had words, you had a short, factual statement that had an
emotional quality to it, but it's doing the same thing, which
is acknowledging what's really going on and then seeing where
that acknowledgment takes you. Because that's really what the
purpose of short, factual statements is. Instead of just hamster-
wheel-mind thinking, thinking, thinking and running off to
the past or the future, it's staying in the moment with what is
going on with you. And if that needs to be done from an emotional perspective that's perfectly fine, too.

Comment: That would really help me.

Eloheim: Good. So there's your alternate version.

Question: Can we ask the Guardians to take all those coats in
the closet, to take them to Goodwill?

Eloheim: You can ask the Guardians to scrape away anything
that you're ready to release. You may be able to release the temptation to anger that, like for your example, you may be able to
release the temptation to anger that you experienced in that
moment, but the Guardians can't come and take anger away
completely, but they can facilitate you releasing that temptation
in the moment. Because you can't just make anger go away. You
transform your relationship to it. And every once in a while,
anger is probably a good thing to have around. It's just if it's
habitual it's not necessarily going to support you, and that's
true for just about everything except breathing. We like you to

be habitual about breathing and heart-beating. Biological functions of that nature are allowed to be habitual. Other than that, habitual behaviors need to be examined. Biological habituation is a positive thing most of the time.

We are allowed to be habitual about the order of the Council at this time. We're consciously habitual about that, just so you know, because we absolutely do not need to make it any harder.

[Turning their attention to Veronica's clothing] This shirt has these things, the pants have these things and every time we move they get stuck between things and it's bothering us! Veronica doesn't get a vote. She knows about the shorts thing. Those of you who don't know, why do you let your legs stick to things? It's awful. We have an awful feeling when that happens. We know we're not supposed to be judgmental and all that and we have joy about chocolate and stuff, but that's a nonrepeater. We would have put our foot down. How ridiculous does it have to get? One of those [scrunch—leg peeling off a chair]—it's over. You people are crazy letting that happen to your leg. There's so many things you could do in this world and that's one of them? We are not into it. We made that clear two years ago. "What the hell! You're going to wear that? No." That sound—and it feels nasty. We like this chair because it has arms, so we're not trading it in. OK. We don't like these strings. We're not going to complain about her clothes anymore. Having a physical body is weird and those strings are making it weirder.

The Girls

What's funny to us is that Eloheim has had so much exposure to the physical body that they can actually bitch about it. Like, seriously? You actually have enough time and practice and experience that you get to have opinions about it? We are still like: "Oh, it's all so fun," and they're like, "Ugh, look at these straps." And we're like: "Oh, let's see what it feels like to wear a skirt," and they're like: "No, you'll hate it." This is a little bit how you guys are when you're thinking of planning an incarnation. "Oh, I want to try it blind." "No." "Yes, I do, I do." You get down here and you're like, "Oh, why did I do this?" So, Eloheim's had enough practice being with Veronica that they're making wardrobe decisions. That's funny. For us, we're just happy to be here and we're happy because it always feels like slumber-party energy and at slumber parties what do you do? You wear goofy clothes and you put silly stuff on your face and you be goofy and you talk about boys. So, let's talk about Eloheim!

Anyway, did we have any sort of thing we specifically wanted to tell you guys about tonight? You know it's going to be some version of "be nice to yourself." We're kind of getting into a rut with that. Let's see if there's something else that would be good. Well, let's just kind of riff on Eloheim's thing. During that segue, part of what they're saying is it doesn't feel comfortable to have this string stuck underneath the leg when we're trying to talk. And part of what that is, is being aware—aware of what you're feeling in your body, aware of what's going on around you, aware of what you're experiencing. On some level, it's kind of being conscious and figuring it out and saying, "Yeah, I don't really feel comfortable here. Yeah, I really don't feel comfortable here." And you're really allowed to make those kind of statements.

You're allowed to say, "I don't feel comfortable here." You're allowed to set that boundary. You're allowed to have a preference. You're allowed to say, "This isn't right for me. This isn't right for me." And you don't have to be cranky and bitchy about it. You're allowed to say, "This isn't right for me," and set a boundary without having to, in essence, work yourself up into a tizzy to do it. You can just say "No. No, this doesn't work for me. I'm not into it. I don't like it." Without having to justify your position. And many of you are used to not standing up to someone unless you really have justification for it. You don't change things in your life unless you really have the justification for it.

You expect to be considered flighty or flaky if you say, "I'm just going to quit my job because I want to try something else." The "I just want to try something else" is your God-given right as a breathing being. "I just want to try something else. I just want to try something else." Without having to have gotten worked up, have the justification, or have a long-range plan, you're allowed to say, "I just want to try something else." And what's nice is when you can say, "I just want to try something else," without your whole life having to turn to shit first. The "how ridiculous does it have to get?" that was referred to earlier in the meeting. Everything doesn't have to turn to shit for you to say, "and I'm ready for something else now." But there is that clinging-ness, there's that sense of lack, there's that sense of: "I've got to somehow make it work out because it's good" that holds you in situations sometimes longer than you want to be there and sometimes has to generate ridiculousness as you create.

You're creating, you're creating, you're creating situations to free yourself from the dynamic because you're ready to try something else rather than just letting yourself try something else without having to create a bunch of static first. And the problem is sometimes when you have to create ridiculousness in order to help you transform and get out of situations you're in that ridiculous then generates more stuff for you to attend to. It's kind of like when you get upset and you fire hose on people and then you have to go around repairing those relationships or being conscious or dealing with the triggers that that generates etc. etc. When you require situations to become ridiculous before you transform them it creates more stuff for you to manage. You can see that, we hope. So there's a place where you can just say I'm just done. I'm just done without it having to be crazy. And that's a kindness. And that's what we would like to invite you to do is to be kind to yourselves by letting yourself off the how ridiculous does it have to get hook and put yourself into the I'm just ready for something different place. I'm just ready for something different. I'm just ready for something different. And you don't have to know what the different is. Going into I'm just ready for something different allows you to open the door to different coming in. So I'm willing to experience something different that allows me to be my complete self and live from my soul's perspective, have fun, or whatever it is you're interested in doing different. OK? So there you are.

Eloheim, part 2

You know you all came for the Warrior's story anyway. Don't try to hide it. There was that whole thing for a while there it was all we just came for the Girls really. Now that the Warrior has this hook and he's telling this big long fairy tale, midnight story thing. Everyone's like, is it time yet? Is it time yet? Tuck me in. I want milk. So the Warrior is going to see the King and he's taking you with him. We dig that dude. We're really glad that you guys had so much warrior lifetime energy to deal with that we had to bring him into the Council to help you with it because there's something distinctly entertaining about his story and his way of being.

Warrior

So, where were we? Off to see the King. We had arrived, though, hadn't we, at the castle. It's always such a joke. You roll up at the castle, as you guys might call it. We tend to ride horses. You get to the castle and all the people there, if you ever had any sort of—oh gosh, how would we say it in your terms?—if you thought other people could tell you who you were, rolling up at the castle or maybe at the red carpet at some fancy event, similar kind of thing, all the people are there deciding who you are for you. It's not such a good idea to let them. They can have their own opinions about it but don't take their opinions as your own. You know who you are. That's the beauty of this entire process. This entire story is all to help you know who you are, so don't bail out in the middle here as soon as you roll up to the castle with everyone taking pictures of you telling you you're wonderful. And in your world they take pictures and they want you to sign autographs and ridiculous, ridiculous, ridiculous.

In our world the women give us that look, the men are jealous, for the most part, or afraid, the guards try not to pay so much attention because they're trying to be cool—and we get off the horses and there we go. Always make eye contact with the kid that takes your horse. One, you want to know which one took your horse. Two, you want him to know you know he took your horse, if you know what we mean. We're not sure you have to do this with valets but we think it's probably a good idea, anyway. You want to know who has your ride, as it's said. Those little stable boys are pretty smart, too, so you want to know which one has your horse but you also want to see what kind of a man he might be. We're always on the lookout for new talent. The nice thing about stable boys, they tend to know what's going on, too. Sometimes you can get a little bit of information that is helpful to your cause. Pay attention to everyone. You never know who you might like to talk to again. You've made eye contact with them, they tend to remember you. That and the fact that you outweigh him by 250 pounds. So, off to see the King.

Now, it's really fun to see the King when you stink. Don't let the king's people try to give you a bath before you see the King because it's really fun to watch the King try not to sniff while you're there. We're telling you all the good bits. No one else tells you this stuff, do they? No. So when you go see the king, make sure you're smelly and it's good if you have mud that drops about and things. It's good. Why? Because what you want the king to know is that you are not just a little pawn in his game to be manipulated to his benefit, but that you are a person that comes from a society that has values and comes from a culture and a community and tribe and you come into his domain but you do not get converted into him or one like him. Not to say necessarily that being like the King is a bad thing but it is to say that you want to take the authenticity of you into every encounter. And the authenticity that we present is that we are of the earth and we are of the forest and that we are of the roughness of the world, and to go in front of the king in cleaned-up clothes without our sharp implements would be ridiculous and it would also strip away the truth of who we are. So we recommend that when you go to see the king you take who you are with you, and if that means you drop mud on this perfect floor, well, there you are. You understand? This is very important.

When you go to see the King the thing you have to remember, as well, is that most likely—if you're us, of course, now some other people maybe this doesn't happen to but we can only speak from our experience—the King is very afraid of you and doesn't want you to know it. And you don't get to where we've gotten without knowing when a man is afraid or not. So don't let the fact that the King—or in your world, whomever you're encountering, the authority figure that you're encountering—don't let their response to you tell you who you are, either. Every once in a while, you get a king who thinks he's a badass. In our experience, not all of them are. But every once in a while, you get the experience of one that is a badass. Those are the good ones. But when you encounter a king who just thinks he's a badass and he doesn't actually get afraid of you, those are the ones you don't want to work for. Why? Because he's not showing you his true nature. We would rather work for a King who's afraid than work for one who's trying to pretend he's not. When you are encountering people who know who they are and present themselves authentically—whether it's a king or a boss or a baker—you can trust the exchange to be high-vibrational or at least conscious or at least not generating more static. So, when you go to see the King, whoever the king is in your world, if you show up authentically you've done your part to contribute to a conscious conversation. If they don't do their half, well, that's something very, very important to know immediately. And occasionally is worth the journey.

In this case, in this time, in this example, in this story of going to see the King, we've got a good one here, although a good king is not necessarily the highest type of person on our list. But in this case, we have a story about a king that we were relatively pleased to go see. We'd had good relations with this one before. Keeps his word. He doesn't get all pissy that we bring our truth, which means mud, into his hall. He doesn't require a whole bunch of bowing and scraping in order to not feel afraid of us. When they ask you to go against your nature in order for them to be comfortable, you should be wary. Whoever it is you're dealing with. If they do not like to be around your true self, you want to know that. The only way you'll know it is if you take your true self into the encounter. Did you hear those words? This is important stuff all mixed into a fairytale but it's still important. All right. So, off you go. Here's the king. This king is the kind of king who says, "Oh, we're happy to see you and your men and we want you well fed," and doesn't make any comments about the fact that he also hopes that we take a bath or two. And he sends the men off to be entertained and fed and he wants to speak to us alone. This is a good king. Do you know how you know? Because he doesn't need to grandstand in front of all in order to feel secure in himself. He doesn't need everyone to see his authority in order to feel that he has authority in the dynamic and he wants to sit down and look eye-to-eye and discuss something rather than just dispense orders. You want to be like this king in this way.

So, we go and we sit with the king in this little side area he has there and his nice women bring us nice food and because we know this hall, we have already sent our lieutenant around to, let's just say, remove the one spying on the side there. You can imagine hearing the sounds of a little scuffle off to the side and the king gives a wry little smile because one, he didn't know you knew about that spot and two, he knows he's called the right person. Why? Because he sees that we're aware of our environment. When you bring your complete self to an exchange, you need to also be aware of the environment you're in. As you bring your complete self, you expand into and start to incorporate more of the world you walk in. Your complete self has the ability to experience more without triggering the survival instinct. The complete self has the ability to experience more because it's why it's here. The narrow self wants the world to be narrow so that the threats are limited. That's what the survival instincts says. The complete self starts to expand into a greater picture, so as you experience life from you as your complete self you're going to experience more of your surroundings, too. This will be a beautiful exploration for you.

Anyway, what does the King want? We know you all want to know what the king wants. The king says that some folks are coming for a visit. Some neighboring-kingdom folks are coming for a visit. They're going to come in a boat. And when they arrive on the shore of his land, he would like to have a show of muscle be present beside him. Now, of course, the King has all kinds of soldiers and men that ride horses and this, that, and the other thing. But the king knows that this other group of people respect men of character. And the king knows that this other group of people are going to be pleased to see a reflection of themselves present in his kingdom. Because the king knows that his court is like the courts of all kingdoms. More about the politics and the presentation than about the presence. So he would like us to sort of stand next to him and be authentic. What do you call it? Emanate your true self.

Well now, this is what we call an easy job. And we'll do this for this king on one condition. We'll do this for the King on the condition that the King also emanates his complete self. Because we don't get into agreements that are half-assed. If the king wants us to be true then we're asking the king to show up with truth, as well. Now, this is challenging because he wants to play politics and he was hoping he could slough off the job of being the complete self to someone else. You can't give away that job and that's the moral of this section of our story. You can't give away the job of being your complete self. You can't hope that somehow hanging out with people who are like that or imagining that you are that way. There's nothing that substitutes for being your authentic self. And we don't suggest trying to be it sometimes and not trying to be it other times. The king can look us in the eye in this moment, but he doesn't want to take that truth of him into this encounter—even knowing that the other people value that kind of honesty. Why? Because of vulnerability. Which you covered last week. It feels weak to be that exposed but we know that that's the only place of true strength is when you're vulnerable enough to be the truth of you. So, we say we'll stand beside the king but we won't put up with any petty bullshit. We will walk at the first sign that he's using us, in essence, to give him street-cred. Because an easy job is easy, but a job that compromises who we are is not worth it—and that's another thing for you to take with you. Compromising who you are is never worth it. It never pays. It never turns out. And it's hard on the physical body.

The King is afraid of us because we will come as our true selves and the king honors us because we come as our true selves, and neither one of those states of being influences us much. It's nice to sleep in his hall and to eat his good food and to look at his beautiful women and, yes, to occasionally take a bath. But none of that can be done under the guise of the King telling us who we are. It is us being true to us in his hall. And this is how you go out into your workplace, primarily, is you go out into your workplace and you are yourself in their hall. They do not tell you who you are.

Now, the next installment of our story, we'll be meeting the neighbors on the beach. There may be wrestling and games of chance. What good is it to meet the neighbors unless you can test yourself and you can win their money? Right? Tune in next week for wrestling and games of chance, and we'll just see where it takes us then. So, the moral of the story? You are your true self regardless of your circumstance and you do not let others, no matter how much they would ply you with compliments and beautiful women, tell you who you are. Knowing who you are and emanating your complete self is the fabric of your being. And releasing that truth to anyone else's power is slavery. Energetic slavery. And the only one holding those bonds on you in that energetic slavery is you. You have the key. You have the key and you have the bonds and you make the choice. And that's that. OK. Goodnight. We will go to the beach.

Fred

There was a time when you didn't know. There was a time when you didn't know anything. There was a time when you were formless. There was a time when you were just part of something that didn't require knowing or not knowing. There was a time when you were just "is." And your "is" state was transformed. You were birthed. You were birthed as a soul and created. Created an opportunity for you to experience. Created an opportunity for you to know something beyond the void, let's call it. Not devoid of but just devoid. A place where there was not change. Let's call it that. You were in a place where there was not change and you moved into a place where there was possibility. And you moved through possibility and have moved through possibility for a countless number of what you would call years and you are doing the dance of possibilities now. This is who you are. You are a soul doing the dance of possibilities and the exploration of all that is.

You went from being "is," to the exploration of "all that is." You went from a passive state of existence into an active state of existence. You went looking. You went looking and you find and you find and you find and you find and you find. And some of the things you find are so uncomfortable and some of the things you find are so delightful and many of the things you find are just sort of boring. But you are an infinite soul experiencing the movement of creation. And we would hope that somewhere in all that you would find the ability to find it all. To find it all fascinating. To find it all possible. To find it all marvelous. To find it all the opportunity you've been given. Every time it feels hard, we hope that at some point you'll be able to say, "but it's also magnificent." At least let those be simultaneously experienced. Hard and magnificent. This is our wish for you.

When you were in the place of all that is and you were in passivity you never imagined it would be different and now that you're in the place of active exploration, it's never the same. We hope that you will hold this precious opportunity in you and let that realization of precious opportunity have airtime in you in addition to the exploration of frustration and anxiety and fear and doubt and all the other things that seem to consume so much of your time. There's a marvelous, precious intensity here that is overlooked so frequently. Your beautiful creation continues to unfold and it is your choice how you wish to know it. You are all that is and is that all. It's so difficult to put into words that you can understand. But there is an invitation. There is an invitation that even in the challenge of it you find the wondrousness. We hope that you're able to give this a shot.

Matriarch

As always, we always just picture this giant white space that curves up on the sides. It's not unlike what we would imagine it would be if you were very small inside Richard's bowl [a crystal bowl played at the beginning of the meeting], but there's more light. And we always just feel this space that you all can infuse your energy into, let's just use that terminology, and this space extends under your feet and up behind you. What we like to do is just send our energy into this vessel so that it circulates, emanates, and embraces you and holds you in what is going on energetically. And really, tonight, we just want to permeate the energetic of your physical form with again this idea of possibility that's been talked about and the idea of perspective. Possibility and perspective.

When you look out at the sky at night and you see all the stars it's easy for you to have the perspective of, "Wow I'm pretty small compared to all of that." But it also, we hope, is amazing to think of the possibilities that exist out there. And we'd like very much for you to have this balance between possibility and perspective where the idea of all the possibilities that exist infuses you and the perspective that the things that are stumbling blocks or challenges or triggers have the proper perspective. We know they feel immense and impossible sometimes, but when you take in the scope of the universe and you take in the scope of all of the expressions you've had, not just as Homo sapiens but all of the expressions your soul has done, that perspective coupled with the possibilities that you can perceive, we hope that empowers you to attend to things that challenge you and empowers you to feel the sense of the scope of your existence. You are not just the limited little being that your survival instinct would like to keep you as. You are a vast, amazing, immortal, energy-force-entity being, love, that was generated in order to explore. And every experience you have is another opportunity for you to explore. Another opportunity for you to fulfill your soul's strongest desire. We invite you to use possibilities and perspectives to support the journey you're on and we thank you for giving us the opportunity to share that concept with you. Goodnight to you all.

July 28, 2010

Summary

Guardians: Brought the group into the moment using the Big toe, left elbow tool.

Visionaries: You are responsible for your reactions to your creations. You create all of your reality, and you are responsible for your reactions to everything you create.

Eloheim: Told a story about going to a concert and being overwhelmed by all the input, then finding relief in choosing what to focus on. Also heard examples of and answered questions about where we find equal signs in our lives.

The Girls: Talked about biological-family relationships and setting boundaries.

Warrior: Continued his story of going to see the king. Accompanying the king to the shore to meet the neighbors, and the games that followed. They advise: The greatest gift you can give to yourself is to be consistent regardless of the circumstances you find yourself in. This doesn't mean the same, this means consistent, whether you're the victor or the vanquished you still act the same. Being the truth of yourself in any situation.

Fred: We are at a choice point. And the choice is to come out of the belief that things happen to us, and to move into the belief that we are the ones making things happen. And then to choose our reactions to our creations.

Matriarch: The entire Council is here to support us in our journey as we walk the path of choosing our reactions to our creations, which brings us toward ascension.

Guardians

Bring it in. Let's be in this moment now, this exact moment. Check in with your big toe, check in with your left elbow, check in with the back of your head. Check in with whatever it requires to be in this moment. Come forward into this moment. Bring the completeness of you into this moment. Bring all of you into this moment. Be present now. Be present now. Be present right here and right now.

The most you can do for this environment, this circle, this world, this life, is to be present in this moment. Bringing that attention into this space is what gives you the opportunity to be who you are. To emanate the truth of you, and to express the completeness of all that you have to offer. Excellent. Well done.

Visionaries

There comes a time when you approach life, there comes a time when you approach even the moment, there comes a time when you recognize that the intensity of density, the intensity of the experience of the Homo sapiens perspective, the intensity of duality, the intensity of this opportunity to be physical, all has actually served you.

For a very, very, very long time, you've resisted, shall we say, argued with, fought with, been stubborn about, the idea that you actually created all this. Even when you buy into the idea that you create your reality, you still argue about the fact that you create the shit you find yourself in. You argue with the idea that you actually create the things you feel uncomfortable about. It's true. No matter how advanced you are, no matter how high-vibrational you've been able to become, there've been aspects of your life that you argue about creating.

The stiffness that you feel in the mornings, the sleeplessness you feel at night, the way your partner reacts to a simple comment that you make. The idea that the gophers ate your garden. There are things in your life that you're currently arguing about.

Arguing about whether or not they are being created by you. And you don't realize you're arguing about it. And we are going to keep talking about this until we sense a shift. Every single thing—you created it. Every single fear, every single anxiety, every single incident, every single accident, every single breath, every single movement—you've created it all. All of it.

And more importantly even than that, more importantly even than the fact that you created it, now, your focus is that you're also choosing your reaction to your creation. And that's really the most important thing we have to talk to you about tonight. You are choosing your reaction to your creation. You are choosing your reaction to your creation. And when you buy into the idea that every single thing in your life is your creation, then the idea that you are choosing your reaction to every single thing in your life starts to become your number one responsibility. And we've talked about "no pointing fingers" as a way to illuminate this to you, and various other ways: "What is true now? Where am I lying to myself?" And all those nice tools are really, really helpful, but the rubber meets the road at the point that you are choosing the reaction you have to every single experience in your life. All of it. And that is where you have to really pull yourselves up by your bootstraps, people.

Because you're also enmeshed in your core shit right now. Everyone we're talking to, all the energy we're tapping into. Everyone has come around on the peeling of the onion again. And here we are back at "go" and it feels like you're starting over, and the reality is you're just having another go around at the core shit. The stuff that you have re-queued, the stuff that you have skipped over, the stuff that you said, "I can't handle it," time and time again. It's all piled up in your face right now, giving you the opportunity to compare you to you by saying, "I am responsible for this creation," and more importantly, "I am responsible for my reaction to my creation."

I am 100 percent responsible for my reaction to my creation, regardless of how insignificant, small, minor, it seems to be. Everything is here for me to learn from and I am responsible for my reaction to it. Even if you can't buy into: "I create my reality." Now, most of you here are able to buy into that. Even if for some reason, you don't want to buy into: "I create my reality," then buy into: "I choose my reaction to this experience I'm having." You can almost skip over: "I create my reality," and go straight to: "I'm responsible for my reactions," if you want to. But it's not actually true, so we'd like to keep "I create my reality" in the picture. But now, the focus is: "and I am responsible for my reactions to my creation. I am responsible for my reactions to my creation." That's one of the most conscious things you can say right now. And we'd recommend strongly that you write that down and stick it on your bathroom mirror. Because you are responsible for the reactions to your creations.

Before the meeting started, you were all having a bit of a talk about money and finances and jobs and work, and feeling stressed about it being whatever's going on. And astrology's happening and all these things are very nice creations. And you are responsible for your reactions to your creations. You're also responsible to set boundaries, state preferences, tell the truth about your creations, and to make sure that all that the creation does, is elicit more of the authenticity of you to be shared. Your creation elicits more of the authenticity of you to be shared. Your creation elicits more of the truth of you to be shared. That's the gift of your creation. The gift of your creation allows you to then choose your reaction, which lets you share the truth of you. This is how you go about emanating the truth of you in the world. By choosing reactions to your creations. Again, the way the truth of you is emanated in the world is through your choices about how you react to your creation. And if you can't take responsibility for your creations, at least take responsibility for how you react to the situations you experience in your life.

We don't know how to say it more plainly, but you need to hear it again and again because it hasn't sunk in yet, to take responsibility on that level. You haven't been taking responsibility on that level all the time. Sometimes, here and there, occasionally. Maybe even consistently, but not constantly. Because what's happened is that you have a conjunction between your core shit and a deeper sense of responsibility about your interaction with your life. There's a Mars-Venus-Pluto-square-eclipse thing for you.

We called you off the landing and invited you to walk up the next set of stairs by saying to you: You can't point fingers anymore. At the same time that everything was circling around that you were going through your core shit again. It's a good thing you're over-achieving light workers, or you might just quit. So yes, whatever your core thing is—you know what it is—whatever it is, it's up. And it can feel very much like, "I haven't made any progress. Here I am back in this same shit again."

And the truth of the matter is that now is the time to compare you to you. And recognize, "Yes, I'm in it again but I'm not in it the same. And yes, I'm in it again but I have the ability to make new choices about my reactions to it. And by choosing differently, my reactions to it, I choose how I emanate in this world." That's how your emanation experiences. That's how you are putting yourself into this world, is by the choices you make in reaction to the experiences you find yourself in. And as you emanate the truth of you into this world, you are showing the world there are options to habitual response. There are options to societal-based reactions. There are options to survival instinct–based reactions. You are offering the world that, by making choices about your creation. And that's just the way it is, folks. That's where you are. That's what you're in.

"I am responsible for my choices about my reactions. I choose my reaction to my creation. I choose my reaction to my creation. And, I created it all. Because it's all here for me." And remember, again, we have to reiterate: When something occurs, you're not wanting it to be somehow different. You're not saying, "I wish it was some other way." What you're saying is, "What is here right now is here on purpose. There's a reason. It's here because it needs to be here."

When you have a wood sculpture and you rub it with the sandpaper, you rub the sandpaper in just the right spot, at just the right speed to get the desired effect. Now, if you said, "Why is the sandpaper here?" and acted like the sandpaper was somehow in an inappropriate place, you'd never get the refining of the sculpture, and this is what you're doing. You cannot refine your existence without addressing these things that are in your lap.

What is in your life is in your life for a reason. Because you and your soul conspired to create it to give you the opportunity to interact with it. And as you interact with it, you make the choice of your reaction to it, and the choice of your reaction allows you to emanate a new you. And as you emanate a new you, you can compare you to you over time, and you can sense progress. And eventually, that movement, those changes, allow you to create healthy patterns rather than habitual responses in you. And as you do that, you move toward ascension, you raise your vibration, you become more conscious, you connect more deeply with your soul's perspective, and you allow yourself to start living from a position of Homo spiritus. And that's really what the hell's going on, just in case anyone had lost track. That's all we have for you tonight. You're welcome. Now go do it, all right?

Eloheim

Well, there's some vintage Visionaries for you. They haven't come around and kicked ass like that in some time. It's like the old days. They've been kind of mellow recently. OK, making eye contact now… That's interesting—who's in the big black chair tonight? Someone's sitting there, but we don't see a body. Who is telecommuting? We're not sure who it is. We're tele-communing…ha…aren't we clever! We're tele-communing. That's funny.

Tonight, we get to tell a story on ourselves. Doesn't happen every week, but it's only fair because we're always telling stories on Veronica, so it's only fair we tell a story on ourselves. Totally busted. So the other day, Veronica took herself off to a concert, and it was Richard's suggestion that we be Veronica's date at the concert. She was going by herself and thought it was a good idea. So, she rolls into the concert and she invites us in to observe the concert. She puts down a boundary, she said, "You can come in and watch the concert with me but you've got to watch it in a way that I actually get to watch it, too. I'm not saying it's your concert now, we're going to time-share the space a little."

So we said: Oh yeah, cool, concert. Never been to a concert before. We came in and went, "Arrghhh!" That's sort of what it sounded like, because there's laser beams and lights and people screaming and the music. Let's just say we had a little bit of sensory overload going on. And the question we asked is: How do you do it? So tonight, we come forward to say we have a better sense of what it must be like to be human, and we understand it can be challenging and we have a better sense of how challenging it can be. We also see more clearly why you guys don't pay attention to a lot of stuff. Because if you did, it would probably feel like that all the time, right? So, we understand a bit more about that and we had to tell the truth about that.

In the moment, we found it very overwhelming and Veronica said, "Look, just focus on the singer. Just connect with the singer and let everything else go." So that's what we did. That was OK, we could do that. So, now we know now why you guys, in essence, have… like those blinders you put on horses, why that's going on. We can see more why, when we say: Color with all the crayons, and you guys go, "I don't want to." We can understand why you would feel, if you open it all, it all might come rushing in.

Now, not that all of that gives you a free pass not to do it anymore. But there is a sense in us now that we have a better idea of what you're dealing with. But we also want to say that even when you're dealing with that, and even though that's very intense and it's a lot of stimulus, again, Veronica gave us the out by saying, in essence, "Choose. Make a choice about what you want to focus on." And the Visionaries very clearly expressed, how, choosing your reaction.... Even in a very stimulating environment, you can make a choice. And along with that story, we just want to reiterate, as you make a choice in that very stimulating environment, don't make the habitual choice. OK, we get that it's very stimulating but we also get that what you've done year after year after year, is make the habitual choice. What that habitual choice has done is make you believe there's only one color in the crayon box. So yes, don't color with all 64 tomorrow, because you probably would break. But be sure you're asking, "Is there more here?"

It would be like going to the concert, seeing the singer, and only seeing the singer. And kind of having a sense, "Maybe something else is going on," but if you don't have that, "maybe something else is going on," you're missing the dancers, you're missing the laser show, you're missing the lights. So, when we came in we took it all in and it was too much, but what you guys do is, probably as a survival instinct, we get it, what you guys do is you're only seeing the singer.

And we're trying to find where you could—not open up all the way, because that would probably be overwhelming—but you can be curious to see if there's anything else on the stage. Curious to see if there's anything else going on. Open about being curious about the possibilities. OK? That's just what we want to reiterate. We're not asking you to blow your circuits wide open. But we are saying, wow, there's more stuff going on here than what you've previously let yourself experience. We don't want you to continue to habituate toward that narrow line.

Plus, we're not sure how you manage it. But that's OK, it's not our job to manage the body, thank God, because we're not sure how you guys do it. It's taken a lot of practice, and it's taken a lot of practice moving through a number of incarnations that were not as stimulating as this one. This is a very stimulating incarnation... you've got TV, you've got driving cars, you've got the Internet, you've got lots and lots and lots of people. That's a lot of stimulus, and that's very different from a lifetime where you live in a village and there are 30 people and you know every single one of them your whole life. The most important thing was how many lambs did we get this year, as opposed to going on the Internet, building websites, doing online banking, there's a lot going on in your lives. Your lives are very, very full of stimulus.

Are you OK, Mary? Mary's just laughing her ass off.

Response: I'm doing the fortune cookie thing, adding, "while you're driving," to the end of every single one of the examples you just gave. [group laughter]

Eloheim: Veronica's reminding us that's what you do with the fortune cookie, and at the end you add, "in bed." And it makes them more fun.

Back to the story, now. You live in an extremely stimulating time and you also have strong desires for it to be even more stimulating. You want your psychic powers, you want your teleportation, you want ascension, you want, you want—you guys even do lucid dreaming! Like you don't even give yourselves a break when you're sleeping, right? This is what you guys are all into. Yes, you live in a very stimulating time. But you also live in a very habitual time. OK? That's what, again, want to illuminate to you. In a very stimulating world, you live in an habitual way. So, try not to do that, is kind of what we've been talking about for eight years. Try not to do that, because the temptation is to say, "All of this is too much, so I'm only going to do this." And then "this" never changes. And "this" tends to be fear-based because it's survival instinct. Everybody knows about that. So, we got to see what it's like, a little bit more, in the human body. Wow! And we also got to see where you guys could keep navigating.

Question: We were supposed to do the equal signs thing. Equal signs are so slippery. About the closest I can get to them, except when I'm watching somebody else, is a little bit in retrospect, kind of get a sense of something going on there. But it's really, really slippery and thin.

 I had a client today who was doubting my ability, and I started to go to: That's right, I can't fix it, I'm wrong. And then I just heard The Warrior saying: "Hey! Don't let her tell you who you are!" I went from being really irritable, it changed the whole thing—her attitude toward me changed and it was all good. It switched. It seems that's what happens when you get conscious about something. It switches.

Eloheim: The energy can switch very, very quickly. Part of the reason it can change very, very quickly is that, one, you've changed, you're emanating a different state. But remember, you're also creating a different reality to the one you're in. So if you're creating from freak-out, you're going to more likely create freak-out. If you're creating from the well-rounded place, from that Warrior place, you're more likely to create more of that.

Response: Yeah. It's no big mystery why it happens. It makes sense.

Eloheim: Well, it can make sense, which is probably comforting to most of you because you tend to have a brain and it is still a mystery. It's a mystery because just like, how does your food digest? We could tell you biologically, but it's still a mystery because so much happens on a molecular level. That's the magic and the mystery and the wonder of it. Let it stay in that realm of "Wow!" because once you think, "Oh, I understand it," it puts a box on it. So, allow it to still be kind of mysterious, but you can start to understand the underlying mechanism.

There's an underlying mechanism in kind of: How it all comes out is the beauty of it.

It's more like a painting, something you revel in, rather than a math problem, you know—a + b = c. It's more like, "Wow, look at that watercolor." Use that part of you to understand it rather than the mathematical, logical part of you. "Oh, understanding's overrated. I don't try to understand anymore. Look at this." Well done. Well done.

Response: I worked on someone's computer on Sunday and there's some equal sign in there. I have a sense of it, but I don't know, maybe because it went extra-long and one of my chairs got broken, but there was a little bit of: "No good deed goes unpunished" equal sign. Not really strong, but there was something else in there too, equal sign.

Eloheim: These are all good examples, although they feel kind of vague, and other people might think they're kind of vague, these are all good examples of you looking for the place, you know, this is the work of consciousness. Looking for the place, "I know there's something else that's happening here." It's that looking, it's like panning for gold—you look at the river and you don't see gold, right? You look there and you don't see gold and you don't see gold, but you get the pan out, you put some of the stuff in and swish it around and you say, "Wow, there's gold here."

There's that sense that you're looking where it's not obvious to be found. That's the example we're trying to come up with. You're using that extra step of consciousness, "I know there's something more here." And by using that extra step of consciousness, that's what helps you grow. Because it takes you off of that habitual path into: "Wait, wait, wait…." And just like the panning for gold and any other example you like, it just shifts your perspective, maybe, out into another direction where you say, "There's something else here, there's something else here, there's something else here."

Question: Sometimes other people have an equal sign that is offered to me. They'll say something or do something or try something, and I don't pick it up as something to share energy with or something to match. I'll say, "Oh, OK," and then they just feel like, "Wow, she just really dropped the bucket." Like I'm not keeping the communication going or something. Or I'm in another world and then they look at me like, "Whoa, can I even deal with her?" It happens a lot. People say something—I'm not real judgmental, I don't really get involved, it takes two to get excited about something. I just go, "Oh, OK," and people think, "How do I even get you involved?" And I think, "Talk about something that's conscious." But the energy of that, it's happening an awful lot and maybe I'm doing a good service to them somehow. Maybe I should dig into it bigger or something.

Eloheim: Well there's a sense of you, it's like a version of you going to the bathroom. It's like, "I don't want to participate in unconscious conversation," and so you don't run away and go into the bathroom as much as you stand there and go, "Next? Try something else. It didn't work actually for me." And sometimes dead silence and staring alerts people to: "That subject didn't work for me." And they can project their discomfort onto you. So you don't take it. Is that the equal sign you're talking about?

Response: Yes.

Eloheim: A thing to do at that point would be to bring up something else. Another subject. Answer the question you hoped they had asked. Or you can even say, "You know, I don't see it that way." Short, factual statement with the truth. If you sit there and stare, it might be awkward, if you care what this person thinks. That's the question: "Do I even care?" It's hard sometimes to answer, let's say you're at a party or some event, you don't necessarily care about that conversation but you're happy to be at the event. It's someone's birthday party, you want to be there and be involved and you keep getting into these conversations that are like... ahhh. And there are all sorts of conversational tricks about finding common ground.

The one that we've also seen work the best is ask them a question about themselves. If they're busy talking about this, that, and the other thing, just ask them a question about themselves. If you're at an event with someone, a pretty safe one that we've found is ask them how they know the person that's having the event. "When did you come to work for this company? How did you meet so-and-so? How long have you known so-and-so?" Just get them talking about themselves. Because if they're talking about themselves, it might actually be interesting and it's not going to be as low-vibrational. To talk about yourself you have to be somewhat conscious about what has actually happened in your life. It might not be conscious about what's going on in your life but, "When did you come to work for this company?" "Oh, I have to consider that, what year was it?" right? It's better than, "Those people in Iraq...." or whatever they're doing. At least they're talking about what's in their own lap, so we're moving toward something else. Most of the time, people will talk about themselves. And you might not be thrilled by a long conversation. The vibrational level goes up and at least you're not talking about something over there, "them peoples." You're talking about something actually going on in the moment between the two of you—and you can always go to the bathroom if it gets too bad.

Question: I had a big, conscious equals sign the other day and it was, of course, around money—my big thing. That winning the lottery or having a large amount of money equals unconsciousness. I was having a conversation with a friend of mine about that and I had watched this documentary the other night, I just flicked onto it, it was called Lucky, focusing on all these people who won the lottery. What had happened in their lives and those it worked for and those it didn't work for. Watching the show, I was watching through completely different eyes than if I had seen it six months ago and all these things were being triggered in me. I spent a lot of time saying, "What is going on here for me?" Because I say I want all this money but what does that really mean? And then talking about it to a friend, she said, "It doesn't mean you go unconscious." Yes, it did mean that, one of the guys who had won millions of dollars said it was a full-time job just keeping track of the money. And I thought, "That's not my thing." So it's still percolating. I was spending a lot of time imagining if I had all this money and I woke up in the morning, how would it feel, and it wasn't feeling great. I then did the short, factual statement, "I feel very nervous, period." Opened up to soul and soul said, "You're so far in the future, thinking about all these things that you would do or wouldn't do, you're not focused on what's going on right now." I thought, OK, well that's being unconscious because of all this money. Anyway, that was a big equals sign I discovered.

Eloheim: And we remember a while back when you had some equal signs that were similar around your sister and how she behaves around her money and how that's what money meant, was the way she acted. So you might want to revisit the way she is wealthy. "I don't want to be wealthy the way she's wealthy." So you might want to make sure that's clear because we're getting that one more time. Just go through it again. It's like the wheel comes around, so stuff you've previously considered, you get to consider again at this vibrational level. And "It's not that I screwed up, it's because I've gone deeper. I've gone deeper, I've gone deeper."

If old stuff's coming up again, it doesn't mean you're broken, it means you're going deeper. So, just allow yourself to go deeper with it. And the temptation is go into: "God, this is back, so I'm broken; this is back, so I've backslid." That's absolutely the opposite of what's true. It's back because you've taken all the steps to come back and revisit it. And when you revisit it, you have the opportunity to go deeper with it. That's where you guys are right now, that's what we see with you, that you have the opportunity to go deeper.

Response: OK. I have been doing that. It's funny, I haven't talked to my sister in quite a while but we both do Farmers Market Tuesday night, and she happened to be just behind me in line pulling in, so I waved to her for the first time in probably two months. And I thought, "Maybe I should go over and talk to her, maybe I should do this, maybe I should do that." I shouldn't have to think about doing anything, I should do my own thing because we're not right next to each other, so it would be a major effort. I thought, why would I even want to do that? What is in there, what is in there for me? So, when you say let it come around and revisit that, you mean...

Eloheim: Yeah. It's up again. "Oh, here's the stuff with my sister again. Compare me to me. I'm not the same person I used to be." Immediately, as soon as you started to talk about it, we got the picture of the king. You're wanting to see the king and you're wanting the king to tell you who you are. The Warriors are saying, "What are you doing?" The picture was you wanting to see the king, hoping the king will tell you something about you that you don't know. She doesn't know anything about you that you don't already know. It's like the king is going to tell you who you are, that you've given her that authority-figure position, where she knows who you are and you don't.

Response: I was thinking: She doesn't know who I am, she really doesn't know who I am. I didn't realize it could be that little... I'm waiting for her to tell me maybe something that I don't see about myself that she might see.

Eloheim: Because you have that mother/daughter figure energy going on somewhere, and that she'll approve of it. "She'll see something in me that she likes and she's pat me on the back for it. Or pat me on the head," even worse. "If I go see her, she's going to give me some kind of dispensation." So it comes around. In the past, you would have gone to see her because you would have felt that you had to, and: "If I don't go see her somehow I'm not strong," or "I can handle her." You know, you've got to get yourself all jacked up to go see the king.

So, you go to see the king in that way, or you can go to see the king like the Warrior goes to see the king. Or you can say, "Fuck you, I'm not interested in going to see the king today." Which is what you chose to do, but when you did that, did it drop in your mind or did it niggle in your mind?

Response: It must have niggled in my mind because we're talking about it now. I went through the whole scenario today, thinking, wait a minute is that…?

Eloheim: It's because you're hoping for the king to tell you who you are.

Response: How do I not do that?

Eloheim: You recognize, "Oh, I think the king knows something I don't. That's not true. It's that habit thing. I've always looked right there and I've always expected right there to tell me this whole story. Now, I'm looking here." And let that tell you more of the story. What's fabulous is when you look here, the focus is suddenly not on that person—they could wander off the stage and because you're so busy looking at all the other stuff that's on the stage, you don't see them leave. They're no longer the absolute pinnacle of achievement, impressing your sister is no longer the pinnacle of your experience as a human.

Question: When she's talking about her sister, it's like she's talking about my mother. I had an experience about month ago that I'm revisiting, I'm there again. I reacted like the five-year-old. So I'm revisiting… do I want to engage with this woman anymore, do I even have to? And I've gone to this place: All she was, was a vessel to get here. And that's kind of how I feel, maybe that is what she was.

Eloheim: Well, it was one of the things she was. It doesn't have to be all. You can just say, "That is part of it. Part of it is she did that for me, I did that for her, we combined in that way. I also have a relationship with her." It's not like an either/or kind of thing. It's like, "All these things are true." You could make a list about: "All the things that are true about my mom. She was a vessel to allow me to have physical form, she is someone I can't get along with." Make this kind of a list within yourself—and it doesn't have to be she slots into one, she's all those things. When you look at all the things that she is, let them have balance within you. It's not like she has to switch roles. She's this and she's that. Let her be all the things she is, and you can also say, "I'm not interested in interacting with any of it." Or, "I'm only interested in interacting with you when you're this way, and when you're playing jealous sister or playing this or playing that, I gotta go. I need to be more conscious than this."

Response: What's really key for me is why am I looking for her to tell me who I am when I know who I am. Then take the finger-point out.

The Girls

It seems like an appropriate time to talk about mothers and sisters. All of you have got a mother, lots of you have sisters. And if you don't have a birth sister, then you probably have someone in your life that kind of feels sisterly to you. Or you have an opinion about sisters in general, or you've seen some, so let's just get on with the idea of mothers and sisters, basically feminine family energy. Feminine family energy. Those of you who are women, sometimes you'll have sisters that you feel so close to that you can't imagine living in a life without them. And some of you have mothers you can't imagine living in a life without them. But unfortunately—or fortunately, we shouldn't make a judgment—there's a lot of pain surrounding the sister/mother relationships that we've observed.

A lot of times you go off into the world and you find sister figures and mother figures that are much more satisfying than the ones you're born into. Part of what goes on with this, is that you're born into birth families with individuals that you've had relationships in past lives with, or alternate expressions. You're born into relationships that need to have some clearing, opportunities for healing—sandpaper is an easy way to say it, you're born into sandpaper families.

Some of you would say, "Why, why, why would we ever be born into sandpaper families?" Why, why, why would you climb Mt. Everest? OK, we're always going to have the same answer. Why, why, why do you think you need to run triathlons? Why, why, why do you think you need to learn foreign languages? Because that's what you like to do, you like to learn. You like to learn. So you come here, you're over-achievers, you like to push the envelope, you like to push, you want to grow, you like to have intense experiences, that's why you come here. You get born into situations where you have sandpaper people that you're living with.

And upon reflection, just like every other lifetime, you say, "I'm not doing that again." And then, sure enough, you just plan another one. We don't like to say you did it to yourself, even though you did, because it makes it sound like there's no hope for you. But the truth is, just like anything else, you're here to learn from people and situations. A lot of times, because of cultural norms, you believe you have to create really deep relationships with those people you were born into relationships with. And we would just like to reiterate that we believe it is very important to have deep personal relationships—and we don't believe it has to be with people you are biologically related to. We do believe it is important for you to have deep personal relationships but we don't believe it has to be with people you are biologically related to. And that's where you get to make a choice. You get to make a choice about creating deep relationships and you also get to evaluate whether the people you were born into relationships with, whether or not you've already learned enough from them.

You'll break up with a boyfriend, you'll break up with a girlfriend, you'll break up with a best friend, but there are really ingrained cultural and DNA-driven pressures to stay deeply connected to biological relatives. And as you evolve, you have to make choices about that. It's another thing that you have to consider: Do you really believe that you have to stay connected to someone simply because you're biologically related?

There's a lot that comes with breaking off from biological relatives. There's a lot of societal guilt, societal pressure. There's a lot of, "Am I going to regret?" and things like that. But if you're building powerful relationships with other people, and that you're creating connections and learning about community, that's really what you're here to learn. And forcing yourself to have them with biological relatives, oftentimes, is an unkindness because sometimes you've already worked out what you need to work out. Boundary-setting, especially with biological relatives, can be incredibly liberating. It can really help you know what boundaries really are, when you set them with biological relatives.

It doesn't mean you have to get rid of all your relatives, it doesn't even mean you're supposed to, it just means you have permission if you choose to. A lot of people don't feel it's even allowed, so it's something to say "Look, if this was someone I just went to school with and knew for 10 years, would I still want to spend time with them? If this is somebody I grew up with, would I still call them? If this was somebody I was dating, would I still date them?" Asking yourself those questions is really important.

If you decide to cut off ties to biological relatives, you have to really be careful because oftentimes the guilt trip thing will come in. So you have to make sure you're making the choice, not because of a hissy fit, but because you know it's a choice that supports your growth. Supports you emanating the truth of you. Supports you being the completeness of you. The temptation is to wait until you throw a shit-fit to get to where you want to be. Instead of making a choice from a position of strength, and that position of strength is saying, "I know what's best for me. I've revaluated this and I'm not reacting, I'm choosing my reaction. The choice of reaction is, the only reason I'm still connected to you is because I'm biologically related to you. That's it and that's not enough for me anymore. It's not enough for me to have an unconscious relationship with you just because we share DNA." You have permission to make that choice and that permission comes from yourself. Now, that's not to say that you're going to; it's just to say to it's on the table, it's one of the options. OK? It's just one of the options.

That said, we still want you to know that we believe that you get an enormous amount of learning from deep personal relationships. So if you decide to fire your own biological relatives, don't be a hermit. Find people that you do resonate with from who you are now, and create relationships with them, so you still get to learn what's it's like to be in relationship, just go be in conscious relationships. That's the gift you give yourself outside of the cultural norms that say if you're biologically related, you have to be close.

Some of you have the interesting journey of having biological relatives that you feel very close to, and that in itself is a journey. But each of you has someone that you're close to, a friend, partner, lover, whatever. You know what it's like to be close to someone. You have to ask yourself, "Am I close to this person just because I think I have to be, or am I close to this person because it actually fulfills us both to have this journey together?"

It's a good question. And also, "Am I running away from something because it's too hard to learn?" Or, "Am I choosing to walk away from this person because it's too difficult to learn with this person?" Because if you're running away from this person because it feels too hard to learn, well, you know what's going to happen? It's just going to come up again. You are allowed to say, "It's too hard to learn it with her, whatever this is that I'm learning, it's too hard to learn with her. Let's set this up again, Act 2, clear the stage, try again, re-do. Bring out a new set of cast of characters to help me learn this thing I want to learn in a way that more accurately reflects who I am now, and is more likely to be able to be learned."

A lot of times, what happens when you're working with biological relatives, the stuff that you're learning is the stuff from when you were five. You're five and now you're 40 and you're still doing your five-year-old shit. If you took that lesson you were trying to learn and you could have someone you could learn it with when you're 40 and they're 40, rather than, "I'm 40 but I'm acting like I'm five, which I've been doing for 35 years with my mom." Well, you can see you have a better chance of success, or a different chance of success, of actually learning and growing and becoming more of who you are by having that experience in 2010 rather than repeating 1980.

It's the "who answers the door" thing, but related to your parents or relatives. A lot of times you're trapped in the patterns of when you were five, six, seven, eight years old. Yes, you can say, "There's something for me to learn here, but my God, me as a 40-year-old trying to act like an eight-year-old with my mom who is now 70, is not working." It's not working and you have the right to say, "I want to learn this some other way."

That might be disconnecting from that relationship for a while or forever. Forever meaning while you're here in the body. We don't know, you don't know. OK? This is loving yourself, giving yourself permission to set boundaries across your life. Set the boundaries you need to set in order to give yourself the best chance at learning what it is you desire to learn. When you don't do that, it's that going-with-the-flow thing. Remember going with the flow? We don't do that. Going with the flow means whatever happens, happens. No, going with the flow gets you where the least common denominator takes you. Instead, you say, "Here's my experience, I choose my reaction, I set boundaries and preferences about it." That's far different than going with the flow. That's actually standing on the bridge, you're on bridge looking around going, "Aha. If I want to get into the water I will, if I want to stay on the bridge I will, just because there's a flow going along doesn't mean I have to get in it."

Warrior

Let's see, where were we? The king wanted us to go off and do something with him and we said, "Why not?" So that evening, we did take a bath because it's not like we don't like to bathe, we enjoy bathing. We just don't want to bathe in order to be someone we're not. It's time to have a bath, why not? And it's nice to bathe at the castle. Why? Because when you bathe at the castle the water is warm. When you bathe in the forest the water is cold, hence, a reason to bathe at the castle. You can be tough all you want but it is nice every once in a while to be kind to your body, yes?

So, off we go to sit in the tub with the beautiful young women—don't call us sexist, it doesn't exist in our time. Beautiful young women filled the tub and we got in. And because we don't have to stand with the king on the shore of the ocean until tomorrow, we even had something to drink. We made merry, as you like to say.

Back to the story, then, but that's an important part of the story. If the king wants you to do something for him, you may as well take advantage of the comforts while you're about it. So off we go. And in the morning, the nice thing is, in the castle, there's just so many people that have jobs looking after people. They're everywhere and so they look after you and they clean things up. But there's certain things they don't get to do, like touch anything that's sharp. But the rest of it they can do, like if they want to clean mud off of this, that, or the other thing. And it's nice because we're not unknown at the castle, so sometimes when we come around, well let's just say it's nice when somebody mends your things, occasionally. We can certainly mend our own things but it's nice when someone else does it. And every once in a while there's a little something extra added in and we enjoy that, too. There is something nice about fresh, what would you call them, underwear. You know the things you wear under, it's nice when your unders are nice and new and clean. And if they smell pretty like roses, well, it helps you remember that you're not alone in this world. You can tell we have fun.

So, off we go. The king is rounding us up and asking us to show up and so we've gotten ourselves together and we're going down to stand along the shore and see who's coming to visit. They come along and yes, they're big and shining and blondish, and they have beautiful boats. They bristle and we bristle and the king talks and the other king talks, and it's all so good. And the king is authentic enough to make the thing all work out and we decide to have games. Now, you like to have games, we know you play games. You play games of chance and you play games of skill and you play games just for fun and you run about and exercise your muscles because it feels damn good to do so. This has been true since you had a body these things have gone on, so this is a normal act of being human. But again, no matter what happens in any of these environments and whether these games extend to the games of corporate America or whatever country you come from, or the games extend to Monopoly with your kids, there's a point at which you have to ask, "Is winning this game telling me who I am? Is how I'm playing the game telling me who I am? Or am I knowing myself regardless?"

There's sense in you that you have to accomplish in order to know yourself. There's a sense in you that you have to achieve in order to know yourself. Your society is based on rewarding the victor and indicating yourself, indicating your worth, indicating your nature by your accomplishments, by your résumé. You're promoted at work when you do well, et cetera. You're paid bonuses if things go your way. What happens is, then you can only feel accomplishments if you make accomplishments based on other standards. You must not fall into the trap that says: "I am only me if I'm accomplishing based on other standards. I'm only me when I compare myself to other standards. I'm only me if...." There's no such thing as: "I'm only me if...." That's just crap. "I am always me, regardless," is the position we'd like you to adopt. You are you if you stand on the sidelines, you are you if you compete, you're you if you are the victor, you are you if you are the vanquished. You are you, regardless, and as you bring your complete self into all these interactions it allows you to emanate the truth of you and to show those you interact with, regardless of what form you interact with them, to show them that you are the truth of you. This is how they know your nature. You've heard the saying: No one likes a sore loser. Of course no one does, and no one likes too much of a braggart for a winner, either. Humility is respected on some level. We don't particularly care for it. We're not into humility, we're not into bragging. We're not into being sore losers. What we're into is a consistent emanation of the truth of us, regardless of the circumstances we find ourselves in. And this is what we invite you to do, too. Consistently emanate the truth of you regardless of the circumstances you find yourself in, choose your reaction based on your higher-vibrational conscious experience of yourself.

So, you wrestle and you're vanquished and you smile and laugh and pat the other one on the hand and you thank him for a well-fought match. You wrestle and you're the victor and you do the same thing, and by your consistency they will know you. And by your consistency you will know yourself. Because by your consistency, when you compare you to you, you can really see progress, because you're consistently showing the completeness of you regardless of the circumstances you find yourself in. You will sense progress in the process.

Earlier, you spoke of sisters and mothers. Part of the problem when you get in those relationships is that as they push and pull, you to react differently based on how they're behaving.

The greatest gift you can give to yourself is to be consistent regardless of the circumstances you find yourself in. This doesn't mean the same, this means consistent, whether you're the victor or the vanquished you still act the same. When you roll the dice and they roll in the direction you hoped they'd roll or in the direction that you didn't hope they'd roll, you react the same.

Not because you've faking it but because anything that is presenting itself to you is presenting itself to you for growth. And it's how you react to it that dictates the growth you get out of it, not the result of the action. The result of the action does not give you growth, it's the reaction to the experience that gives you growth. That's the gift you give yourself. The Visionaries explained it so well that we don't need to go into it again.

Now, moving along with the story right? One of these men on the other side—let's call him Eric—Eric has a proposition. He would like us to come along with him on a little adventure. One of these "Let's just go and rape and pillage" kind of things—for the fun of it, he says. He doesn't use the word "fun," but it's the best translation we've got. "Let's go rape and pillage for the fun of it" is basically what he's offering, to shortcut the whole thing. And in the moment of making this, we're sitting around and there's much merriment after the games of the day, much drinking and eating, beautiful women, the fire's roaring. You can imagine the picture, we believe.

And Eric calls us out, in essence, in front of everyone. He says, "Come, let us go together, now that we've become friends and brothers, let us go together to see this other neighbor and take what is theirs." It happens, right? We're looking around and we're thinking, "Well, we've got it pretty good now, and we've had it pretty good in the forest, and we had it pretty good before we were in the forest. And we're not really feeling like we need any pillaging because we can't really carry any more sharp things, and we've got a new pair of underwear from the gal last night, and things are pretty flush in our book because it doesn't grow it flows, remember? Especially when you have to carry everything you want, you don't want too many things. The old horse can only carry so much after we get on it, right? So, there he is and he's now standing and asking us, "Come with us, we'll go together, we can leave on the tide," and all that crap—you've seen it in movies, you know what it's like.

And all our men have started to bristle now, because they know the truth. The truth being that conquering does not conquer the self. Just like you going out and getting a promotion does not make you a better person. You piling up a bunch of money doesn't give you ascension, right? Eloheim has talked to you about this very well, money is not rare. Consciousness, ascension, Homo spiritus—those are rare things, money's not rare, but he's calling us out. All of his men are making hoopla about the whole thing, and all of our men are starting to slowly slide their knives out from under the table, because it may come to that, it may have to come to that. And it is now our place to speak again. And because cliff-hangers are part of every good story, we will leave you with that. Ha!

So maybe, during the next seven days, you might contemplate how you would handle the situation. And remember, it's not that situation where we are, it's that situation where you are. When you are called by another to behave in a way that you know is contrary to your growth, and you are pressured by society to do so, what do you do? And next week, we'll see what goes on next.

Fred

You really are on the cusp of something here, you really are at a point of change, you really are at a point of choice, you really are at a fork in the road, you really are being given the opportunity right now to make this choice. To make this choice, to make this choice, to make this choice. And the choice is to come out of the belief that things happen to you and to move into and surrender to, in essence, the belief that you are the one making things happen. You are the choice point, you are the chooser, you are given the gift, you are given the gift of choice.

It's a universal idea, this free-will idea, this grand and beautiful concept of you being given the gift of choice. It's been laid in your lap, laid at your feet, hung around your neck like a beautiful necklace, the gift of choice. That's what you have, the gift of choice. This is something you can say to yourself: "I have the gift of choice." You don't understand, maybe, the magnitude of this gift but nonetheless it's there, it's yours.

"I have the gift of choice, what will I choose? Will I choose to surrender to habit, will I choose to surrender to cultural norms? Will I choose to surrender to the pressures of my society? Or will I choose to emanate the truth of me?" The gift of choice is yours. You have the gift of choice, and this gift of choice is not a common thing because you're in a duality-based society. When you are a soul, when you know all, when you know each other, the gift of choice is irrelevant.

But what you've done is put yourself into limitation, and in the state of limitation the gift of choice is freedom. It's so hard to explain. It's the key to the jail door. So many of you bemoan the fact that you're here on the planet and you struggle and it's energetically impossible and you wonder, "Why did I ever come here?" and "It's so hard," and "I'm stressing," and "My family…" and this, that, and the other thing. And the key to the door of the prison you've locked yourself in is the gift of choice. The choice to react in the way that you decide fits. Fits the truth of you, fits the emanation of you, fits the gift of you. That's what you have here, the gift of choosing. It's a gift, so choose. And don't choose once but choose all the time. Choose, choose, choose, and choose again. Isn't this one of the things that you've been taught?

That's been upgraded now, instead of choose, choose, and choose again about looking for consciousness, it's choose, choose, and choose again about your reaction to everything you experience, because that is the gift you've been given. And it is the ramp, or the path, to Homo spiritus. You all want to know how to get there, the doorway has been opened, the carpet has been rolled out, and now, you just need to walk it.

Everything you have been taught up to this point is where you make the consistent choice of the reaction that you want to have to the situation you find yourself in. You couldn't come to this moment without the lead-up. If we said to someone who's just thinking about their spiritual journey, "Oh, you just choose your reaction," it wouldn't make any sense to them. But you who have all sat here and have worked so hard know the magnitude of that statement.

You wanted it, it's here. It's laid out for you. Will you partake? It is your choice, of course.

Matriarch

Ah, yes! As we sit here with you and we share this moment, and we recognize the journey you've been on tonight, it really is the journey of so many lifetimes but it also is the journey of tonight. From the Guardians all the way through the Council until now. It has been a journey of becoming clear and ever more clear about the choice you have laid at your feet. Dispensation bestowed, we don't know the right word, but it's such a precious opportunity. It's such a precious opportunity to be given this gift, this—we just don't know how to say it right—let's say it this way: If someone said to you, back when you were younger, "Would you like very much to have the opportunity to go study abroad for your junior year?" And you might say, "Oh boy, I've always wanted to be in France and learn French. But I just don't know, I'm kind of afraid, I don't know what it will be like. And maybe I don't have enough money and I don't know whether I want to be away from my family and friends for that long." Yet you keep coming around and circling around to: "I have the chance to be in France for a whole year, I don't know, but I have the chance, I don't know, but I have the chance...." Right?

You've all done this, on some subject you've had this. And what if you just decided it was worth the risk? What if you just decided that it was OK to let go of one side of the swimming pool in order to feel what it was like to swim? And this is really what it feels like here, choosing your reaction to every situation and being conscious of the fact that that's what you're doing. Not pointing fingers. Taking responsibility. Panning for gold, like Eloheim was talking about. These things give you the opportunity to be the completeness of you, to integrate with your soul and to live as Homo spiritus. It really is the final step, and we will help you each week as much as we possibly can—the entire Council—to give you the opportunity to actually do this, but you're the only one who can choose to start walking down that pathway.

So, we leave you there. We leave you at the door and we walk down the pathway and we stand, you can imagine us lined up on the side of the path, ready to support you on every step and inviting you to just let go enough to see what's new when you do. And we'll be back to do it some more.

August 4, 2010

Summary

Guardians: Opened the meeting by encouraging us to bring our attention the moment and be present.

Visionaries: Discussed emotive states and the difference between emotions and feelings. Emotions are habitual, feelings are in the moment.

Eloheim: Expanded on the discussion of feelings and emotions, and took questions to help illustrate the concept.

The Girls: Had a humorous time trying to eat a goldfish cracker. Brought the discussion of feelings and emotions around to self-love and the difference between vulnerability and weakness. They advise: Recognize and express your feelings and let that give you vulnerability rather than weakness.

Warrior: Continued the story of going to see the king, and dealing with Eric, illustrating unconsciousness versus consciousness.

Fred: Explained that by discerning the difference between emotion and feeling and delving into feeling in the moment, we allow our soul's perspective into our being.

Matriarch: Invited us to allow ourselves to take the time to revel in the feelings of joy that can be associated with physicality.

Guardians

As always, we ask you to bring your attention to the center of the circle, to the center of you. Bring your attention to the moment, to this time, to this place. Be present, be accountable for the fact that you have arrived here, you've logged on, however you're doing it, and allow yourself to actually engage in the experience. Be present, be ready, be available, be open, and allow and allow again for your presence to be reflected, your presence to join in the energetic, your presence to share in the dynamic of exchange that's going on. Allow and allow again to come into this time together.

Visionaries

Early this morning we, through Eloheim, were having a conversation with Veronica and the information we discussed was very helpful to her and we thought perhaps you'd like to hear it, too. Because it really comes down to this: There is a difference between emotions and feelings. We're making a discernment there, we've decided it's important for you to recognize that there are two different things occurring and it's important for you to see that very, very frequently, they're all mixed up together like one of these ice creams where you get the chocolate and the vanilla and they all swirl together.

The issue at hand is that emotions are typically habit-based, culturally-based, past- and future-based. They are not the same as what we're going to identify feelings. Feelings are based on what is actually going on in the moment. So, we recognize that you have an emotive response to a situation. What we want to help you with is recognizing when that emotive response is a habit, and when it's actually a reflection of the truth of the moment. We know we've talked about "the math problem" example before, and we know we've given you many, many options about being in the moment. But a lot of that discussion is very intellectual and it doesn't actually acknowledge what goes on within you when you're presented with an experience that draws out an emotive response in you.

As you have an experience, the kindest thing you can do for yourself is to ask, "Why am I feeling this way?" To be acknowledging the feeling you're having may not be actually representative of what's going on in the moment is going to offer an incredible amount of freedom for you. Because as you experience having feelings rather than emotions, you're going to actually have a conscious experience of the dynamic you find yourself in.

Emotions very often draw you out of the moment, where feelings are going to deepen your experience of the moment. An emotion tells you that you need to be jealous or fearful or envious or depressed or confused—lots of those kinds of generalized emotions. You've all felt them. A feeling, on the other hand, gives you the opportunity to actually be completely present and reflect upon what's going on. It's a bit like the tool "who answers the door," but instead of it being an intellectual exercise it's an emotion exercise, emotive exercise. It's hard because you always say that emotions are feelings; there's not really a third term that encompasses the fact that you're having an emotional response, so we're trying to make up some different language here. We might have to work on the terms a bit but basically we think they work all right if you say, "How am I feeling?" and you don't settle for an emotion.

Eloheim has said to you many times that they're not impressed with emotions, that they're not romantic in that way, and what they're really meaning by that is, typically your emotional states are habits. They're habits, they're patterns, they're culturally driven—something occurs and you already have an emotion that is pre-programmed to be assigned to that situation. And if it's not assigned to you by your culture, it's assigned to you by your family of origin or your role, or it's assigned to you by habit or things that have happened in the past or projections of things that could happen it the future.

A lot of times you'll be in a situation and the dynamic will draw you out of you, draw you out of you. Your feelings are an accurate representation of what's going on. Your emotions will draw you out of the accuracy of the moment, through habit mostly. So, sometimes you just say, "God I just feel sad or angry and I don't know why." And a lot of times it's because you're being triggered into an emotive state and you're going habitually into the rut of whatever pattern you're most accustomed to, instead of addressing what's actually going on.

Now, there's a strong pull from the body to go along that rut, just like being unconscious, and we've talked a lot about that, too. The idea that there's this ditch and you've been digging it, it's much easier to keep digging that ditch than start a new one. But if you keep digging the ditch, the scenery never changes and that means life never changes. So when you're in an emotional response to a situation, you have to make the choice to say, "Even though it's very compelling to be sad, mad or whatever, I want to actually reflect upon what's actually happening here," and the body's going to make a demand on you to not change. But you've had a lot of practice to deal with the demands of the body to not change, so we trust in your ability to say, "Hang on, hang on, hang on…." And you know the feeling of "don't change," so you can invest in, "OK, that's just a red flag now. That 'don't change' feeling is a red flag to indicate to me that something important is going on here. There's an opportunity for growth, there's a chance here for me to know myself more."

Now, for you women, oftentimes this brings up sitting by the campfire, and we're going to remind you of what that's about. The idea of the woman at the campfire is this idea that back and back and back in your DNA, is programmed the idea that if your man brings the efforts of his hunting back to someone else's campfire, you and your kids might starve. So, you're heavily invested in him coming back to your campfire all the time, so you sit around the campfire going, "I hope he comes back, what if he doesn't? That one down there, she's just a campfire hussy with her low-cut campfire hussy clothes," or whatever you've got going on. "She's got the one shoulder campfire hussy clothes going on."

So, you have this intensity around "I have to be jealous, I have to be envious, I have to negotiate my position, I have to look at other people and keep an eye on what they're doing." And a lot of that is still in your DNA, so survival-instinct kind of behavior, for those of you who are women at this time, can be really intense for you, and this whole emotional response tends to go along with that a lot of times. And maybe it's true for men, too, but of course, because we work with Veronica, sometimes it's easier for us to understand the feminine perspective on things. But there's a lot of that: "If I don't protect what's mine, I'm going to lose," so that emotion of "protect what's mine" is very easy to access. So when something happens, it's super easy to go into "protect what's mine" instead of what's actually happening.

And you can make assumptions about what's happening based on the idea that you're automatically going to go into "protect what's mine" rather than analyzing what's really happening. Or "somebody's criticizing me" and you just assume somebody's criticizing you, and you get defensive, instead of listening to what they're saying and hearing that they're actually criticizing you or that they're just sharing something and you're taking it as criticism. "I feel criticized, I'm defensive, I'm angry, I'm sad." You automatically go into those emotions instead of asking, "What's really going on? What am I feeling here?"

What's interesting is when you go deeply into feeling, you know, on the one hand you could be the woman by the campfire who goes into jealousy, lack, rage even, and on the other hand it could be compassion, right? If your man—in whatever capacity that looks like in 2010—if your man goes to the next campfire, you could look at him and recognize, "Wow, you know, old widow woman down the street really needed his help in this moment and I'm actually tempted to be jealous that he's helping her fix her screen door instead of looking at him and saying, 'I'm partnered with a man whose generous with his time and his abilities and who cares for other people.' " But the temptation is jealously, right? The temptation is, "Oh God, I have to protect," instead of actually letting yourself feel in the moment.

If you don't let yourself believe that you have to protect the future and instead examine the moment, we think you'll more often find yourself in positions of gratitude, ease, and more of a relaxed state because you're not protecting or projecting the future. You're allowing the moment to reveal itself. And when the moment reveals itself, your depth of feeling is very profound, and of course, when you're in the moment you also have access to your soul's insight. So you're also getting a twofer because you're letting yourself have the depth of feeling and you're allowing your soul to access the depth of feeling. So not only do you have depth of feeling but you have soul's insight on top of it. We think this will be powerful for you and we hope our explanation illuminated it clearly.

Eloheim

Hi. Making eye contact, we see eyes. OK, the Visionaries told you this story about what we were talking to Veronica about this morning, and it's a really interesting concept to us. We told you we went to the concert and got overwhelmed. We also got a different picture than we had before about what it's like for you guys feeling-wise, so that's why part of this subject has come up. The idea of involving you all in a different way with your emotional body. Your emotions, your feelings, like they explained the terms—you don't have that many. What we want to help you see is that you can allow yourself to have the feelings that the gift of density gives you. And the gift of density is that you feel very strongly in density without the habit of emotions taking it away from you.

The habit of emotions take it away from you because it's like the horses are out of the barn. You've seen these cowboy shows where the barn's on fire and they open the doors and the horses run and run and run, and it's like, "We don't care where they go, we've just got to get them out of here." In essence, that's the energetic similarity behind what happens when you guys allow your emotions to take over, because the next thing you know, you're three ranches over, pissed off, tired, angry, broke, whatever. And you're like, "What the hell just happened?" And how many times has it occurred—and it's probably a huge number—that you get yourself back over to the barn and you say, "Oh God, I had a strong reaction to that," and the other person says, "I don't even know why you were mad I was trying to give you a compliment," or "I was just trying to explain." What do you call it? Misunderstanding. If your emotions take over, you're three farms down, and if your feelings take over, then what happens is you can be vulnerable.

This is the other thing, remember we talked about weakness and vulnerability? As a reminder: Weakness is when the truth is you're embarrassed, ashamed. Vulnerability is when you sit in the truth and it shows you; sit in the truth and allow the truth to show you what it shows you. So if you combine the vulnerability with feeling, you're unassailable because intellectually and emotionally, you're in your truth. The Warriors are going to talk about this when they tell their story later, about what happens when you sit in that space—when you're in the space where you're vulnerable, present, and you're allowing the feelings that you have to be present rather than the emotions that you're tempted into, to run the show.

For Veronica, it was very clear because she had something happen and there were a lot of feelings, a lot of emotion, and a lot of reaction, and she was able to actually see, just like the Visionaries had that ice cream analogy, that ice cream cone with the mixed flavors, she was able to see that where she was in emotion she was very, very disturbed and where she was in feeling it felt very, very profound; but it was as though she was switching between the two constantly during the conversation. So, parts of the conversation were like, "Holy shit, this is really amazing, to have this conversation to feel closer to this person and have this happen," and then on the other hand her heart was beating and she was sweating and she was nervous and her stomach was roiling and she was thinking, "How come one minute I feel good and the next minute I feel bad and then I feel good and then I feel bad?" Eventually, she had to have a little cry because it was all too much.

And she was able, after our conversation this morning, to say, "Oh my goodness, when I was in this side of it I was in the feeling of the moment, which was, 'Wow, this person is really telling me something deep and profound about themselves which was an opening and a friendship.' " On the other side it was, "Oh my God, what does that mean about me, what does that mean about the past or what does that mean about the future?" There was a lot of protection, back and forth, all that stuff. And in all of that was the physical discomfort she was in. It was all happening simultaneously and it was very confusing. So that's why this morning, before she even got out of bed, we said: This is what's going on. And so, she was able to say… it divided it for her, and we hope it divides it for you guys because there's definitely two, at least, different avenues of reaction you can have. That emotive experience, there are two different things: what we're calling feelings and what we're calling emotions. They are two completely different ways of emotive interaction with the moment. That's not too subtle, is it? OK, good. We were a little concerned this morning.

So, when you find yourself in a situation, again, this is a way to be in the moment, another way to be in the moment. But we think it's most closely related to "who answers the door." Because when you ask, "Who answers the door?" and you finally say, "I'm going to have the 2010 version of me answer the door," you answer the door and then the emotion can start up and you go back to the 5-year-old, the 10-year-old, or you project to the 50-, 60-, 70-year-old. So you get to "who answers the door," and then you get to deal with the emotional response your body has to what happens. So: the knock, knock, knock; you sort it out; and then Boom!; and then you get to sort it out again. And we hope this helps sort it out better.

For us, we see it as though maybe you have these cords, string, ropes, where they're entwined and you're pulling one and you're sorting out how it got all twisted around something else—for us it's a bit like that. We see it as though you're saying, "Oh God, all the cords are tangled,"—like Christmas lights, that's the one everybody knows—and you say, "What happens that they do this?" You know, it's like January to November, all the Christmas lights are sitting around in there together and they come out as this big wad. It didn't go in as a wad, right? It's the sock in the dryer, too. It's the mysteries we've inserted now—you know what it feels like when you pull those lights out of the box and you scratch your head and you start sorting them out, and it's a little bit like that in dividing up what we're calling emotions and feelings. We think there's a big pay-off, so we hope that will be fun for you guys to explore.

For Veronica, it was absolutely liberating because she was able to say, "Oh my God, all of that confusion was because I was not in the moment," even though she knew she was focusing on being in the moment. The conversation happening and she's being in the moment, being in the moment—her emotional system wasn't. Her attention was but her emotional system wasn't. And we don't know whether we've made that discernment before between, "I'm really here, I'm really here, my big toe, my left elbow, I'm really here, I really here, I'm really here and my heart is racing and my stomach is roiling even though I'm here," and that's because the emotional idea wasn't there. OK? Got it? Questions?

Comment: I wanted to relay an incident that happened to me this weekend in regard to that. I had an ex-brother-in-law call me and tell me that his brother, who used to be my partner, was

threatening to commit suicide and would I help out by calling him and checking in with him because the brother, Alan,
would no longer speak with Eric but was just threatening by
email. Eric is in China and Alan is in Baltimore.

So I answered this call, which is weird because usually my landline is turned off but I was waiting for someone to call me to do
a reading so the landline was on, so obviously this was supposed
to happen. So I took a big deep breath and thought: Do I really
want to get involved in this? Then I thought: OK, I'll call. So I
called Alan and he ranted and raved and told me that he loved
me and that he would see me on the other side and that he was
going to commit suicide tomorrow, which I thought was weird.
If he was truly motivated, wouldn't he just want to do it now?
He hung up on me and I thought: OK, I'm not going to call
you back because you hung up on me and so I'm going to call
Eric in China and let him know what's going on.

So, I called him and I wasn't even thinking about the money
in doing that, but anyway, that's another story. So I called Eric
and I let him know and Eric and I talked a bit and we decided
that if you want to take Alan seriously then you need to call the
police or do whatever you need to do to alleviate your mental
suffering, then you should do that and Alan would then know
what the consequences of making those kinds of threats were.
We kind of left it like that but it was very involving in a way
that, I mean, I never talk to these people but I was able to have
compassion for both of them in the moment and to try to
work it out and it did sort itself out. Alan texted me the next
day and apologized and Eric called and thanked me and I felt
really good about that, but then I was angry. I wasn't angry
in the moment while it was happening, but all day Monday
I was pissed at 15 different people, not just Alan and Eric, I
was pissed that other people who were only tangentially related
to them. The whole thing really stirred me up and I said you
know, you're really pissed about a lot of stuff, you really need
to take a break and try to just sort this shit out. So I did, but it

was weird to me that I didn't go to the emotional thing right off the bat, I saved it for later, so I'm not truly through with that but it was a really bizarre process.

Eloheim: What did you end up doing with the anger?

Response: I went to yoga and worked through my body. I worked through the angry parts of my body and saw where it was settled in my body and then I did some breathing stuff and then I went to bed. I was just kind to myself.

Eloheim: It's interesting, you're really illuminating our point with your story because what you're saying is, "I had this emotion make a request to be in my body and to have me experience it," and you caught yourself, you noticed it, and you did the things that you could do to kind of discharge it. Because we do know it gets involved in your bodies, right? It's a body thing, intensity of density, you're here to have a body and bodies have emotions and reactions and it physically experiences. And you said, "I'm going to let my body work out what's going on." Now what we want to know is, did you let your anger fire-hose on any of those 15 people, or did you just keep noticing that you wanted to?

Response: I warned someone that I was angry and I said it's probably not a good time to be talking, so, no, I didn't. I mean, if that person had continued then it would have happened. I just said: I'm really pissed off today.

Eloheim: That's consciousness in action because we would imagine 10, 15 years ago, maybe even 6 months ago, you might have been like, "I'm angry and I'm going to be angry at anyone who crosses my path and I have every right to be angry because it's a legitimate emotion to have." And that's where the math problem comes in. We say: What's 9 million times 8 million? And you guys won't take the first answer that comes to mind. But you'll take the first emotion that comes in. It's similar to the math problem where you remind yourself, "Oh yeah, that's right, the first emotion that trips along isn't necessarily the one I want to run with," because in your case you could have made everyone you know mad that day because you were so mad. That's really conscious to say, "I'm mad today, so I don't think I want to talk to you." And Veronica will say it like this, "I'm not fit company for anyone today. So you don't want to come around me today because I'm not fit company because I'm working some shit out." So, it's incredibly conscious and if anyone pushes, well, "I warned you, did you think I was lying?" Great. And so you're over being angry, after you did that.

Response: Yes, I'm over it. I was surprised that I actually saved the anger for later, that seems…

Eloheim: Well, part of what we're getting is you were kind of in shock that these people had reached out to you and you were being very conscious and you were being very careful, there was a carefulness. And the carefulness put you in a conscious place, almost like you're tiptoeing through it, and then once you tiptoed through it you had all that backlog of emotionality that wanted it's, you know, wanted some breathing room, too. It's a little bit like when somebody gets hurt and you have to rush them to the hospital and you're very calm through the whole thing because you know you have to do xyz. And then as soon as they're in intensive care, you break down and cry in the waiting room. It's a little bit like that. And we think also part of it might have been, "What the hell?! I'm not giving up! I'm doing all these hard things all the time so I'm pissed off at you for giving up and calling me to tell me about it. Calling me and telling me about giving up, what the hell?!" There's a little bit of indignation.

Response: Yeah, and you're 63 years old; if you think you should give up, maybe you should give up.

Eloheim: This is a cry for help, we can tell. Not like suicide is a funny subject, but when you look at your idea that you create your reality, that you're a soul having a physical experience, that you've had a series of incarnations, that you're not broken and over if you kill yourself. It's not like the lights go out and it's all over with. On some level you can say, "Well, that was a choice." You know, like, "There you go, making a choice, and it's not the choice I'm making." Everyone, probably, has had those thoughts, like, "I just don't want to do it anymore." And the people who decide to, they decide to. And sometimes the people who don't are like, "Great." There's a sense of, "I'm still doing this, be stronger, at least be as strong as I'm being. I haven't given up yet, and you're going to call me and tell me about it when I haven't talked to you in how long?" We can see where anger would come out of that, you guys can see where anger would come out of that? Yeah, understandable, but it sounds like you processed it in a very conscious way. So there you go, gold star for you. More questions?

Comment: There was an announcement today that Warren Buffet got Bill Gates and youtube.com of the most wealthy families in the country to volunteer to give away at least half of their wealth during their lifetime or after their death, and I just think that's pretty remarkable, that's probably revolutionary in the history of mankind. Where in the past it's been the wealth gets concentrated too much in too few hands and there's revolution or violence. And this is like, wow, they're just going to redistribute voluntarily.

Eloheim: When you start to look at people who are ultra-wealthy saying, "I have enough," because that's what that act says, "I have enough." Veronica read an article, we think it was Mr. Buffet saying, "I have enough and all my family members have enough and I can give away the rest," basically was what he was saying. The "I have enough" energy has not been in your society for a very long time. The idea that "I have enough" goes contrary to the survival instinct because the survival instinct says, "You're never safe, therefore you never have enough because enough helps you feel safe, but it doesn't make you safe."

So when you get into the billions, it's a little easier to modulate that survival instinct, at least for some people. So of course, it takes the ultra-wealthy to maybe do that, but that they're doing it is an incredible energetic. It's an incredible energetic, it's an incredible example of the idea that rich people aren't all "bad." Because a lot of people have the idea that "If you're rich, you're bad," or that "You got your money through illicit means," or that "you're this, that, or the other thing." There's a lot of judgment around wealth and wealthy people, and that keeps a lot of people from gaining wealth because they think wealthy means bad or evil or corporate raiders or stocks were sold short or something like that. It's like, "Something bad happened for you to get rich."

So there is a lot of hesitation in what you might call the middle class to really become wealthy. They want to be wealthy, don't get us wrong, but they never let themselves move toward wealth because they've got judgments about what wealth is. So here you have some ultra-rich people saying, "Yeah, but we're going to do it this way now." It will cascade, not only supporting programs and people that could use funding, but it will also shift the energetic. That's a radical energetic shift, which is welcome. A welcome, radical energetic shift. And it's another wake-up call, you know, we had that thing happen in Haiti and you look and say, "Look at how they live," here's another version of that: The billionaires are giving away their money. "Look at how they're living, they're living differently than I thought, they're living differently than me." That's always helpful, not how the other half lives but how anybody lives. It's more conscious and it brings up opportunities for you to look at how you react. What does it bring up in you, how did you react to it?

Response: That they're giving voluntarily for the good of the group, very hopeful, wow, there's hope for the world.

Eloheim: There's hope for the world if the billionaires will share. Right, so that's really fun for you to sit with, and of course, that's your creation. You created that, you created the fact that in your play 40 billionaires gave away a bunch of money, and your reaction was hopefulness. There are lots of people out there that hear 40 billionaires give away a bunch of money and their reaction is, "The SOBs should give away more."

Response: When you look at remarks about them they say, "Oh they're giving money to population control, isn't that terrible, pro-abortion," and people are already bickering about it. And I'm thinking: Oh man, here they are giving away all this money and if they read of these things at the end of articles about them—how did they get the money?—it must be discouraging. But they would not unless they were enlightened enough to go way beyond that. If I was giving away half of my money and then I look at someone's reaction "Look what she's going to spend it on, I didn't agree with that," I would feel kind of bad, but that's me.

Eloheim: And that's a perfect example of what happens when you're letting the external world tell you who you are rather than the other way around. So there's that and then there's the: "Well, maybe they're enlightened enough to handle it." Who knows? They may be doing it for the publicity, so that people think they're nice, because they're sick of people telling them they suck and they think that if they give away half their money, fewer people will tell them they suck. Maybe they're doing it because they get their names on buildings, you don't know why they're doing it. But in your creation they're doing it because it gestates a sense of hope in you.

Everyone is going to have a different reaction to it and everything else, and that's the beauty of this. So for you, it gestates a sense of hope and it gets you to look at, "God I'm finally feeling hope, and these other people are still bickering." And then you get to see whether their bickering gets to tell you the truth of you or you tell yourself the truth of you. That's the gift here, so yeah, they gave away billions of dollars but that's the gift you got.

We don't want to take the time to go around the circle right now, but it would probably be helpful—because almost everyone's got money issues of one kind or another—to reflect upon what it brings up in you to hear that these 40 ultra-rich people are giving way a bunch of their money. And then don't judge what comes up, just allow yourself to sit with what comes up, and we're hearing from where-ever, "I wish they were giving it to me, I wish they'd give away more, and how did they get it?" is one of the big ones. How did they get all that money, even when Warren Buffet announced he was giving all that money away, Veronica was reading an article and even he said, "Our society overvalues what I did, what I did paid really well, and it didn't make it any better than a teacher or anybody else, it just happens to be that our society pays really well for what I did." Frankly, Veronica couldn't even understand what it was that he did because it had to do with stocks, so she was like, "Wow, cool, you're giving away a bunch of money."

But it would be a gift to you—maybe call in your homework—to reflect on what it feels like to know that that is occurring. What that feels like, and once you know what that feels like, what does that teach you? It's like a short, factual statement. "The 40 rich people are giving away a bunch of their money, period. What does that do in me?" And then follow what that does in you and see what judgments, assumptions, projections you have about it. That's a good place to do feelings and emotions, too, because you had emotions about it and you had feelings about it and sorting them out. And your emotions came with, "How do they feel with all these comments? They might be enlightened enough not to need to worry about these comments, or hopefully they never read them because won't that make them feel bad about this great hopeful thing they did?"

We think that might be fun for you guys, so we invite you to see if you enjoy doing that and we can talk about it some more next week.

Response: With the sun filaments coming out and causing the magnetic waves to flow against Earth, there have been all kinds of predictions from earthquakes to tsunamis and hurricanes, the regular horror stories, and I do have people sending me things and wanting to talk about that on the telephone and it's pretty hard to funnel them into: What are you doing now? What's in your lap? Could we have some more tools?

Eloheim: The interesting thing about that, you know, when people have disaster projections, here we go not being romantic, we're warning you up front, we are fit company but it falls kind of in that category. The question is: Why do you care? The question is: What difference does it make? Are you going to change the way you're living between now and tsunami day? How's it going to change your life? Are you just going, "The sky is falling, the sky is falling." You can say, "OK, what if a tsunami is coming tomorrow, what are you doing about it today?"

It's that old thing, if you knew your life was going to end tomorrow, what would you do in the next 24 hours? If people are so convinced that something "bad" is going to happen, what are they doing with it? Sounds like they're calling up and trying to freak out with you on the phone instead of trying to attend to what's in their lap. Obviously, you just got to say to them, "You sound really afraid, what are you doing with that fear, what is it teaching you, what is it revealing to you? If today is the last day of planet Earth, which it's not, but if today is the last day for planet Earth, what are you doing with that? Are you feeling regret or remorse, if today isn't the last day of Earth, what are you going to do tomorrow? What's Saturday going to be like? What is the fear that you're experiencing teaching you? What is true now? You sound afraid, what are you doing with it?" You know, you're asking for consciousness about the emotions: What are the feelings rather than the emotions?

Response: Thank you.

Eloheim: OK, that was easy—short and sweet. Anyone else got a short-and-sweeter?

Response: You gave us a weather report for a cool and wet spring, you were so right, I want to know if you're going to give a report for August and September?

Eloheim: Let's just look at the seasons here. What we really see happening is that summer is going to be kind of like now. But you're going to have, what do you guys call it, that Indian summer thing and it's going to be hotter. So instead of it peaking in the July/August time, it seems that it's slow but stronger and it's going to be one of those things where you going to go: "Has it ever been this hot in September? Why is it hot in October?" We just feel the months kind of got pushed. Winter got stretched and spring is kind of now, and then summer's getting pushed later. And then you probably will have a very cold winter again, but it may not feel as long. We feel like the winter will be more of a bitter cold but it won't be so long and wet like you had this time. You know, last time it seemed like it never ended, in fact, it feels like it's still happening to some people—this one here [Veronica], she's convinced that if it's not 95 degrees it's still winter. She said to someone the other day, "Some day, summer's going to start," and they're like, "It already did," and she's like, "No, I don't care what the calendar says, has it been 100 degrees?" Veronica and her weather challenges...

But yeah, we see that most likely you're going to continue to have a mild summer, have a very warm if not hot early fall and a very cold winter. When it finally comes it will be very cold but it won't be very cold for very long. You're just in for it again, basically. But spring will probably come early next year, and it seems like spring will be of a more normal pattern. You've had two years of whacked weather, so, you're interacting with your creation, so put in your order. Short, cold winter. By the time it finally it finally gets cold, it'll be well into it. It's going to be weird, we really sense it's going to be weird, like, "Yesterday I was wearing shorts and now I'm wondering where my sweaters are." It feels like it's going to change really fast, when it changes.

It's interesting because it really does feel like this graph that goes up and down and we'll see if it's right, but Christmas will be cold like it always is, Thanksgiving may be actually really warm. Which you guys will probably really like, a warm Thanksgiving you guys can go out and play football in the yard. Right? And that, of course, is for California, we're not talking about all you people all over the place, we're just talking about doing California, mostly, North Bay. Our weather reports don't extend beyond Sonoma county line.

So the Girls. Ready? [long pause] And for those of you who aren't here in the moment, they're passing around a packet of those crunchy goldfish crackers. [laughter] Alright, we're really going now.

The Girls

OK, we want a fish. We never get to eat, you got one? [spits out cracker, group laughter] Wow! You like those?! Wow, wow, wow. OK, we spit it on the ground.

[Watch video of The Girls and the cracker on YouTube: "ELOHEIM: The Girls Eat a Cracker 8-4-10"]

We'll get it later, we're going to put our feet up so we don't step in it. We felt that all the way down the back, you know how you get chills, we got those all the way down. OK, that was fun. Oh. You can imagine that's the first time we've ever eaten anything. We just saw you having so much fun with them, we thought this is loving yourself, eat one of those cracker-y things. We think Veronica thought they were OK, she's had them before, so anyway, we're glad you guys are having those. You can keep them over there, we're going to sit over here.

You really do have to put an enormous amount of stimulation into your systems to even notice, we're noticing that. Like when Veronica went to the concert, she's like, "wow," we're going, "argh." Eloheim took one for the team that night and we're were all like, after Eloheim came back we were all like: How was it? Are you OK? Can we get you anything? And Eloheim was like, "Oh, shit! You guys don't go, if she asks if you want to, say No!" So we all went: Yeah, OK. So when we had the goldfish, damn, it was intense, so anyway, [clears throat] we're trying to come back here and be present with you. We know you guys are all like, "What can we feed them next week? What shall we think of, let's plan." [group laughter] Anyway, back to the subject at hand, which we're not even sure what it is.

Feelings and emotions, that seems to be the theme tonight. And the other thing is, that whole not being romantic thing, we want to address how love fits into it. Because there's a sense of, "I love you but you confuse me." Right? And the "I love you" is the true feeling in the moment and the "you confuse me" is the emotion about projecting in the past or the future. So there is a sense of saying "I love you" to someone and it's incredibly vulnerable. And in the past, that vulnerability made you feel weak, but remember, we've discerned between those two now. So, the ability to say, "My feeling is love for you in this moment," and to sit in it, knowing it's your truth, is incredibly powerful. And also, "My feeling is distrust, my feeling is unease," whatever your feeling is, that's all true.

So, the sense of being able to authentically represent your feelings and when that makes you feel vulnerable, to recognize you're strong. That's the new game in town. Recognize and express your feelings and let that give you vulnerability rather than weakness. And that's really hard because a lot of times, telling someone you care about them or love them or want them in your life in new way especially, making those steps with people can be really, really intimidating because of your fear of how they'll react. But the truth of the matter is expressing your feelings and then going into vulnerability is an unassailable position. It's just what's true. And if you're not projecting into the future then you don't have to project into the future. They may project into the future and you can say, "I'm not attached to the future." You can say, "At this moment, this is how I'm authentically expressing myself to you."

What has happened in your society is, saying "I love you" means "I want to be with you and I expect these kinds of behaviors out of you and you can expect these kinds of behaviors out of me," and there's all that stuff going on. But you can say, "I love you, I appreciate you, I'm glad you're here, I'm glad we're friends," whatever you want to say to someone. If it's an authentic feeling, then it's in the moment; if it's an emotion, it's tied to the past or the future or behaviors that you expect out of that. And when you're in feelings, you're in the moment and you're vulnerable. If you're in emotions, you're not in the moment and you're in weakness. Right?

And that's really an enormous amount of discernment for you to make but the difference in how you will perceive each of those states is huge and it's an incredible gift of loving yourself that you can give to yourself. It's a real strong way to love yourself, is to let your feelings be acknowledged and even expressed, and let your temptation to emotion be modulated, or noticed and attended to.

Because just like you have more crayons to color with, there are more feeling states to color with than you're aware of, but you tend to sweep them into emotions. Sad, glad, depressed, angry—right? And those are such general categories of experience, whereas feelings are extraordinarily varied and nuanced. So that's the gift we have to give to yourself tonight, is to be in the extraordinarily nuanced array of feelings that you have to give yourself by catching yourself when you're short-cutting into emotion. And really selling yourself short. Yeah?

And we had a good time with the fish even though it was something we would not do again. It certainly was an experience to be had, we'll tell you that right now. And the Matriarch's like, come here honey, we'll just hold you. And we're just going to let her because you would do it, right? For any reason what-soever, "Just hold me mommy, I went and had a fish, it was orange." OK, you got it? Good, you're welcome.

Eloheim, part 2

Wow! Where is that damn fish. Oh, good, it's over there, it swam away. Well now, that was just a whole thing there, wasn't it? We're not doing that, we're having chocolate, are you kidding. The tongue was so stimulated that it was overwhelming, like when you guys hear the fingernails on the chalk board, when you get that feeling, it was so much stimulus that is actually gave that feeling through the body, all the way down the back, yeah, chills. Just think, you could be having that much fun with your fish. We're going to have chocolate because we've worked it out, we don't want it to be fancy. [eating a chocolate bar] It's not over stimulating in the way that the fish is and it's not complicated like the M&Ms were, but we did kind of get lost in the moving of the tongue back and forth.

OK? You know what's happening now. Is it time for the Warrior to tell their story?

Warrior

Yes, you've had your fun. When we last left you, we were at the table with the king and his new friends from across the water. And as we recall, Eric and his friends had decided to tell us we should go pillaging with them. Right? That's where we left it. We wonder, we probably don't have time to talk about it, but we have wondered what you did with that story. Did you think we were in a trap of some sort? Were you concerned for how it was going to all sort itself out? Did you think about it at all? Yes, yes.

All right, so, Eric stands up and the splashing of the ale is almost obligatory when challenging the other warriors to go pillage with you. So, we're here at the table and we have our arms here and we're eating the food and he stands up and makes this grand pronouncement blah, blah, blah; and the king is there. We sit just to the right of the king, of course, and the king is noticeably tense, let's call it, because he's invested in the projection of what's going to happen. Mr. King doesn't spend much time in the moment, we'll tell you that right now. So we're there, we're eating, Eric is doing his splashing-of-ale challenge. The men, if you could see under the table, have all pulled knives because they know it's best to be ready. Because this may not go exactly the way other people would like.

So we take a moment, they're all exuberant you know, because they're drunk and excited and blood-thirsty, and they want to go and pillage. And we sit; we sit with their challenge. Let's not be kidding ourselves, that's exactly what it was. It's one thing to play dice and cards and wrestle, it's quite another thing to prove yourself on the field of battle or field of pillage. And they want to measure themselves as comrades. Who knows? They might turn on us there. Couldn't say. We haven't actually made real good friends with them yet.

So we sit there and we just wait. And the king gets more tense and the men continue to eat, but we know they're ready. We've been here before. And Eric and his friends were kind of hollering and hooting and now they're growing quiet, and all the servants have gone quiet and you can hear the crackle of the fireplace, and a dog or two snuffles and resituates itself, but the tension in the room grows thicker and thicker and thicker. And then we look up from our meal. We look directly into Eric's eyes and we hold his gaze and then we say, "No!" and look back down at our meal. To this, of course, there is shock, and the king gets more fidgety, and Eric starts boasting.

You don't let them tell you who you are, ever. No one can tell you who you are. That's the moral of tonight's story, keep that in mind. Now they're going to start goading us. "What, aren't you strong enough, aren't you brave enough, don't you think...?" All that stuff. The temptation is to defend yourself verbally.

Of course, we're not at fisty-cuffs yet, hopefully we won't get there, but we might. The temptation for you, when you're in a similar situation, is to start to do your but- and-because thing. To defend yourself, to justify your position, to explain it, to try and win them over to your side. We couldn't give a shit whether Eric and his buddies are on our side—because you have to remember, we don't have a side. We have our understanding of ourselves. Not their projection of who we are. You get it?

So, Eric continues his boasting and we continue to eat because, after all, part of going to see the king is that the food's good and you don't have to kill it yourself, nor do you have to cook it. We suggest, when you go to see the king, you take advantage of this fact. Eric now has worked himself up. His face is so red, he's just so furious with something. We know what he's furious about: He's furious with the fact, unconscious as it may be, that his manhood is in question now. Because he's used to expressing his manhood by going out and walking all over other people. We're expressing our manhood by sitting in our own energy. We don't need conquering to prove who we are. He feels like he does. So now we're at odds, we weren't at odds until this moment. At this moment, we're at odds because now he doesn't see us as someone who's like him, and that's when he's most dangerous. Because he may need for us to be like him in order to be comfortable in our presence. The king is shitting his pants. Not literally, but close, because he's seen this whole thing fall apart now. Because we are going to be true to what's true to us rather than go along with what this guy has dreamed up.

It's interesting when you're in a situation like this where someone else's knowing of themselves is so predicated on others actions. There's not a lot you can do but be the example of the truth of you to them. Now, we're going to give Eric a back door, we're going to give Eric another choice. Why? Because we don't want to have to kill the guy. The king certainly doesn't want us to kill the guy, and as you go out into the world emanating your truth, what has Eloheim taught you? You emanate your truth simply by being you. You show people there are other options by emanating your truth and being you, right? So we're going to give Eric another option and we say to him, "You don't want to go there. You don't want to go there this time of year, you don't want to go there," whatever reason we think of. We just think something up, in the moment, doesn't matter what.

Not why we don't want to go there. Why we don't want to go there is because we're not into it. If we give him a reason why we don't want to go there, do you understand the difference? "You don't want to go there this time of year," and then he has a back door. He has a way to save face and say, "Oh, you're right, the heat of the moment came upon me." He's young, he may not take the back door, so we're going to give him another one. "You don't want to go there, stay here with us and we'll do some kind of exercise," we'll dream something up, doesn't matter because in this story it's only an example of illuminating to you how you can be your true self out in your world. And in your world, as you experience people like this, whose opinions of themselves are based on how you act, the best thing you can do is emanate the truth of you and give them options if it's coming to a head. You don't want to... we don't even know what situations you get into, but the truth of the matter is, when you are faced with someone who wants their opinion of you to be your opinion of you, you are most challenged to emanate the truth of you. And in that moment, when you emanate the truth of you, "No" is a complete statement. It's a complete sentence. And it doesn't need to be defended, but you can present options to them for making different choices.

So in our story we're going to let Eric say he took the back door, because if he doesn't take the back door, the story ends really quickly. Our guys jump up over the table, kill his guys, it's over. That's not a very fun story. Plus, there's a lot to clean-up, and we're wearing our new underwear. We're not really in the mood to get it all bloody, so there you go. Plus, then the king shits his pants and then we have to leave the castle, and actually we were sort of hoping to sleep in that bed because we kind of like the looks of that girl over there, and that's just the honest truth. So we're moving the story along in the direction that feels good to us, what do you think of that for creating your reality?

So Eric decides, "Oh yeah, you're right." "The wisdom of the king's men," you see, then he flatters us. The wisdom of the king's men show and then he expects us, again, expects us to be who he thinks we are, or to respond to his impression of us, and this is something you have to get into your systems. You can enjoy flattery but don't let it tell you who you are, just as you can experience disparagement but not let it tell you who you are. You know you better than anyone else can know you. So he flatters you and tells you, "Oh the king's men are so smart, so wise, we shall stay here and on the morrow we shall go hunt something." Better hunting it than hunting each other. That's the way we look at it.

And the thing about this story that we want you to really settle in with is that we emanated the truth in the moment and we held to what we knew was true. We did not extrapolate into the past or the future. We did not get emotional, the feelings of the moment were, "We're not interested in pillaging, we certainly not interested in going anywhere with these guys," and we are not afraid in that position, come what may.

Now, the boys all took out their knives—why? Because you have your tools ready when you have this kind of circumstance, because you are rubbing up against unconsciousness. The best tool to have at hand when rubbing up against unconsciousness is consciousness. In this case, our tools are sharp and pointy, but your tools are just as effective.

So we're off on the hunt the next day, and at this point in the story we're going to bring in Eric wanting to be more conscious, OK? So, the hunt is going on and the men are having a great time and we don't know what we're after, say boar, it's always a good one because they're dangerous—very, very dangerous. And Eric comes beside us as we watch the men run and do their thing and says, "I thought it might come to blades last night," and the response is, "If it had, I would have killed you without a thought." There's the truth. Because what he's saying is: "I thought I was going to be unconscious," and you say, "My consciousness would have put that down." You see? And he says, "I know that would have happened, I agree with you that that would have been the case."

In our land, men are not known for their steady minds, they're only known for their bravery. Bravery's another word for unconscious, bravery's another word for: "I'll just do it and see what happens. I'll go with the flow of my emotions, I'll just run in." Courage is feeling the fear and doing it anyway. Bravery is just cannon fodder, a lot of the time. That's the discernment between the two terms, not everyone defines them that way but that's how we define them. It's interesting to have brave fellows around, every now and again they live through it, they typically have good stories, but we'd rather have a bunch of courageous men by our side than one brave one or one hundred brave ones. Bravery's overrated, in our book.

And Eric says, "I would like to join your men, I would like to ride with you, I want to know more of how you can be you." And in that moment, you can make your choice. And this is what Eloheim has taught you well, as you emanate options into the world and then you allow people to approach you and ask you questions about it. To tell you, "I want to know more of what you know." And the beauty of this is you know the journey has not been easy and you know the journey will not be necessarily easy for them, so it's not exactly flattering, it's more of the idea of: "Do you have any idea of what you're getting into? Right? It's, "Well, if you would like."

We tell Eric that if he would like to ride with us, he's welcome to. And at that time we have nothing to ride off to, so let's be in the moment and hunt boar so that we eat well tonight.

Because we're not projecting into the future about what's going to happen with this guy. We're not projecting into the future about what the king's going to say. He came to us with an open and willing heart to learn something new, and we are willing to offer what we have. Not because we're perfect, great, better, but simply because he's saying, "You have something I'd like," and it does not harm us to share it.

In fact, when you teach what you most need to learn, at some point, you've learned what you most need to teach and you're able then to share what you have, not from a place of arrogance but from a place of: "This has been challenging but it's helped me when I compare me to me. This is what has helped me." Not: "I know what's right for you." But: "This is what has helped me." Please discern the difference there and please recognize that we're not going to leave you with a big old cliffhanger this week, but our story is not done because now we have Eric and his men and our guys, and now we get to see what it's like to mix consciousness with unconsciousness. You all know a lot about that and hopefully next week we can share some more with you. Until then, you are welcome.

Fred

This discussion tonight can feel very mental, and we hope you do not leave it on that plane. Do not allow your brains to tell you where to stop and start with this idea of emotions and feelings, that's not the point of this, the point of this is to create a big crack in you, to crack you in two, open you up so your soul can get in deep. To allow your soul to experience the intensity of density with your soul's perspective.

That's the whole point of all of this. And the opening that's being offered to you when you discern between feelings and emotions is a way to go deeply into the feelings. You will be able to have a more profoundly deep feeling state occur when you get the emotionality out of it. We believe you'll be quite shocked at how profound this tool will be. How much more of your soul's energy and insight will be available to you when you get the emotionality out and you let your feelings be accurately represented in the moment.

Your soul waits for the opportunity to have room in you and you have been piece-by-piece clearing out the unconscious aspects of yourself in order to make room and space and make the invitation to your soul to more deeply interact with you. And this is one of the ways that you have not yet experienced your soul deeply interacting with you because, let's say the soul gets to be part of the feelings and the soul does not get to be part of emotions; and they're mixed together like that ice cream cone, so the soul's not actually having a straight line into the experience. We have a very strong suspicion that as you access your feelings more accurately, that you will be able to experience your soul's perspective more profoundly. So we invite you to find the truth of this tool and apply it in your life.

You have the ability to discern between emotions and feelings in this way and we invite you to play with it and enjoy it so that you can emanate more accurately the absolute authenticity of you. Because that's really what's going on here, is that you're emanating accurately the authenticity of you, shared with your soul, so that you might combine your ability to eat these silly goldfish crackers and your soul's ability to comprehend the universe. Can you imagine what that must be like? Well, that's what you're doing, combining those two things, that ability to be in density and that ability to be in expansiveness at the same time. All while walking round going to the grocery store. We just want to, in essence, take off the top of your heads and push all this stuff in there. We do our best. Good night.

Matriarch

Let's have a feeling together. Let's have a feeling together, don't project. Just allow yourself to have a feeling about what you're feeling right now. Feel it. Feel what you're authentically experiencing right now. Just allow yourself to open from the center of you. It's as though you're turning yourselves inside out in order to access the deepest part of you where these feelings have been accurately stored but covered over—buried, if you would. Just turn yourself inside out in that way and let yourself see what's really happening there. What you're really feeling, what your authentic emanation is, the truth of you. The truth of you from an emotive place, and then allow yourself to drop down even deeper, deeper into the lower chakras, the places where density is most dense, and let those turn inside out and feel what you feel there, too.

And we invite you to see where the love for yourself resides, the love for the physicality, the love for the dirt and the grime of it. Remember when you were a child and getting dirty was fun, getting in the mud puddles was fun, and rolling around on the ground was such a delight. You didn't think about staining your clothes or having dirt under your fingernails or messing up your hair. You just let yourself revel in it, revel in the physicality of you, and that's what we invite you to remember, is that reveling in the physicality of you, generating feelings of love for your body, love for the planet, love for nature, love for just the fact that you breathed today. Those feelings are also feelings that have been covered up by emotions, by emotions of responsibility, the emotion of "got to do." What about the feeling, the utter joy of expression?

Be sure to let yourself tap into that feeling state as well. Ah, thank you for sharing your feelings with us. And we say good night to each and every one of you.

August 11, 2010

Summary

Guardians: We come together to explore knowing. We come together to explore the truth, and we come together to deepen our experience of the physical in order to invite the soul's perspective to participate with us.

Visionaries: Delve deeper into the subject of emotions and feelings. The deep knowing of you is facilitated by the clarity you have regarding the difference between the experience of emotion and the experience of feeling.

Eloheim: Took questions regarding emotions and feelings, and used them as examples to go deeper into the subject.

The Girls: Emotions and feelings: The nuances and the aspects that you find yourself experiencing when you experience feelings are going to be far more varied than what you've allowed yourself to experience when you experienced emotions. The emotional state is low-vibrational, therefore limiting. The feeling state is high-vibrational, therefore expansive.

Warrior: Continued with his story of Eric and his men joining the group, and some of the situations that resulted from Eric not being his true self, hiding from his desire and need to express his lack of understanding. Also, more exploration of emotions and feelings.

Fred: Explained that your crown chakra is the chakra that acknowledges the entry of the soul's perspective into the physical form. That's the place where you make that connection, it comes in through the crown. They hold open the portal between our crown chakras and the soul's perspective so that we can experience our soul's perspective more easily.

Matriarch: Explained that what they do is, in essence, hold the mirror of the truth of us up, and also hold us like babes in arms, embraced, to reiterate the security that we can feel within. The truth of us being reflected.

Guardians

Bring your attention in—so easy to do after hearing those lovely sounds together. Bring your attention together and in, and focus on you knowing you. You knowing who you are, you knowing what you are, you knowing all there is to know. This is, of course, not understanding. This is not a mental process. This is a knowing, and knowing is spread across the mind and the body and the soul and the physical incarnation in all its aspects. That is knowing. You know it from the tips of your toes to the roots of your hair. And everything in between. And everything else, too.

We come together to explore knowing. We come together to explore the truth, and we come together to deepen our experience of the physical in order to invite the soul's perspective to participate with us. This is why we come together, and in order for that process to be facilitated, you must bring yourself into the now and allow yourself to have the experience that's offered. Allow yourself to participate to whatever level you're interested in participating. That's the invitation extended. And know that whatever level you've been able to participate, there is another level waiting as you shift and change.

Visionaries

Last week, we spoke about emotions and feelings and the differentiation between those two states in response to stimulus. We imagine that each of you could probably give us a story or two about what that's been like for you, and maybe Eloheim will invite you to participate in that way. But we wanted to discuss it a little bit more in depth because this is not something that only deserves a few minutes of your contemplation.

The deep knowing of you is facilitated by the clarity you have regarding the difference between the experience of emotion and the experience of feeling. The invitation to know which you're in, the invitation to discern the difference between the two and the invitation, then, once you've made that discernment, to stand in feeling and allow yourself to be infused in the now with the feelings you're experiencing.

Of course, what that means is that your feelings don't take over, they don't run the show. They aren't taking you down the road, dragging you around, driving you to fire-hose on people. What they're doing is deepening the experience of the moment. They're giving you those new color crayons to work with. They're offering you the opportunity to facilitate extreme knowingness of yourself and they open up the opportunity for you to commune with your soul, which, of course, raising your vibration, brings in more consciousness and gives you an opportunity to receive ahas.

Feelings, not emotions, as was discerned last week, feelings, are a deep and powerful pathway to ascension. They're a deep and powerful way to ascension because they give you the opportunity to be powerfully in the moment. Being powerfully in the moment opens up the opportunities for everything else we've been working toward. So, it is your doorway, your gateway, your pathway, whatever you like to see it as.

Emotions will trip you up. Emotions habitually drive you. Emotions cause you a lot of drama. Emotions cause you a lot of suffering. Frankly, emotions tend to lead to suffering. So, staying in the feeling state, infusing the feeling state with your consciousness, which allows you to experience the feeling state even more deeply, is what we really want to remind you, and hope that you're working with. And when you find yourself experiencing feelings, allowing yourself the knowingness that the feeling state you're in is infusing the experience of the moment.

A lot of times, we sense that you really aren't clear on what it feels like to be in the moment. And sometimes you can be in the moment in a way that's easy—if nothing is triggering you. But to be in the moment when triggered is something you're not very practiced at. When you're triggered, you may feel present but oftentimes you're in the past or the future when triggered. Allowing feelings to guide you and separating feel-ings from emotions will allow you to be more present in the moment. It will allow you a foothold, a handhold, a grasping point toward the moment. And as you stay present with the feelings you're experiencing, you allow yourself to be present to the truth of you.

So again, emotions are habitually, biologically, culturally based. Feelings are what's actually occurring in the moment. And they can be so incredibly, radically different. And when they're mixed together they can really throw you off your center. And as you discern the difference between these two, you will be able to make enormous strides. Not only in becoming less of a sufferer but in becoming a more conscious, high-vibrational, and ascended being.

Again, taking responsibility for your reactions to your creations fits in nicely with this, because your reactions to your creations are often an emotional state. Your decision—or a biological reaction, maybe we should call it—your decision to discern in that biological reaction, what is what we're calling emotions, what is what we're calling feelings, allows you to infuse that moment with consciousness, to root yourself in the moment and then to stay in the moment, attending to anything that arises. This, of course, gives you the opportunity to manage your reactions to your creations in a new way.

A few weeks ago, we said your reactions to your creations are 100 percent your responsibility. And now we say one of the ways you can analyze your reactions to your creations is check in to what are emotions and what are feelings as you react to your creation. We wanted to tie those two things together because you see, we've moved off the landing and we're walking up the next set of stairs. And as we walk up the next set of stairs, we want you to be sure that there are tools coming to support that aspect of your journey. And as you come into a place where you start to default to feelings, when you start to actually live in feelings rather than letting emotions run the day, you're going to really have profound comparing-you-to-you experiences.

Back when we started talking about being a victim and a creator, that's one very powerful level of the spiritual journey. And this one is another very powerful level of the spiritual journey. It's like a graduation, in a sense, when you start to default to feelings and you crack or break the default to emotions. For Veronica, we know that it works best if she speaks about this; others might meditate on it; or whatever you like to do. But finding the way that really illuminates to you the fact that there are two difference stances you can be in. And there can be multiple emotions presenting themselves and there can be multiple feelings presenting themselves about the same stimulus.

So, the stimulus occurs and you say, "Wow, I'm tempted to fear, I'm tempted to hate, I'm tempted to anger, I'm tempted to feeling like I felt when I was five. I'm tempted to, I'm tempted to, I'm tempted to…." And then when you let yourself say, "But what's actually going on? What am I actually experiencing? If I do my big toe, if I do my elbow, if I start to come into the moment? What is actually my experience?" The feeling you may feel—curiosity, intrigue, fascination—and yet all those others emotions are trying to hold your attention and are quite good at holding your attention. But none of them accurately represents what you're experiencing in the moment. That is what a feeling is, what you're actually experiencing in the moment. And that's where the truth of you lies. That's where the completeness of you is. That's the presence of you, that's the knowingness, that's the space that you can actually use as a handhold.

Emotions are like climbing up a wall and whenever you grab, it just crumbles away from you. It's not real because it's not based in the moment. A feeling is a strong handhold that you can put some weight on. What will be interesting is when you default to feeling and the feeling is a sense of bliss, serenity, what some people like to call love, and fascination. That's the default feeling that you will get to as you work this process. But now you're still having to discern between emotions and feelings and probably take a pretty strong stand with yourself about not following the temptation of emotions into habit. That's what we have for you for now.

Eloheim

Here we are once again it's Wednesday. Let's make some eye contact with you beautiful beings. Feelings and emotions. We're not done with this one yet. Anyone want to talk about it?

Question: I appreciate what they were talking about earlier, telling us the difference between a feeling and an emotion. I thought I was doing pretty well and then a big trigger hit. My dogs started barking at the dogs next door because the fence was put up poorly with spaces in between. So these are all historical things, I realize that. And I went back to that: Oh my God, the dogs are going to break through our yard again and kill my dogs. They're gonna get dead. And I screamed as loud as I could, "Noooo!" And then of course the dogs were quiet. And then I thought: Oh my gosh, that was the trigger. That was a really big trigger. And that HUGE outburst was emotion, not a feeling. But the feeling was fear and the emotion was fear and anger and frustration. Is that right?

Eloheim: Well, the emotion was fear, frustration, and anger and connected to the dogs getting dead. That was all the emotion thing. And the momentary feeling, we would say, had more to do with the idea of, "This is a problem and I know it's a problem and I haven't done anything with it." Like, "I know the fence was put up poorly. I know the dogs might get through and here's a problem that needs to be solved." Yeah. So all the emotion component of it was projection. Because nothing had happened, when the overwhelming reality of the moment was, the only thing happening was the issue with the fact that the fence wasn't secure.

We would wonder who you were pointing fingers at over the fact that the fence isn't right? Is it your fault...?

Response: My neighbor.

Eloheim: You're blaming the neighbor. So your feeling was probably a lot of blame the neighbor. Blame the neighbor and the dogs are going to die. And all this is emotion. Blame the neighbor is a fact. And you were pointing fingers. So, blame the neighbor and, "maybe I could blame myself." Or take responsibility for, "Yes, the neighbor's fence is no good, but I know it and I haven't done anything about it." Right? There's a little of that tucked under there. Like, "Oh my God, the dogs are going to die and I didn't do anything about it."

Response: Yeah. But I was surprised at observing myself screaming at the top of my lungs, and I was totally exhausted afterward. I came in and said to myself: This is so interesting, I am totally exhausted. It totally drained me.

Eloheim: Part of that is what you were saying no to, more than even saying no to the dogs being hurt or the neighbor being a shitty fence builder or you not building the fence properly even though... more than any of that, the "No" was almost like a no to that creation. It was like, "Wait, wait, wait, stop the presses. I see where this is going and I'm saying 'No.'" And that's part of the reason why it was so exhausting, part of what happened is your body went, "Wait a second." It was a lot to physically stop, in a way. It was like, literally, the car's rolling down the hill. Nobody put the brake on and you're trying to stand in front of it. And it was like, "I can almost barely get the car to stop." That's the feeling of it emotionally, or the physical feeling we're getting from you.

Response: It was huge! I know I was triggered from the past because of the dogs got into the yard a couple of times and I know I was triggered because the guys tried to build the fence the best they could, but they left spaces. I was triggered by all these things and I really thought I'd done better than that. But I know I have to keep going and learning.

Eloheim: Well, it's not so much you could have done better than that. We would say it this way: You accessed a deeper position on the subject. You went deeper with the aha. You went deeper with the evaluation of the situation. In the past, it was one way and today it was very, very different reaction. So it's like that onion thing. We've said it 100 different ways but the reality of the situation is, you accessed a deeper part of you, and afterward you immediately spoke about the fact that it was a trigger, you reflected on the fact that it was a trigger. All those things are very conscious and show progress. And in the moment, you had the experience you did. But we really find it interesting, and we're getting it very strongly from you, about the guys… you know even you said, the guys fixed the fence as best they could but they left spaces.

Response: Because they didn't know that it was important.

Eloheim: Yeah. And you know it's important. So we're really getting—even though we know you have an enormous number of things you are doing with your life—there's a part of you saying, "and I should have fixed that. I should do something about that. Those dogs are important to me. That fence is not right." There's almost a sense of brewing guilt. Like, "Something's going to happen and I'm going to feel guilty." So the finger-pointing thing is very funny because the essence of it is you're pointing your finger at yourself. "I didn't do anything in time, and in hindsight I'm going to say I knew better." That's what we're picking up from you.

Response: Sure. That makes sense. So was there a feeling in there or that was all emotion? I'm trying to discern between feelings and emotions.

Eloheim: Yeah. The emotion thing was the fear and the they're going to get dead. The emotion was all of that reactivity. The feeling was more of what we keep picking up from you, which is the: "I know that fence isn't right. I know that fence isn't right." Because that's like a short, factual statement. "I know that fence isn't right and the dogs today reminded me of it. And now what?" Because it's like, "Oh my God, fix the fence." It could be a big job or it could be expensive or it could be whatever. But there's that underlying thing niggling at you: "I know that fence isn't right."

Response: So, just as an add on. A tree fell down through the fence. My neighbor had fellows come to fix it. They didn't know it was important. But when they were putting up the fence, I said: Please make sure there are no spaces. I did what I felt was my best to let them know. I tried to do what I could do without appearing a really bitchy, terrible person to express my needs.

Eloheim: And all that's emotion, too. There are all those emotions in there. "I'm a bitchy person. I tried to do my best but…." There's that victim thing. "I tried but it didn't work out. I didn't want to look like a bad neighbor." You're sharing very forthrightly, but there's probably more in there. And all of that is emotion. All of those are emotions. In the moment, the truth is, "I feel uncomfortable saying this, but I know that's a problem. And that's a problem for my dogs and it's a problem for your dogs and it needs to be changed."

Sometimes, it's really liberating to just say the feelings. Say the feeling so you don't feel the emotion. "This is uncomfortable for me to say," instead of going to "Do they think I'm a bitch?" So, the feeling is what's happening in that moment. What's happening in the moment is the dogs fighting through the fence. It's not the dogs are knocking down the fence, it's not the dogs are dead, it's not the guy's a shitty fence-builder. It's not that damn tree, why did it fall down in the first place and cause this problem. It's: "The dogs are fighting through the fence. How can I attend to the fact that the dogs are fighting through the fence?"

And it's really liberating because if you stay with the feeling that "the dogs are fighting through the fence and that's what I need to focus on," then you're going to attend to it more readily, more quickly, more efficiently. Right? If you're paralyzed in your brain about: "Oh my God, they're going to die," and bad fence-building, or wherever you went with it, you're not focused on attending to animals that are upset. But if you're focused on the upset animals and you get them safe, then you can say, "OK, now, what do I want to do about this?" It also gives you the opportunity to be attentive to what's really going on, which is more helpful, especially in a situation like that. Because some animal could have gotten hurt, you could have gotten hurt. You know, if you were in fear and distracted by your fear and uncertainty and upset, you know, it could go… down the road. That's the thing about emotions. It's a good example. Thank you for sharing it because it's a good one. Anyone else got one?

Comment: I'm glad for that distinction. I was at the airport on my way back home and I realized I didn't have my wallet. I dropped it in the shuttle bus on the way to the airport. The people I told I didn't have my wallet were surprised that I wasn't freaking out. I was aware of my discomfort, which I think is the feeling of the idea of having to plan how to spend the night and coming up with money for getting home and stuff. But basically, because I'm training myself to be in the present moment, there was no problem at that present moment. I was able to tease the airport woman that I was just coming back from camping and I could set up my tent right there. I think that when I am in the emotions of shame or constriction or something like that, it's just becoming more clear. And then there isn't all that time in confusion just by having that distinction.

Eloheim: Yeah. And that's what we were trying to illuminate about the dog story. Same thing you're saying, about that time not in confusion. When you attend to the fact that the dogs are fighting, you're not confused because it's clear what you need to do. And you had the situation where it wouldn't serve you in the smallest way to freak out. Because then you're distracted from attending to what's occurring and you're out of the moment. And when you're out of the moment what do you cut yourself off from? Insight. Soul's perspective. High vibration. Consciousness. So there's a real big payoff for being in feeling because when you're not in feeling, you're taking all of your assets off the table. And you're freaking out. The emotion is kind of a freak-out space. And the emotion oftentimes takes you back to when you're 10 or 20 or 30, instead of where you are today. So you can see how it really rips everything away from you, strips you back down to where you were before you did all this work. So, you're going to do all the work and learn all this stuff and build yourself up, then when the moment happens, the triggers happens, you want to bring it all to the table. Bring your tools to the table. And by bringing your tools to the table, you get the reward of your work, which is to have that response from your soul-level support show up.

Trigger, discernment, discipline to stay with the feeling, and then you get all the information that can come from the soul's perspective. That's how we're seeing it working now. You know, we're always making new layers to this but that's the new layer. The new layer is that discernment, "Am I in an emotion or am I in a feeling?" Veronica had an example where she was feeling. She had fear, she was remembering her birth father looming above her, getting ready to hit her. And she had the idea of being completely alone. All three of those emotions were vying for her attention. In the feeling, the feeling was simply a sense of curiosity and "I just would like to know the answer to this question." But the emotion was a huge amount of loss was going to be happening. You can see how radically different those two states were. And when she stayed with the feeling of it, she got an answer, and she had an experience with the answer that was very constructive. But you can imagine what happens if you stay with the emotion there. And remembering that you're creating your reality from the moment you're in—if you're creating from an emotional state, you tend to get emotional results. If you're creating from a feeling state, you tend to get more feeling. Once you get in them you tend to stay in them. But it's very important at that trigger point, at the bottom of the V, at that trigger, that you use discernment. And that when you use that discernment, you move then and you tend to stay on it. You tend to stay on the course that you pick once you make the discernment. Mostly because the feeling state is so much more high-vibrational, and high vibration kind of feeds on high vibration. It's perpetual motion, really.

So, once you get into a high-vibrational state, your body goes, "Thank God." And it helps support you to stay in the high-vibrational feeling state. When you go into the emotional state, the body freaks out. Because, really, you're in fight-or-flight at that point. So the body is adding its tumultuousness to things. You can see when you get into feeling, it can feed on itself. And you know emotional states feed on themselves. Mob-mentality is a perfect example of that.

This one's important, folks. That's why we're taking whatever amount of time to talk about it. This is important. And your practice at discerning. You know, a good one is in the car and the guy does whatever the guy does in front of you and your reaction. We've talked about it before. Who answers the door? It's kind of a "who answers the door" thing. You have a reaction and it's instantaneous. That's why we said: Fear is a choice, not a mandate. This is another layer to that. This is another layer to that idea. That we're bringing on line the ability to discern what we're calling emotions and what we're calling feelings in order to help yourself root yourself in the moment. And to perpetuate what it feels like to move in the moment that way. Would anyone else like to talk about it before we move on?

Question: Would it be safe to say that emotions are unconscious habits?

Eloheim: Yeah, they're really unconscious habits. Very, very habitual. Quite often, very unconscious and they're the automatic response, let's say. And you know, we have the famous example of the math problem. If you have an emotion, you assume it's right; but we do a complicated math problem, you'd never assume that the first answer that came into your head is right. But the first emotion that comes tripping along, you guys are like, "Well, I felt it, so it must be real." Well, yeah, it's real, but do you want it to be in your reality? We're not denying that it's a real experience, but here's your reality and you get to dictate what's in your reality. OK?

Question: So if you get triggered and you go into your emotions, and you even become that whatever-aged person, might be multiple ages, but if you're able to catch yourself in it… Because I know that mad is an emotion but you can calm yourself down to: "I feel mad," and then go into a solution. So, are emotions sometimes good for pushing you into a solution or should you say, "Shit, I got triggered." Because you don't want to be triggered at all, right?

Eloheim: Well, you can't help but be triggered when you're in the human body. It's just a fact of life, at this point. Until you're Homo spiritus, triggers are going to be a reality, so you can't say, "I don't want to be triggered." You say, "I'm going to deal with my triggers in a new way." And you can say, "I caught myself being mad," and mad as an emotion takes over, you can get out of control, it can run the show, you can fire-hose on people, that's mad as an emotion. You can have a feeling of, "This isn't okay with me." That can be the feeling because that can be the truth in the moment. But "this isn't okay with me," is here [gestures in], mad is out here [gestures out]. See the difference? So, "This isn't okay, I'm going to set boundaries, I'm going to state preferences. I'm going to make decisions about 'this isn't okay.'" You see the difference? Yes.

Question: I feel that the use of neutral observation, once a feeling starts, that it keeps me out of emotion. So I'm wondering is this a tool.

Eloheim: Yeah, neutral observation is a great tool. For those of you who aren't familiar with neutral observation, it's the idea that, not deciding ahead of time if this is bad or good, but saying, "This teaches me something." So that was the main point of neutral observation, was to get you out of duality. Now, if you get into a feeling state and you use neutral observation to keep you in that feeling state instead of going into duality, which would be emotion, it can be used that way, definitely. Because it helps you stay out of duality—neutral observation. And then you infuse that space you find when you're neutral with: "What's really going on here, what is true now?" What is the feeling you're experiencing? And then you allow that to perpetuate. Sure, if that works for you, it looks like a good use of that tool. We're mixing and matching the tools, folks, we're mixing and matching. It's like your wardrobe, sometimes you wear that necklace with a different pair of pants and it's okay. If it still goes, it still goes. Anybody else?

Comment: I really like your distinction. My husband and I were up in Shasta; we're looking for a place to live up there and a lot of stuff came up. I was already feeling uncomfortable going up the mountain with him. When we got to a certain place, I was looking forward to a walk to clear and I really wanted him to enjoy this walk. We get up there and the place is totally closed down because of all the water that they had, this area wasn't walk-able. I went right into everything—depression, resentment, mad—a variety pack. It was curious to me because I said "I'm done, let's just go, I'm done." And I expected a reaction and he didn't react the way I thought he would, it was weird. He just said, "Well wait a minute, let's just look around." And I'm going what is this? And then I thought about, you know, I was mad, I was feeling mad but the tone of voice that I used was actually just like, you know, I'm sad, I'm done. And I think he was reacting to the sadness and wanting to make me feel better. So we ended up going up the mountain and there was still some tension but I was able to come to the realization of what had happened dynamically. When we started back down, I asked him what he wanted to do, he wanted to visit a place he'd been before. Then, he was going into that emotional state saying, "I don't know where I'm going, it's been too long," and because of what happened before, I was going, "I recognize this." So I just kept it kind of upbeat and just said, "This is an adventure." And the whole time, it was absolutely amazing. We got there and he was still fearful and he didn't know where the place was that we were walking to. But holding that intention, holding that feeling of, "I know what he's feeling, I know the emotional component, and I can hold over here that feeling of openness and adventure." And it had an effect. I could almost see that emotional field of his until he was very relaxed.

Eloheim: That's great. Emotions are contagious. They really are, we know that for sure. It would be interesting to see how feelings spread. Because emotions jump from person to person very quickly. Feelings may not do that exactly, because feelings are more of an emanation. It's more like you telling yourself the truth and you become different within, and we don't know what that will look like in community. But we imagine it'll be interesting to observe because what you're doing is infusing your emanation with more truth. And again, that's sort of like if you were a light bulb your wattage goes up. So you start to broadcast something that's different. But it's quite different than that sort of virus kind of a way that emotions spread. It'll be interesting. We'll let you guys tell us what you find about that.

We have come to the part in the meeting where we have to do math. We have 39 minutes more to get four more council members involved in the meeting. We probably have a few more minutes, don't you think? Anybody have a question?

Question: I've been having an interesting experience at a job. It's a network-cabling job, it's a great big cabinet shop full of men, one woman, and me. I had a little bit of a feeling thing go on with the boss, he's a little unusually weird. Apparently, he says one thing to the office manager and something else to me. We had a nice long meeting, the three of us decided what to do, and then he showed up one of the days I was working there and he said, "What are you doing here?" like we never had the meeting. He kind of flipped out a little bit, but I just thought the whole thing was fascinating because I was really sure of who I was and what had happened. And then he got over it really fast.

Eloheim: We want to interrupt your story because we want to make a comment about that. That is a perfect example—who said you don't want to be triggered? That's a perfect example where the trigger was the best part of the story, because if the trigger hadn't happened, there's no story. Right? The trigger happens and that's what creates the opportunity for knowing something happened. Right? If the boss had just come in and everybody had been, "da da da da da," you would have learned about network cabling, and just how much more of that do you have to learn? So instead, you got to learn about comparing you to you, staying in your truth, being in your presence, not letting his opinion tell you who you are.

Response: Don't let the king tell you who you are. I love that. It's so liberating for me.

Eloheim: Veronica's getting chills all down her arms and interestingly on her scalp which feels really cool. It's like, you know, when they wash your hair at the hairdresser, it's like that. If we could make that happen on a regular basis we would. Is there a button for that? We want that to happen more. Veronica is just dying right now.

Anyway, what we were trying to say is yeah, you went to see the king. You see, this is what you guys also do when you create triggers, you give yourself the opportunity to compare you to you. You give yourself the opportunity to feel progress. Remember when we said, when you're grateful for your triggers you know you're really moving down the path quickly? When you're grateful for triggers, period. When you say, "OK, that helped." It's not to say, "I want to be triggered because I don't want to be bored," because triggers are still uncomfortable most of the time. But it's that point where you say, "That trigger gave me something. I took something away from it. I didn't just take emotional upset. I parlayed my feeling into progress." And eventually, like the Visionaries said, your feeling won't be upset and suffering. It'll be serenity and bliss. Not yet, maybe, but pretty much closer than we've ever been before.

Now, one of things Veronica caught herself doing, she had a big trigger, did the feeling thing, and she's in the other side of the feeling. Like, the feeling happened, stuff occurred. Feelings happened. Feelings were worked through. At the other side of that. After the conversation, after the situation, you know, we're here now, we're not wherever else we've been. There's this thing of saying, kind of wanting to clutch at it. "It worked! That was so much better than what it's been before. I want to clutch at it, I want to hold it. I want to get past it to where it feels natural and normal." And we told her—in the bathroom of the Chinese restaurant, just in case you guys want to know, we often talk to her in the bathroom of restaurants—that this is graduation. This is not something to be rushed through. This is so that it sinks in, don't rush through this feeling of "OK, it worked. Good! It worked! Okay!" There's this sense of wanting to skip what happens when it works. And skip into: "It's over, thank God I made it through." Like it's boot camp and you made it through the obstacle course. OK, go ahead with the rest of what you were going to say.

Response: The other little thing—a lot of the guys there, I ask them a question and they tell me a ten-chapter story. It's like nobody ever listens to them, so they're going to take this opportunity to tell me all kinds of things that aren't related to my question. And I was kind of wondering if that was related to maybe the monsignor life or the herbalist.

Eloheim: It's related more to the fact that you seem like a person who has answers. That emanation thing, remember we said, don't shake the people by the shoulder and tell them you have answers. You wait for them to ask you if you have answers. You come off as a person, especially in that environment, as someone who has something that's interesting and different. And yeah, they're probably not listened to and you seem like a person who could hear them. Not just listen to them but hear them. We hope you guys understand the difference. You come off as someone who can hear them. And the fact that you can relate because you've worked in construction, worked in that kind of a field and you don't come off all girly-girly, so you feel safer, but you're a woman. There's a lot of dynamics going on there, so this will be fun for you.

There's a sense that when you're there and these people want to have these kinds of conversations with you, to allow yourself, not as an ego thing, "Look how cool I am," but it's a compare you to you, "Wow, they really want me to interact with them. I'm being invited to interact with these men." Where in the past there may have been professional jealously, there may have been: "I don't want anything to do with you," there may have been: "Get out of my way." There may have been a lot of other things. Now, you're getting: "This is someone who can hear me." And they may not know it consciously, probably don't know it consciously, but you can see how they're responding to the emanation. And that's a perfect example of what we've been telling you guys for a long time. People are going to say, "You've got something." How they do that, for a man to want to tell you a big, long story, is not exactly the most common thing to happen in most people's lives. Right? Like, how many woman are going, "I just wish he'd talk to me." Right?

You got it? We made some progress on that subject? Go out and have some fun with that and we're probably going to talk about it some more next week. Remember when we did four weeks of fear? We talked about fear for four weeks, nothing else.

Why? It was that important. We can do three weeks of feelings and emotions. This is that important. We don't necessarily have to spend the whole meeting on it next time, but if you have something come up that you feel like sharing, be ready, because we're going to open up space for that unless something really different happens in the next seven days and we have to skip it. But we have a sense that there's going to be room for that. OK? Yeah? Thank you for those who shared and those who added just energetically because we really want you guys to start living in serenity. We've chipped away at it. Boy, if you talk about the marble sculpture, we've been chipping away at it, big chunks have come off. We're revealing the finer features of it now. OK, enough said.

Let's see, what are we going to do here? Very soon, you know who's going to come [Warrior]. Where did they leave off? Oooh, Eric was going to join their band, right? Their band of merry warriors. They're going to like... we should shut up right now. Going to eat chocolate, don't you mind us. They're [Warrior] really scary. If you guys could see them…. Veronica doesn't invite us to show up in the physical. We had to make a deal about that a long time ago. She was like, "Why is it that everybody's story is the apparition appears at night in my bedroom? No, absolutely not! You are absolutely not appearing in my bedroom at night. Off the list!" This was years ago. "No! All I need to do is wake up and see you in my bedroom. I'm gonna scream. No, it's no good!" She's not into the physical appearance thing. It's interesting how people think that certain things would be so cool and Veronica says, "No, that's not cool. I'm not into it." So we listen, most of the time. We listen until we don't. She absolutely gets to have her free will and we absolutely encourage her free will in certain directions at times. Or you wouldn't have Fred. You like Fred, right? OK. Well, Fred would not be here if we hadn't said: "We know you don't want to do it, but by the way, it's time."

You wanted to get off the landing didn't you? If you

wanted to get off the landing, you had to have Fred. The Visionaries—they took a year-and-a-half to come. We took five years to come. It was predicted we would come; five years later we managed. A year-and-a-half later, she actually started working with us. And then The Visionaries, they were predicted; a year later, they came. We've been on a roll ever since. We just kept pushing them in.

Question: Is that fear or really good boundaries [on Veronica's part]?

Eloheim: It's fear and it's seeing how powerful boundaries are. Fear generated the boundary and you can see how powerful boundaries in free will can be. It's also her own spiritual path. Her own journey of making peace with being a public figure, mostly. It has to do with core emotion, too. But yeah, making peace with being a public figure and making peace with all that it entails. Which is a developing process. Okay? We're all good on Veronica's stubborn nature?

The Girls

We're being serenaded by guitars. The people next door are playing their guitars. We can hear them practicing. They're not even playing, they're sort of strumming randomly. Which is nice. We're not picky because after all, when's the last time we heard guitars in the body, right? See how we can delight in something that can make you arrrgh! We're delighting in it. There's a choice there between a feeling and emotion. You like the theme? We're on the theme.

The really neat thing about all this is when you actually experience feelings, you get to experience a wide range of them. Emotions are actually quite narrow. They're very loud and they're big. But they're very narrow in the sense that there's not that many of them. They aren't nuanced, right? Anger, dread, fear, passion maybe, we don't know. But there's a very small palette, let's call it, and when you start to get into feeling-land, it starts to become richer, more varied. There are opportunities for more variables to present themselves.

Now, all feelings eventually lead to what we call bliss or serenity, whereas all emotions basically are fear. So there is that kind of narrowing-it-down of it all. But the nuances and the aspects that you find yourself experiencing when you experience feelings are going to be far more varied than what you've allowed yourself to experience when you experienced emotions. Again, because the emotional state is low-vibrational, and low-vibrational is very limiting. Whereas the feeling state is high-vibrational, and high-vibrational is very expansive. So it makes sense, it falls into the rest of the things we've been teaching you guys, or sharing with you guys.

The opportunity is for you to have wide, varied experience of feelings, and that experience feeds you in a new way. And being able to leave behind the narrowness of emotion and to wallow in the experiences of feeling. Not only does it make the moment more pleasurable, it also gives you the opportunity to experience an ever-expanding palette of things to experience. So when you get into the feeling state, instead of it being just blue or green, it gets to be sky blue or royal blue or you-name-it blue. Right? It starts to become these nuances, these nuances of feelings are available to you. And we expect that you'll start finding yourself being able to discern between the nuances of feelings you find yourself in just like you can discern between different colors of blue.

And that's the fun bit, right? What you're doing is taking yourself out of the limitation of Homo sapiens and allowing yourself to experience the variety of Homo spiritus. And of course, since the Homo spiritus state is infused by the soul, and the soul is infinite and immortal and very expansive, it makes sense that the feeling state would also reflect that. The feeling state is like bubble bath and all that yummy stuff, whereas the emotional state is very stark and it's very limited.

And it's very train-track-y. Here's the train, here's the stops, which stops are you getting off at? Whereas the feeling state is like running through a meadow filled with millions of different kinds of flowers, and which one am I going to smell today?

There's all kinds of options and openings. It's like a kaleidoscope, looking through at all the different colors and combinations and nuances for you. So there's a lot to be gained and a lot to be taken from the feeling state that the emotional state is just void of. Yeah? Pretty cool huh? Yippee! All right, that's about what we have for you tonight. Have fun with that. Meadows, flowers, yippee! We've run through flowers, metaphorically.

Warrior

So, we were telling a story, we believe. Yes, that's where we were. And in the story we left off with Eric wanting to hang out with us. And yes, we're sort of glow-y in the way Eloheim talked about earlier, they want to come hang with us. And considering that before that, they wanted to go and rape and pillage the neighbors, we think that was a good outcome. Emanating the truth, speaking up, allowed for a different alternative to present itself.

Now, some might think, "Oh God, now you're stuck with Eric and his band of marauders." Eric and the Marauders. That might make a good band name. Eric and the Marauders—oh, the potential. For a limited engagement, Eric and the Marauders, every Wednesday night.

So, Eric and the marauders, because now we have to call them that, because it's too cute to pass up, want to join our band. Now, you have to remember that we are not that many in this story. In this story, we are twelve or so, we are not a huge group of men. But Eric and the marauders want to join in, and the thing about Eric and the marauders is that they are almost equal to us in number. That immediately causes a little bit of a thing. Because when you have equal numbers it's very easy to believe that you have equal representation of how things will be led. And Eric and the marauders are coming along because Eric is all keen to see what we know, but his marauders are a little confused as to why he would make himself subordinate to us. Put himself in a position of less authority. His men are confused by this. Now, because Eric is just a kid in his spiritual world, he doesn't tell them, he just expects that because he's made the decision, they'll follow along with no problem.

Now, this isn't the army. This isn't something where someone tells you an order and you just obey it. We're twenty guys walking through the forest. Let's be real.

The only hierarchy that happening is the one that created from respect or fear, or both. So, Eric didn't take his marauders opinions into account much when he took them off of their boat and fed them for a while and now wants them to go through the forest with us.

[The video camera fails at this point]

We have an emergency, we need another battery for the camera. OK. We're going to let Eloheim come in so Veronica can see what's going on. We'll be back.

Eloheim, part 2

[starts the process rolling to fix the camera, and asks if anyone has a question while the technical issues are being resolved.]

Question: Off topic completely. I've been practicing therapeutic touch to smooth out energy fields of people, and I'm wondering about the effects of people who use marijuana—medical marijuana—the effect on their field. How their field might feel different and how I could work with that?

Eloheim: OK. Medical marijuana, in general, is a positive thing when it is used consciously—just like anything else. When it's used as an excuse to tune out, it is not very helpful. It may be helpful for symptoms, but energetically…. Marijuana and other narcotics and prescription drugs and even caffeine can create different states in the physical body. Those physical states, of course, have an impact on your physical field. Now, when marijuana and other substances are used consciously, so you can experience states that you're not experiencing without them, so that you can try to new things, so that you can experiment—OK. But when you put yourself into a position where you're doing it to get away, to tune out, so you don't have to think about something, so you're doing it to be unconscious, then what it tends to do is shrink your auric field and make it… you would feel it as rough. Pebbly would be the right word, that's the sensation we're feeling. Like the outside of a building when it's stuccoed or something.

What's the verdict, Ms. Mary? The camera, apparently, has died. The camera went to heaven. The sound should be OK. They have sound, they just don't have a picture. Let us just hold it one more minute to let Veronica have a moment with it. This is what she's thinking, just to share her little process with you guys. She's had this camera for eight years, it was $800. She wants it to work. She doesn't want to buy a new camera. More than the problem of buying the new camera—you know what the question is? Which one to buy? "Fuck!" Is what she's saying. "Fucking work so I don't have to find one that works." It's a good thing you people can't see her because she's sort of attacking the camera.

OK, go on with your question.

Response: Let's say people who are using marijuana to be more in the moment, not to escape but to more feel everything, and their field feels a little different. I'm just curious.

Eloheim: If they're consciously using it to seek alternate states, if they're consciously using it to learn more about themselves—but there's always a residual effect of using that kind of stuff that can be in your field. So, there's a difference between using it consciously and unconsciously, we covered that. There's a difference between using it to escape and not escape.

And there's a difference between: "I can't reach these states on my own so I have to use it." There's: "I have to use it," and then, that can turn into dependency to reach altered states, and we think that's what you're feeling. That thickness is like that dependency of that tool to reach the altered state.

So, there's the opportunity to use it to achieve that state and there's the opportunity to become dependent, not addicted, but dependent on it to get a certain place. It becomes disempowering at some point. There's a return on investment that can kind of go like a mountain. So, watching where you get something you weren't able to get before, and it's new, and getting to the point where: "I know I can't have this unless I do." When people do it in an addictive way, it feels pebbly, and that thick feeling is almost a barrier they're putting between them and the reality of achieving alternate states.

OK? Makes sense. It can't be a replacement. Even when you see the shamans using mind-altering substances, they're not not shamans without it. They're just achieving something different with it. It doesn't take away your power to be that, it enhances it until it doesn't. Because even a shaman who might take a mind-altering substance can't live on that mind-altering substance, or you're not having the experience you're having.

OK, we've got to get back to the Warrior. So, everyone can close their eyes and see the story of the Warrior in their minds.

Warrior, part 2

OK, we're back. So, the camera broke, who gives a crap? It broke, it didn't break, you'll get a new one or you won't. We're still going to show up. Back to Eric and the marauders joining the merry band, and out we go.

Now, what's interesting here is Eric, well, he didn't tell us that he didn't talk to his men, but we could see it and we knew that it was going to brew. We knew there was going to be a problem because you have to remember, just before Eric decided to join our band, what were we doing? We were competing in games of chance and other things, right? So Eric's men knew that our men had a cohesiveness. Our group had an unwritten structure to it. His group was far more "Do as I say." They did not gel very well with our group because the leadership styles were so different. They kept looking for guidance. Eric kept saying, "We're going to go this way," not explaining. We don't have to explain anything. They're not our guys, anyway, and we don't know them. We're not going to bother to get to know them until we get to know them, if you know what we mean.

It was not pretty when it came to an end. And in this case, what you have is an example of this emotion/feelings thing. Because the men got hot-headed. They grumbled and they did not want to play nice. They started to feel betrayed by Eric, they started to feel misled. They started to feel like, "When are we ever going to go home, why are we here, what are we doing?" Those are emotions. The actual feeling was simply, "What the fuck?" But instead of that, they went with all those other things we described. Eric could have simply stepped in and said, "Look, we need to do this for a little while," but he didn't. He didn't, he didn't, he didn't, he didn't until one day, we were off doing something important, and all of his guys decided not to help. It wasn't pretty for them.

The result is the emotions kept them from having an experience of camaraderie, which is one of the reasons they came along with us. It denied them the opportunity to learn, which is another reason they came along with us. And it created a situation where a couple of people didn't quite live after that. Oops. Which sort of pissed off the rest of them, we have to say.

Now, we didn't kill them. We were just doing something. We had a job to do and they were supposed to help and they didn't do a very good job of helping. And that's what happened. The moral of the story is: Tell the truth. Part of the reason Eric couldn't tell his men what was going on was that he didn't want to admit he didn't know everything. He didn't want to admit that there was a place for him to learn. He didn't want to admit that, and because he didn't want to admit that, he denied them the opportunity to have authentic presence in the band. Authentic presence with us. And it cost two of them their lives. So now, Eric is even further diminished in the hierarchy of the no-hierarchy of our experience. He's even more diminished in their viewpoint because they've lost two of their comrades. And they're still wandering around the woods wondering, "What the fuck?"

The opportunity here is to remember, you don't want to be an Eric wandering in the woods, not admitting to yourself that you want what's being offered. You see, there's that part of you that will sometimes say, "I want something but I don't want to admit I want it." Again, it falls back into the weakness/vulnerability thing. I'm in a position of weakness or I'm in a position of vulnerability. Vulnerability is based in truth. Weakness is based in lying. "I don't want anyone to know I need to learn something, therefore, I'm going to be in a position of weakness." Rather than admitting there's something to learn from these men. "We're going to go with them, and yes, they're going to be in charge of what we do." Eric felt diminished by that, but knowing he wanted it, not informing his men.

He was a mess. He was a mess. Some of you might say, "Well, why didn't you step in and tell him how to be?" Well, it's the same reason you're not advised to run around shaking shoulders and demanding people behave in a certain way. The truth of the matter is, you have knowledge and they will come to you if it's your turn to share it with them. After this little mishap, Eric did not come to us, but his men did. One by one, here and there, and say "We don't want him to lead us anymore." Some of them didn't want to be there, some of them wanted to come with us. Until finally, Eric isolated himself through his own inability to tell the truth about the situation he found himself in. Through his own inability to discern what was going on with him, emotion or feeling. Through his own inability to offer the truth of him to the situation. He ended up isolating himself.

Now he could have been a boy, let's say, instead of a man. Or he could have hidden from the truth of the matter. And it will be very interesting to find out what he decided to do, and you'll find that out next time because it's more fun when it's a cliff-hanger, right? Yes, we know you like those cliff-hangers. All right, that's it for tonight. But the moral of the story? Don't be an Eric. Vulnerable. Tell the truth. Be honest about your feelings. Be willing, be willing to admit when you want to learn something. Open to the fact that you don't know everything. That one you're pretty good at already. And allow. Allow yourself to be in the presence and the moment of the situation at hand. That's it. No problem. What is it? Six or seven steps. You'll have it down by next Wednesday. Good night.

Fred

We're going to open tonight with the idea that your crown chakras are very activated by this idea of feelings and emotions. And many people would think, "Oh wait, that shouldn't be, because it should be more of a body experience. Maybe the power chakra or heart chakra. It's emotions, it should be all about the heart or love," or something crazy like that. But the truth of the matter is, what's really being activated is your connection to your soul. That's what's really being activated at this time, is your connection to your soul. And as we are the member of the Council that resonates with the crown chakra, it makes sense for us to bring in that energy and connect you more deeply with your soul's possibilities. Because as you bring the truth of you into the moment, and you allow feelings to help you access the ascension process, and you connect more deeply with your soul, your crown chakra is the one that does the job. Your crown chakra is the one that acknowledges the entry of the soul's perspective into the physical form. That's the place where you make that connection, it comes in through the crown.

And as the crown chakra resonates to our frequency, what we can offer you is some clarity about how it works. And the way it works is this: The crown chakra opens to the reality of the soul's perspective, and as the soul's perspective, in a sense, starts to descend into the physical form, your ability to stay in the feeling state is sort of the lubricant or the causeway for the soul's perspective to actually infuse the other chakras. To start moving into how you see. To move into how you interact with the verbal. Move into how you interact with your heart. Move into how you act in your power. Move into how you interact in relationship, and eventually, to move into the way you feel secure in this world.

So, the crown chakra is the portal to your soul's perspective, and feelings are the causeway that gives it the opportunity to infuse you. And as it infuses you, it broadens your experience of this world as was shared earlier by the Girls. And it facilitates that place in you that allows triggers to become handholds, triggers to become the pathway or the guiding point to serenity or bliss. It takes the triggers and turns them into serenity. That is the pathway that the crown chakra opens up and offers to you.

That's the journey that you're on. That's the gift you're being given right now. And that's why, as we come in—someone asked earlier, "Why did Fred have to come?" Well Fred—that's us—had to come because you were ready to start building the bridge more deeply between the physical form and the soul's perspective. And we're incredibly able to hold that portal for you, so that you don't have to keep opening it and re-opening it re-opening it as triggers and responses and emotional states create a closure. Because triggers take you into a lower-vibrational state if they're reacted to with emotions. And in that case, most often what was happening is the upper chakras were sort of closing down. We're trying to use language. It's not very language-y, but we're trying our best to share with you that the portal between you and your soul's perspective wasn't kept open. Because you kept shifting between unconscious and conscious, low-vibrational and high-vibrational states.

We came in to facilitate creating that portal and holding it open, so you could practice with discerning between emotion and feeling. Practice holding a higher-vibrational conscious state without having to also keep that portal in place. That's why we're here and that's what we're doing, and that's all we've got to say for tonight.

Matriarch

As Fred holds open the portal, we hold you. We just hold you. We always see you in a big basket in our arms. And all this stuff that goes on, your emotions, your feelings, your chakras, your triggers, comparing you to you, and the progress you've made. All those things that happen, they happen within the basket or vessel of the intense loving presence that we hold. And we don't hold an intense loving presence for you as if we are giving you something. We're not giving you love, what we're doing is holding the truth of you loving you, for you to see. For you to live in, for you to be in, for you to experience.

In essence, we hold the mirror of the truth of you up, and we also have you like a babe in arms, embraced, to reiterate the security that you can feel within. That truth of you being reflected. It's a big job, but it's our only job. The rest of the Council have all these different things they do and it's wonderful. But always—not just at the end when we talk—always, we hold you reflecting the ultimate truth of you to you, while embracing you and offering the true security of the essence of you as your gift. That's what we do, because apparently we're doing job descriptions at the end.

Good night to you all and thank you, thank you, thank you for coming and showing us the truth of you. What a joy for the truth of you to be here tonight.

Good night.

August 18, 2010

Summary

Note: During set up, we had a number of technological challenges. The Council incorporated our experiences into their message.

Guardians: Silent energy work.

Visionaries: "I am new" – watch the tendency to match energies with previous instances of an experience. The intensity of the moment. "Do you have the courage to make it about you, to think about yourself instead?"

Eloheim: Insight into the composition of the Council; how and when each member came in, how they communicate through Veronica, how they communicate with each other. The overall mission of the Council is to balance our physical experience of being Homo spiritus.

The Girls: "Why we tell you to love yourselves is because no one else will. Somewhere in your energy field had to be a constant reminder that it's OK to just love yourself. That even though you think you suck, that even though your life is hard, that even though you feel like you've been in suffering and habit and confusion and angst and all that stuff, there is still room for love, of you to you."

Warrior: Spoke about how we relate to weapons, both in our alternate expressions and our current incarnation.

Fred: "The opportunity to work with you all and to experience the physical form is a great honor and it's a great path for expansion for us."

Matriarch: The Matriarch's section was not recorded.

Guardians

Silent energy work.

Visionaries

It's a good example, fussing and blustering and all that with technology—or whatever your version of the thing that's driving you crazy this week is. It's a good example of how you can be pushed and pushed and you use your tools and you bring yourself back to the center and back to the center and back to the center and back to the center and back to the center so many times that at some point we understand when you just kind of want to say, "Forget it. I quit. Let me out. Stop the bus." And what we want to remind you of is even when it becomes so frustrating and so difficult and so challenging and you just really want off the bus we always want to bring it back to this fact. And the fact is that you're letting yourself have these opportunities where you feel sandpaper, where you feel frustration, where you feel anxiety, where you feel fear, where you feel hopelessness even, you're letting yourself have these experiences from a completely new place, and if you don't compare you to you and if you don't give yourself that courtesy you really will go down in a frustrated hole.

You want to continue to remind yourself it's not the same as the last time. And it can't be the same as the last time because the last time you weren't you. You were a different version of you. It can't be the same. And this is a real nuance-y aspect of compare you to you that this experience with the camera difficulties gave us the opportunity to have with you, which is reminding yourself that you are new all the time and that when experiences occur—especially when they're experiences that are similar to experiences you've had in the past—that's a perfect moment to remind yourself: "I am new. I am new and what is happening here is not the same as before." Because that's really what we see happening for a lot of you, is when something occurs to upset you, to frustrate you, to anger you, to make you feel off balance, your tendency is to match energy with previous instances of the experience. And as you match energy with previous instances of the experience, one: you're leaving the moment, and two: you're actually changing your vibration to something that doesn't actually experience itself as the truth of you. You're moving out of your current vibration in order to resonate with the vibration of a previous instance.

Even Veronica just said, "It reminded me of when I didn't have help." So that's the space that she was arguing with, fighting with, being challenged by when the camera wasn't working properly. And of course that space is not the space she's in now. So it was the dynamic of remembering, being reminded of, what it was like say, a year ago, and then trying to be in this moment and also projecting into, "What if it doesn't work, what if we can't get it fixed, what happens then?" So it's a really good example of what happens when you have a trigger and where you go. It's a little bit of who answers the door, but it also illuminates the reality of the moment, which is if you can stay with what is going on right now you have the best chance of moving through it with some grace.

It's very hard. It's very hard and we know it. But the alternative is such suffering—and we bring this up all the time to you guys. The alternative is suffering. So yes, it's hard. Yes, it's hard to continuously remind yourself to be in the moment, be in the moment, what is true now, what is actually happening right now, who is answering the door, what's going on with my big toe, come back to the moment, receive insight, open to new ideas, in the moment, in the moment, in the moment. And one of the reasons we bring that up so much and always constantly say it is because if you're not in the moment you don't have access to the highest version of you, meaning your soul's insight. But if you're not in the moment you actually don't have access to the current version of you, either. And every moment that you're not in the moment you're diminishing the—let's see, the best way to say it is something like this. Let's say you can be

100 widgets, that's working with your soul's perspective—100 widgets—and if you're in the moment but not yet connecting to your soul's insight, maybe you're 65. And if you're in an experience where you're in the past or the future it plummets. It plummets down to like 12. The difference is huge. So where am I in the widget scale? It's important to inquire about that.

It's important because the difference is so substantial and you owe it to yourself to say, "I want those 40 points. I want them." Because this challenging thing will not get easier by going into the past or the future. It will not get easier by going into the past or the future. That we have confidence about. Where it will get intenser—and we know that's not a word but we don't care—the intenser place is the moment because what happens is when you take that much intensity and you don't dilute it off into the past or the future you have to deal with all of it at once. And that's part of why Veronica got a little snappy, is because she couldn't attend to her experience of the moment with input from the rest of you. It was too much. Because trying to stay in the moment with the quantity of things that were being attended to was already almost overwhelming. And this is another reason why you guys dilute off the moment into the past and to the future, because dealing with it in a higher-vibrational, conscious way and receiving insight from your soul and having all of that come in is more intensity than you're accustomed to and it can feel over-stimulating, overwhelming.

The moment isn't the bunnies and rainbows spot, and a lot of times in some of the literature that's out there they say, "Oh, just be in the moment and all will be well." Well, that's crap. Be in the moment and you will start to experience the intensity that's available to you as a Homo spiritus individual. And it is intense and it does ask a lot of you, but that's why you have lots and lots of tools to support the journey through it. The moment isn't necessarily going to be silence. It's not meditation. It's an opening to an enormous amount of insight, an enormous amount of information and an enormous amount of opportunity to live differently in the next moment, to create differently for the next moment, to move differently into the next moment. That's where the access point is, and you guys are used to living in the past or the future where it's all more like make-believe, and so the intensity of it can be mitigated very, very readily because if it feels too intense you just make-believe off into a different memory or a different projection.

The other night Veronica was thinking about something and we asked her, "Do you have the courage to think about yourself instead?" It's an important question. Do you have the courage to think about you instead of thinking about this other situation? Do you have the courage to ask yourself what is true now, what is going on right now, what is true for me, where am I lying to myself, those questions we ask you guys all the time. You see, it's nice to think about this, that, and the other thing even if this, that, and the other things sucks and is shitty and is awful and is bad memories and people you don't like and people you don't even want in your life and people that aren't even in your life—that is less intense sometimes than attending to the moment that you're in. And the moment that you're in, of course, is the doorway to everything else but it also can be a lot. But it's your invitation.

So, do you have the courage to think about yourself? Do you have the courage to focus on what is true now for you? Do you have the courage to be in that space? And of course, courage is: feel the fear and do it anyway. It's not: it's easy. It's not: it doesn't hurt. It's not: it's not hard. It's: yeah, it's all those things and I'm going to do it anyway. Why? Because I want healing above all else. I want healing above easy. I want healing above no difficulty. I want healing above numb. I want healing above all else. It doesn't mean healing is hard but it does mean healing is typically intense. But it has a very intense payoff as well. And you're in a very intense time where you're transitioning from one intense thing to another. And intense sometimes feels overwhelming but intense also can be lots of life, lots of living.

Intense is the feeling when you go bungee jumping or jump out of an airplane, that's an intense feeling and you like it. You like intense feelings. So intense isn't wrong. It's not wrong but intense is a new way of being when that intensity, instead of being externalized, "I'm jumping off a building attached to a bungee cord or a parachute," instead of it being an intense action it's an intense integration. Instead of it being externalized intensity it's internalized intensity. When you go around taking responsibility for your reactions to your creations and asking yourself what is true now, where am I lying to myself, etc. etc., all these invitations we've extended to you all these years, there opens up to an intensity that you will integrate. And as you integrate that intensity it will ask a lot of you but it gives a lot in return as well.

So, next time you're tempted to be in the past or the future, we invite you to say: "Am I courageous enough to be with me now? Am I courageous enough to attend to my concerns about me? My fascination about me. My insight about me. Am I courageous enough to do that?" And you will find that the answer to that question is very revelatory because you may do it for a second or two, and then off you are in the past or the future again, and then you can look at that one more time. So, are you courageous enough to make it about you? And most of you that are here with us tonight have already gone through the: "You're a selfish bitch" thing that people like to lay on you when you start focusing on your own journey. But are you courageous enough to deal with your own reactions to you focusing on you?

The Girls said it best when they said, "How can I love myself when I know so much about myself?" And we'd like you just to let that sink in. Part of what happens when you're in the moment is you're aware of who you are in a new way and that awareness of who you are in that new way is you knowing all what's in the nooks and crannies of you, and it can be challenging to love yourself when you know all the secret hidden things that no one else knows about you. But all those secret hidden things are opportunities to grow and opportunities to appreciate and opportunities to check out where you have judgment and opportunities for so many things. But when you start to really stay in the moment with yourself and you start to be aware of things about yourself that you're uncomfortable with, well then you have this new opportunity to say: "And I can love myself anyway?" And notice how we made our voice go up and there's a question mark at the end because that's the exploration for you. And that's what we want to leave you with as we go tonight, is can you love yourself anyway once you're courageous enough to make the moment about you? It's a big deal. It's a big question. It is not a small thing.

Eloheim

Good evening. The reality is sometimes things just suck and that's true. Sometimes things just suck and it's intense and it's hard and we get it. We get it. Sometimes you just want to put your head under the blanket and you just want to say, "Nobody knows where I am, they can't find me." We understand. But you're always there. You're always there. So it doesn't matter who can find you. You're always there.

Like Veronica threatened to walk out. Can you imagine, one, how hilarious that would've been. She would've been freezing cold by the time she got to the end of the block. She would've been like, "I'm cold," which of course would've been lovely. And she would have been right there with herself. You know she would just turn around and come back and say, "Oh shit, let's have a meeting anyway." So that's why she doesn't leave is because she knows she'd just come right back. With that said, there is a high degree of challenge going on right now. Apparently, she's not the only one experiencing it.

There's a high degree of challenge going on and we want to just acknowledge Veronica's challenge out loud because it's kind to do so. So you can all be witness to this information.

When we started working with Veronica years and years ago—it's going to be eight years of public meetings next month, every Wednesday—when we first started working with Veronica, when you do the compare you to you thing, there was an enormous difference. And those of you who've been around, maybe next month we'll do how many years people have been around. But there are those of you who have been around for a while, five years, four years, longer. So, comparing you to you, using Veronica as the example and the work we're doing together, it's different. You haven't even been around that long and you know it's different. Part of what has gone on in the last year—John has the dates of when we started bringing in all the Council members, the Visionaries were first and that was on June 10, 2009, so just over a year ago we started bringing in new Council members.

Let's just say it this way: Veronica makes it look easier than it is. She makes it look easier than it is and that's part of her personality and that's what makes her her in a lot of ways. But what we're asking her to do by working with the entire Council is to stretch not just her own spiritual growth and not just how the frack to make the technology work, it's not just that, but what we're doing is we're asking her to resonate to a different frequency in different parts of her body.

We told you guys some time ago that the different members of the Council resonate to different chakras and that if you have something going on with a specific chakra you can call on the specific Council members to help you. Cool. We don't know if you guys do that ever or sometimes, maybe every once in a while or whatever. But what really has to happen here is that Veronica, in order to carry the Council's message, has to resonate to those frequencies often. Which is a way of saying we'd like her to do it all the time. And she was able to carry our energy in a way because she was always very verbal and of course we're the throat chakra, so it made sense to her. We didn't take a real quiet, shy person and make them a channel.

We took someone who is an extrovert, a shy extrovert but an extrovert nonetheless, who was very comfortable being verbal and said, "OK, good, be a channel." That's all well and good, but then you start to work with— let's say it this way—chakras that are more triggering, more of a challenge, the heart chakra, the sexuality chakra, you name it, they're in there, those two especially. And then you ask those chakras to be elevated vibrationally by carrying the information of the Council and carrying the vibration of the Council. And then we bring in the Warrior, which challenges her on a whole new frequency of different information but also of acknowledging the truth of that energy in the world. A lot of you guys are peaceniks or hippie types and it's like, "Oh, well, I like to believe in bunnies and rainbows." Yeah, everybody wants bunnies and rainbows. But the reality is not everybody's living in bunny-and- rainbowland. So to have that in her body was extraordinarily challenging and it still brings up some things.

So, why we're sharing this both for her and for you guys is to say that the carrying of those frequencies and to be constantly pinged on all those different levels all the time, she has not yet been able to say it to herself in a way that reconciles with her never-ending battle against feeling like she has to be Wonder Woman. "Wow, I'm carrying all this and I'm Wonder Woman and I can't be both and I don't know how to do it." There's no book. There is no manual. And she doesn't know how to do it most of the time. So she also has recognized because we talk about this a little bit but it's hard that now that the whole Council is in place, now that we've been able to bring the energy in and start to get it more vibrationally meshed, things are going to be expanding, changing, there's going to be more, there's going to be more information, there's going to be different ways the information's going to be coming through. And so a part of her is just going, "I don't know what I'm doing now, how can I know what I'm doing then?"

So an aspect of the technological nightmare you two have

been dealing with for the last year is that as it gets better then it's more likely things get bigger. That doesn't mean that she's breaking things, other than a minute ago when the camera went flying. It doesn't mean she's breaking things purposely. It just means that is a very good externalization of the internal turmoil that goes on in trying to get all of the cords and cables of the energetic system of infusing the Council into the physical form lined up. And a lot of times this is exactly what it feels like, something like this, that's what it feels like for her to try to do it. And she'll get the yellow one sorted out and she'll be, "Oh God, what's that do? But look you still have all this." All the while trying to get the dishes done and the food bought and the water and the garden and regular life stuff.

So we're taking this little break tonight just so she'll know that it's OK for it to be hard. And you all get that, but she doesn't get it. Because again, this is a perfect example—next time you guys need an example of compare you to you, perfect example—because instead of it being good old buddy Eloheim who's been around forever, she could literally channel us in her sleep, it's not that, and she still makes it look as easy as it did when she was only us. Externally, right? Every once in a while you guys probably have a sneaky suspicion that something might be going a little odd when she's almost throwing up, can't walk, and is coughing. But most of the time we would imagine the way you guys perceive it is, "I went to channeling." Right? "Went to channeling." And Veronica's like, "Don't let them see it, don't let them know." Last Thursday she couldn't walk, she couldn't function, she was freezing cold again, it was hard. It happens. A lot. We're going to work with her on that, but what we needed to do tonight was acknowledge what's going on with the technology, what's going on with the work, and what's going on with her internally. Because although we talk to her all the time, it's different when it's witnessed. So, we thank you for witnessing.

It's a journey and for us, the difference between five years ago and now. A lot of you might've heard this story but we'll just tell one little quick one so you can have a good example of comparing you to you. Back in the day when Veronica was channeling here in Sonoma at someone else's house, she'd show up for the meeting, about seven people would come, and she would be so terrified that there would be no information. That people would ask questions that there would be no answer to. "How can I know how your dead grandmother is doing or how can I know what's going on with your left kidney?" That line between "I don't know anything about this yet somehow the words will come out of my mouth that this person will be helped by," it was very hard to walk that line. What we would do back then—of course, eyes closed—is someone would ask a question and we would just have her picture a ticker-tape machine like they have on Times Square where the words go by in lights, and she would just have her eyes closed and we would just put the words on there and she would just read them off. And she just read them off until at some point it just started to flow and she didn't have to read them anymore. But she knew no matter what we would put the words up and she could read them. Here we are five years later, and we're talking about her and she's not having a problem with it.

So, there you go. Compare you to you. Perfect examples of compare you to you. If you don't compare you to you no one else will! We sound like the Visionaries now. But we mean it. The greatest kindness you can do to yourself, especially right now when you're integrating the intensity of the moment and the soul's perspective, is compare you to you. If you slip out of the moment and you can't grasp it, you can't be in it, you can't stay in it because you don't have practice, understandably, then what you can do in that time is compare you to you. How is that for acceptable non-moment activity? Compare you to you. And at least half of it you are in the moment because you have to be in the moment to get your current version. But again, what is it? It's being courageous enough to make it about you instead of having it be about somebody else. And that was huge. When we made that inquiry to her and she sat with that it was very large to say, "I see that thinking about this other subject was an escape from attending to the moment." Questions?

Question: Since we're on the subject of talking about the Council and Veronica, can you share any insights on the composition of the Council, how they came to be with Veronica? We haven't really gone into that much. Also, how does the Council communicate?

Eloheim: The first thing that happened—just to kind of make sure we tell the whole story and some of you probably know this one—but the first thing that happened was that you guys took the information that we had been giving you for years and you just took it to a level where you needed new instructors, frankly. You graduated from high school and you needed professors in college. That's the easiest way to say it. So you called in the Council as a collective entity of people who have been joined in this way. So, check you out! Create your own reality. It's very powerful. We'll probably never forget the night the Visionaries came in. You literally pulled them in. You said: "It's time for something else."

What happens is, the Visionaries act as one of our guides is the best way to describe the relationship. And we've told you this before that the Visionaries came in because they literally hold the blueprint. They hold the vision. That's why we call them the Visionaries. It's not like they're known by that name on their resume or something. We just went, "What's the way to talk about them?" And it's like they hold the vision of the thing. That's why they'll be very emphatic about, "This is the way you should be doing it." In the very beginning they would say, "Do it this way!" and we'd be like, "Yikes, free will! What the hell are you doing?" And they would push right up against the edge of what is free will and what is not free will with you guys. Because as we explained, we think we called them the architect. They've got the blueprints. "The 2" by 4" goes here!" There's no: "Oh, you want to have your own experience?" No. The 2" by 4" goes here and then you build the rest of the house and you learn a lot by the 2" by 4" being there, so put it there. That was their energy. They came in in response to basically us saying, "We need more. We need more. Help us give more."

As you guys allowed that to come in, it kicked out so much in your energy field that we had to have the Guardians come in and start cleaning things out. So the Guardians were in response to pushing the Visionaries into your field and the Visionaries kind of like, if you put the 2" by 4" here, then whatever was there first had to go. "Oh, you mean the 2" by 4"'s supposed to go here? Well, I had a metal piece of something or other there." "Well, get it the hell out." And that's the way the Visionaries were. You guys remember. You guys were scared of the Visionaries. You guys think the Warrior is bad. Shit, at the beginning, the Visionaries made everybody crap their pants.

And then the Guardians—it had to go. We had to bring in an entity whose energy field was very, very cleansing. Very, very vacuum-y. Just to get that stuff out. Because the tendency you guys have is to release but it kind of hangs on. What's that Peanuts character, Linus? The one that always has the dust cloud around him? Pigpen. There's always a dust cloud, and that's sort of what you guys do. You release but you're like, "I might need you. You were sort of helpful in a suffering sort of way, but who knows I might need to suffer next week, so you just stick right there." And then the Guardians came in and what did they say? "Let it bubble off and we'll scrape it away." Remember they used to say, "We'll scrape, we'll scrape." So Pigpen is the perfect example of what is the tendency, because remember, if it hasn't killed you, you probably needed it. Right? If it hasn't killed you, you probably needed it, when the truth is, if it hasn't killed you, it's probably helping you suffer.

So the Guardians really help get the suffering out of the way.

Then the Girls came next. The girls had to come in because after all that you needed to love yourselves. There was this sense of: "Oh my God, I'm being completely re-wired. Oh my God I'm letting go of stuff I thought I needed." So the Girls came in to kind of lighten the energy because you figure with us, the Guardians, and the Visionaries, holy shit, that's an intense masculine presence. And what are they doing? The Visionaries are yelling at you, the Guardians are taking away stuff, and we are going, "This is cool!" And you guys are going, "This is cool?" So the Girls came in and lightened the energy, they brought a feminine presence. And what they did and what have they done every week since is remind you to love yourself—and came up with all kinds of different ways to love yourself and reminded you that it's hard to love yourself sometimes. So they come in and they love, love, love. But it's not bunnies and rainbows, everything's smiley love. It's the reality is yes, you know everything about yourself and we are challenging you to love yourself anyway. So the Girls came in and supported that.

Then it was the Matriarch. We'll tell you right now, why the Matriarch came next is because it was just so nice having the Girls come that we just thought more lovey-dovey would be good. More lovey-dovey and also that sense of overarching feminine energy. The Girls are playful, perhaps even sexual, they are very light, but that mother, that vessel. We're pretty sure they explain it but every time they come in the way we see it with Veronica is literally like Richard's crystal bowl that he plays, it's as though the whole room is one of those and you guys are just sitting in the bowl. And their energy just infuses that whiteness and they just hold you. And sometimes Veronica's body opens up so much that she feels all of you inside of her. And sometimes when the Matriarch talks, you know some of you have done the whistling with Margy, sometimes she feels that in her head as they are talking. So there's this very strong resonance because they're creating a field for you all to be in. So, there is this sense of, "Holy shit! I'm channeling all these beings, I don't know what the hell is going on, other people I know that have tried this have literally had to go off-grid because they couldn't handle it." So what do we do? Bring in someone to hold. And it's nice at the end to have that "It's all going to be OK" sort of feeling.

That leaves the Warrior and Fred. So yeah, yeah, the Girls came in, the Matriarch came in, everyone was feeling all lovey-dovey and then, boom! Let's drop the hammer. And the hammer of the Warrior—we talked a little bit about it a minute ago—and the reality of the Warrior is that you live in a world that is populated with conflict. The temptation as a light worker is to try to ignore that, and on some level that's life-saving because if you are trying to raise your vibration and you're trying to be involved in a lot of conflict that almost doesn't go together. But at some point after you've become a certain level of conscious, you have to acknowledge the shadow, you have to acknowledge the places within yourself that you can't love because you have judgment about them, frankly. So that had to be attended to. That shadow side had to be attended to. And the Warrior's also anger and how do you attend to the fact that you are angry? And the Warrior's also how do you attend to the fact that you feel like a victim and the places in your life where you have been "victimized," especially as a child, or in her case as a wife, where there was a lot of feeling of being under a man's thumb in a way that didn't feel good. And the warrior brings in that energy that says: "I'm not under anybody's thumb," and it's like, "Wait, wait, wait. How do I not be under someone's thumb without having to kill them or hate them or be angry with them or want to scream at them?" Where is that place where you just say, "What are you saying to me? Do you think you can talk to me like that? Who do you think you are? Get away." That energy wasn't present in most light workers and it wasn't present in Veronica in a lot of ways. And it has been the most challenging one to carry because it asks so much of her on a spiritual-development level.

Comment: I thought you were going to lose a lung the first time.

Eloheim: Yeah. It was very hard the first time the Warrior came in. And then she put her foot down and she said, "No, I'm not doing it. I'm not doing any more." And we respected that for a long time—a few months or something—and finally, we just said to her, look this is the deal. We have to complete the energy of the Council so Fred has to come in. And she was challenged by that but actually Fred's not so bad because Fred only comes in this far. So, her head feels like popcorn's popping the whole time but his energy's not that bad now that she's used to him a little bit. So that's why each one came in and how did they all get called in or whatever. The need was needed. It's the same way you guys create your reality: The need is needed and you magnetize the need met. So you needed these sorts of influences, so those influences came in.

And how do they communicate with each other? The same way you communicate with each other when you're not in body, which means, in essence, it's like you meld and you know each other and you un-meld and it doesn't have to be in language but you guys wouldn't really know how to communicate other than with language. So let's imagine that you meld with someone, you know all their thoughts, they know all of yours, and then you separate but you take with you what you gained from that melding. It's intense. You guys would never be able to do it because you don't love all the spots in yourself yet, and if you don't love all the spots in yourself you sure as hell can't let anybody else see them. So that's off the table for now. But we are working on that. But that's one of the reasons why you can't have telepathy—not on any deep level. You can think of someone and they can phone you, yeah, that's great, but to actually have merging telepathy, the whole time you'd be freaked out that they see you so deeply and truly. But when you're not in physical form and you're not in duality and you're not in judgment and you're not in fear and you're not in survival instinct that's just the way you communicate.

So the Council, do they get together? They don't have to "get together." It's more like an energetic is spun out by you guys coming together with a desire for a certain level of information combined with where we see Veronica taking the information because she's like our guinea pig. So we see where she takes the information, we have private sessions and we feel what people are doing, people send emails, whatever, and it's a symbol then to here's what's going to be talked about. And as soon as it starts to roll out well the other ones usually get on it.

Now who comes in and tells you the thing at the very beginning? The Visionaries! Why? Because they hold the blueprint. So they unroll the next level of blueprint and say, "This is the truth of it," and they show you where all the sticks go. And the Girls come in and say, "Don't forget to take a coffee break!" And the Matriarch says, "It's all going to be so beautiful at the end." And the Warrior says, "Are any of these contractors giving you shit? We'll take care of them." Do you get it? Does it make sense? We're building something. The Visionaries have the vision of it. We run around kind of being the cheering squad. Fred, we're not sure, Fred just kind of floats around. He's like one of those super geeks, super IT tech kind of guys. He just comes in and says, "We must have the cords run this way." We're like, "Perfect, we'll do it. No problem. Go away. You're a little bit creepy." He's getting better but he was kind of creepy in the beginning. We know it. He knows it! He's like, "I just don't understand. How do they do that? I'm going to go over here." But you are going to hear more from Fred. Fred is going to become more and more important to the overall mission of the Council, which you probably now want to know what the overall mission of the Council is. Because we know you, John, because you've been around for a long time—and John's writing in his notebook.

The overall mission of the Council, in addition to supporting you living from your soul's perspective and working with you to have ascension and all that stuff, is to balance, to balance, your physical experience of Homo spiritus. To balance your physical experience of Homo spiritus. Which is why we were talking earlier about what Veronica's going through, because a lot of times she does it first because we're with her all the time. So she's our guinea pig, like we said. And balancing the physical experience of Homo spiritus, it's a little bit like we were just talking about the parts of you that you don't love. Because some of you would be very good with the heart chakra or very good like Veronica with the throat chakra or very good with the root chakra, not so many of you actually, but that's OK. That's a rough one, we know. But can you do all of them all at once? No. We don't know anybody who can, so you're being very honest by shaking your heads "no." That's the role of the Council. And really, we said 2010 is the year of the physical and we will look at 2011 again as we get closer to it, but probably this last quarter of 2010 moving through 2011 will be the year of balance. And it's the year of yes, you're strong with this one tool or yes, you're strong with this one chakra or yes, you're strong saying what is true now when it has to do with how you feel, but if you think something disturbing you can't say what is true now. And if someone cuts you off on the freeway you can't say what is true now. So it's like could you say what is true now no matter what kind of stimulus you're getting.

A lot of you have a kind of trigger and a tool that you like for that trigger. What we're going to work toward is, can you use that tool no matter what the trigger is? Because most of them work for any trigger but we have segregated them and said, here's a good tool for this and here's a good tool for that—but that balancing.... You'll start to realize that you can use tools for any kind of trigger—emotional, physical, mental, spiritual, financial—and you can use the same tool for it because you're using all the chakras together. And again, when we say chakras we just use that to indicate the different aspects of the way your energetic [is] in the world, the way you move your energy in the world. You have to balance those things out in order to move in a balanced way. And this is why sometimes it feels herky-jerky in your spiritual growth because if it has to do with the chakras that you're strong in, you have a better chance of having a balanced, ascended, Homo spiritus, graceful, easeful response to it. And if it has to do with chakras that you're not that strong in, you're more likely to go into low vibration, unconsciousness, the past or the future, fear.

Question: Does the Council create a lot of interest outside of the realm? Is it a big deal for the Council members to be doing what they're doing?

Eloheim: It's important for all the Council members to be doing what they're doing. The whole idea of ascension from the physical form, the whole idea of Homo spiritus is a big deal, in general. And the Council's working with you guys and that's a big deal but it's not as thought it's like—it's important but it's not epic yet. You guys starting to live as Homo spiritus, that's when it's going to start to feel epic and it will start getting more attention. It's a little bit like you're still working on your PhD, and when you actually do your dissertation and you have your PhD and you start to publish papers and get some notoriety for "Look what I learned," that's when you actually get notoriety. You're still in your PhD phase. But comparing you to you not very long ago you were in high school. So you're moving at a pretty good clip. But right now, in its essence the Council is like your thesis advisor. You roll in and you say, "Yikes!" and they say what they say and then off you go.

So it's important to keep reminding yourself to compare you to you. We just cannot emphasize that enough. It's really the greatest kindness we can suggest you do to yourself. You know some people like to meditate and some people like to do this, do that, do everything, but you can do compare you to you in any situation. You really genuinely can. And it genuinely is one of the kindest things you can do. Did we answer all the aspects of your question?

Question: From the Council's point of view, do they wonder why a billion people aren't listening to this?

Eloheim: From the Council's perspective one is equal to 20 million. There is no sense of if you had 20 million it would be better than one. It's just not the same, because you're not in duality. Their perspective is "Can it be done? Can the energy be evolved? Can the ascension process happen?" It's just fascinating to see if it works.

Now, on that level or on that subject would it be nice if there were 200 people instead of 20? On some physical levels it would make it easier on Veronica and on a lot of physical levels it would be very challenging for her. So it's a pay-off both ways. For you guys would it be better if there were 200 than 20? Well, you would have to get a bigger room. Change would have to happen and that probably will happen in 2011. By the end of 2011 we expect that it'll be different than it is now. It has to be. Because you guys—literally, the PhD candidates—at some point there are more high schoolers and more college students. And just like how many people get a PhD compared to how many people get an AA. It's not necessarily everyone's focus. Can it help them? Well, the argument could be made that getting educated at college could help you, too, but not everybody does it. It's just the choices that people make.

But you have to remember where that analogy breaks down is that energetically, vibrationally, one person walking in the ascended state is energetically transformational for tens of thousands of people. So it's different than you get one person who has a PhD in medieval anthropology or something and yeah, that's great and it's good that somebody knows that stuff, whereas a PhD in "Ascension" you are emanating such a radically transformational idea into the world simply by breathing that it can have a strong impact on the way people perceive the opportunity that is available to them by living on planet Earth. And that's really the "service" that light workers will end up doing, which is not service at all because all it is is breathing, it's the effect of being an ascended light worker, is that you emanate out the idea, the notion, that there's more to Earth than just waking up, going to work, coming home, putting the kids to bed, and going to sleep. There's something more going on. And a lot of people don't know that.

A lot of people really think: "My greatest goal in life is to have enough money to not have to worry." That's where people live. A lot of them. And, "God, it would be sweet if I wasn't scared all of the time. And maybe could get more sex," right? Literally—stuff, sex, money, safety. You give people that, they think that's all there is that's available to them. And for very, very many incarnations you thought that, too. So don't get cocky! But you also recognize that there's this something called serenity and yeah, stuff and sex and security are interesting, but serenity is fascinating. "Serenity is the true rarity and I'm curious about it and I'm sick of suffering." The reality is you guys are sick of suffering or you wouldn't be sitting in this room. Maybe that's a way to sum up what you do. Are you sick of suffering? OK. Don't think it's going to be bunnies, rainbow, easy, or even fun, but we think all of you can agree you don't suffer as much as you used to.

When you suffer, it's intense, but you don't suffer as much as you used to. It doesn't abate the intensity when you're in it. What it does is it reduces the frequency that you're in it, and when you are in suffering it's extra intense because you have so much time when you're not that it stands out. It's like being in a noisy room. A little bit of extra noise you don't notice but if you're in a quiet room and noise starts, you notice it immediately. That's really the truth of the matter. That's really the truth of the matter. Does that cover all things that you wish to know? It's been a while since you've done one of your let's get deep, deep, deep. But this is good information that's probably time to have out in the world.

Question: I was listening to some information on an Internet site, and I brought it up to Veronica that it sounded like someone had been eavesdropping on our meetings when they were asking for tools. Could you talk about how the information about your tools became so readily apparent to other light workers?

Eloheim: We don't know how they got it but what we can talk about is why we use the tools. One of the reasons we use the tools is because we realized that you guys come with this question, whatever the question is. We've got 60 or 70 tools, so it's not like it's rare. You come with a question and it's like, "I need an answer to this question." Well, the answer to the question is not the words. The answer to the question is addressing the energetic that you want to shift. So we come up with a way to shift the energetic because we can feel the energetic. The tool shifts the energetic and then you assign different words to it because you have a different interaction with the experience. That's nothing unusual. Other people could probably do that, but that's how we do it.

You come to us, we hear your words, but more than anything we're looking at your energetic. We've always told you that. We're looking at your energetic, we're experiencing your energetic, and we're analyzing how can we shift that specific energetic. And when we shift that specific energetic through a tool then you can use that tool for other situations that generate the same energetic. You see, that's why they work in different places. What will be interesting is when physical, emotional, spiritual, and financial situations, when the energetic that you feel is the same because you're not isolating it in your body or your field. We'll use Veronica as an example. If she can talk about a problem—whether it's physical, emotional, spiritual, financial—if she can talk about it she immediately feels better because that's running it through the chakra that she's most familiar with. But like you said the other day, "What if you feel it?" and she's like, "Hell, no. I don't want to do that," because that doesn't work as easily for her. But that's actually a good insight, the idea are you just thinking about it all the time. Well you guys, we've been trying to get you out of your brains because every single one of you is good at thinking.

So you can think about stuff any old time and some of you can talk about stuff any old time, but what about the rest of the ways you process information? Because Homo spiritus, if nothing else, is balanced. Homo spiritus is firing on all cylinders. That's ascension. You caught everything up and everything is going together. And that's why we've been—sometimes it feels a little bit like spinning plates, like that one needs a really good spin—but what you're doing is you're bringing it all into…. We don't know exactly how to—there's not a real good example of what you're doing because it's really quite unique. You're giving the opportunity for you to become something that you've never experienced before. Consciousness-based operating system, serenity, balance, wholeness—none of that is going to take away the intensity of being human, but you're going to have so much of a different experience with the intensity of being human that you will have a new way of being. Just like the Visionaries were saying: The moment is an intense place. Sometimes the moment can be quiet, but quiet, of course, just means you can go deep. And when you're in the moment and seeing places where you're ashamed, seeing places where you don't love yourself, or seeing places where you're not being courageous, seeing places where you're lying to yourself, all of that lives in the moment. So when you're in the moment you're with all that stuff, and then how you attend to all that stuff is what you're doing with the ascension path.

So the idea of the quiet of the moment used to be because your brain is not talking. "I'm in the moment, I'm not thinking about the past and the future." OK, but. You bring all the rest of the Council members on board, there's a hell of a lot going on and then insight from your soul comes in, hello! Showtime. In the old days, the moment was quiet and peaceful because mostly it was just not talking. Now the moment is intense, and it's like watching TV in black-and-white and then watching it in color. The same thing is going on but you're having a much deeper, more varied experience. So it's good we're talking about this. We talked about being on the landing and then going up the stairs, and now it's like, "Welcome to it." This is what walking up the stairs looks like. It's a lot of responsibility, taking responsibility for your reactions to your creations, looking at feelings and emotions and deciding which is which and where you're in one and where you're in the other, and now the idea that the moment is an intense place and there's a hell of a lot going on. You can imagine that just like the Council members can each talk about a specific subject from a different perspective, you can imagine being in the moment and having your body give you feedback about that moment from those different perspectives. Similar kind of a thing.

Comment: I would like to say thank you to you. I thank Veronica but we don't really get the opportunity to say thank you to you.

Eloheim: You're very welcome. We've mentioned before, but it's worth repeating, that it's part of our spiritual development to work with you guys. It's not as though we're finished and we're just sitting up there being like, "Oh, we know everything and we'll just dab it out to them as time goes by." It's not like that. We grow as you grow. And a perfect example of that is watching the Girls try to eat that cracker. If you don't think that was a new experience, we're going to back you up a little on that thought. So you can see, that's growth. When we eat the brownies, when we drink the water, when the little thing breaks off and we're playing with this thing, silly as it looks, that's a growth. We're having an experience of transformation by playing with a plastic bottle. And you guys think being physical is kind of boring. Well, we could probably play with this bottle for three days.

So the point of it is that we are growing with you. We are growing with you. So thank you for giving us the opportunity to grow as well. And sometimes we hear people will say to Veronica, "God how can they be so patient with us?" Because it's all fascinating to us. We'll try it 8 million different ways. Why? Because each one of them is just as interesting as the one before. We're trying to remember if we've gotten impatient with you guys. Maybe once or twice. One night we sent you home. One night we sent them home because somebody who's not here anymore, she moved away, said something that was absolutely so full of victimhood and everyone sort of, the way we felt you guys that night was everyone kind of: "Oh well, let her get done with her question." And we just lost it. Because we were like, "You can keep each other energetically responsible. You can be attentive to the fact that she's part of your creation. You don't get to go unconscious and pretend like, 'Oh, I can't wait until she shuts up.' " So we don't remember exactly what we said, but it was something like, "Go home and think the fuck about that." And it was the shortest meeting on record. Yeah, that was an intense night. So all of you people who are new and haven't been around for years, yeah, you think you've seen it. The night that Eloheim quit. It's only happened once in eight years, though.

Question: Are you up there or are you in a different dimension or on a different plane? Where are you?

Eloheim: It's a hard question to answer because, first, we'd have to have definitions of all those places, and then we'd have to see energetically which one makes the most sense. But the truth of the matter is that we have not lost sight of the truth that we are all one. So we exist with you on a soul level and we experience you as experiencing the passage of time in the physical form.

And it's almost like watching a movie to us because it's all such make-believe that it's like this fake thing going on, but then it's real and intense and there's suffering and joy and love. And it's real and intense and we watch it and every once in a while that's why it's a good reality check for us to have certain experiences because it helps us say, "Wow, that's really, really physically happening." And it's so different for it to be physically happening than it is for it to be soul happening.

The difference between those two states is so radically bizarre that that's actually why, one of the things about this Council coming in is it allowed us to move into a different relationship with you guys. And we say we're like Norm at the Cheers bar. Instead of being the "teacher," now we feel more like the pal. And that helped, too, with Veronica's energy, the way we melded with her more. We started melding with her and then we brought the Council in. And it took us—not that we don't have things we can teach you or show you or explain to you—but it shifted us out of being some people kind of thinking we're up here, we wanted to shift more and experience the physical form more and experience physicality in a different way. Bringing the other Council in allowed that shift to happen as well. So we can't really say we're on plane 5232A or whatever, because we don't know what any of that actually means.

But we can say is that we experience the physical form with Veronica all the time. We are experiencing it with you guys more as we have eyes open now, we can walk around now, we can eat, we can drink, we can experience things in a physical way that we never experienced before, and we also get to experience the way the rest of the Council experiences physicality because they experience it, too. The Girls sit sideways in the chair, the Matriarch expands out the heart chakra, the Warrior plays this movie while he tells his story, Fred has the popcorn going on in the head, the Guardians are scraping this brown shit off you guys all the time, and the Visionaries, they just have their blueprints. Their blueprints and their script. So there's this very precise way about them. When they go to do a speech, boy howdy, not only do they have the script there but they have it memorized, too, because they know just exactly what they want to say. It's very precise.

So we get to experience them experiencing you, experiencing different information, experiencing Veronica's physical form because you have to remember, on a soul level, nothing is half-assed. Nothing is half assed. Everything is done red-lined. Why? Because if you're infinite and immortal and you have nothing else to do and it's all fun and fascinating, you guys would have it in fifth gear with your foot on the floor, too. And if you don't believe that, we just don't know why you're here because we know that one's true. You guys will put the pedal to the metal given any opportunity to—that whole climbing Mount Everest thing. Each one of you has an example in your life where you've done something similar to those people who go climb Mount Everest. Showing up here every week for five years, that's climbing Mount Everest, we just want you to know. It's a big fricking deal. Being on Earth is sort of pedal to the metal. This is like old times. We're talking for an hour, no problem, it's like old times. But we've talked for an hour, so if you guys want to hear from anyone else tonight, we've got to go.

A couple of things are important. We had a check-in on Veronica, which is always a good thing to have at least once a quarter. We had an overview of what's going on with the Council at this level because we're new today. A new overview, that's always important. We had going forward with the Council, ideas. And something else just happened that was important, too, and we can't remember it. It was time to kind of all say, "Where are we? Where are we now?" Oh, we know what it was. We go to talk for an hour. It's been a long time since we just sort of hung out and rapped with you guys. We like it.

The Girls
OK. OK. We know we're not supposed to spend a whole lot of

time tonight because we're in a hurry or something like that, but the reality of the situation is this. Why we tell you to love yourselves is because no one else will. Really. People will say, "Oh, you should be loving yourself," or they'll send you a Valentine's Day card, or sometimes you'll remind your friends, "Oh, be kinder to yourself." But how often? Let's be real. Somewhere in your energy field had to be a constant reminder that it's OK to just love yourself. That even though you think you suck, that even though your life is hard, that even though you feel like you've been in suffering and habit and confusion and angst and all that stuff, there is still room for love, of you to you. And that's really why we came into this circle at this time. There will be more that we will do but until we get the love quotient up a little bit, we can't shift out of it. You guys needed to love yourselves more. You guys are willing to push yourselves, you guys are willing to drive yourselves, you guys are willing to be intense with yourselves, you're willing to knuckle down, you're willing to do all these ways of asking a lot of yourself, but what you hadn't been able to do, what you hadn't been able to do, is remember to love yourself. And that's one of the main things that we're doing in all different kinds of crazy ways is to remind you to love you. Because if someone doesn't remind you, the tendency is to forget to. Because loving yourself has never really had a lot of payout. You've gotten shit from people because you've been full of yourself or selfish or self-centered or all those kind of negative ways of being perceived as loving yourself, but the truth of the matter is to be Homo spiritus you have to love yourself well because only through loving yourself will you forgive yourself for the things that you've done that you feel are unforgivable. Love is the path to transforming the places where you feel unforgivable.

You know there's that thing in religion about your sins being washed away. Well, as light workers most of you don't prescribe to that idea that "someone else is going to wash away my sins." But those things that are """sins"""—in big quotes, triple quotes, just to make sure people know that we're not meaning you actually are a sinner—are the places where you have decided you can't love you. That you're unforgivable. And that's what we come along to help you remember—that that's not true. That even in those places there's something there, something redeemable, something that you can grow and learn from if you don't decide that that is not possible. As a whole being you will love your whole being. That's our goal. We know we can't stay long. So that's all we've got but it's important, so we're glad we had a chance to say it.

Warrior

We know that the evening grows short, and we actually are going to let our story be on hold until next week when we can tell it properly because right now we just want to talk a bit about what it's like for us to experience the physical form with Veronica. You have to understand you were illuminated about how Veronica experiences us and we imagine some of you have the same issues around the idea that anger and aggression and hatred even and mayhem and all those feelings that you have and you suppress or you try to deal with and/or your experiences of alternative expressions having those experiences that you have to deal with can be very challenging to someone who believes in a high-vibrational, peaceful way of being. That makes sense, we hope, for everyone. But when you look at the experience we're having, imagine what that's like. Because we come in and we are accustomed to taking our challenges out in a way that is externalized. You guys primarily handle your challenges in an internal way.

So we look at you and we think sword, no; knife, not so much; gun, pretty useless. So it requires of us a transformation of our energetic from an external leaning out way into an internal experience, which is an enormous period of growth for us as well. And that's why we're telling you this big, long story because in the story we have the opportunity to say, "This is what we did and this is how you do the same thing." And we're both learning because we are getting to infuse you with the energetic of handling things in an external way and letting you have some comfort with that part of the truth of you and then you're helping us to bring it into an internal position, which offers us a transformational place and also allows you, through recognizing that the external urges and skills you have can be applied to the internal journey in an honest way, in a way that's constructive.

So you see that those urges and the way you've worked in previous experiences, alternate expressions, are not keeping you from becoming high-vibrational but they're actually serving you in becoming high-vibrational. So instead of it being like something like the Girls were talking about that you can't love, you can see how it's turned inward and become something that helps you to love yourself, to respect and honor yourself, and to become aware of the magnitude of your magnificence.

So it's an out and then in, that's our journey with you, is to show you and let you kind of try on how it feels to externalize these things and then to show you how, even in your world where hand-to-hand combat isn't very common, you can internalize and infuse yourself with that intense skill level, but used in a way that supports the way you're growing, the way you're experiencing being physical. So we move it out and then we bring it in. We move it out and then we bring it in. We move it out and then we bring it in. And the out part allows you to heal the aspects of yourself that you've been very uncomfortable with and the in part allows you to take that intense ability and apply it in a way that's actually working with the battlefield you're on, which is the internal process. And we tell you this story because it's fun. It's fun to tell it in a story format. It's fun to give you the opportunity to experience the truth of you along with a little fairytale. Grown-up bedtime stories. You're entitled. Why not?

So when we talk to you about our weapons and our swords and

our blades and all that stuff, we talk to you about that because we want you to know the reality of that part of you. Every alternative expression you've had up until this point, and maybe even including this point, included weapons. It doesn't mean you have to run out and get a gun and a sword, but it means you have to make peace with the reality that they have been part of your life. You have to because if you don't then there's a part of you you're not loving. It is a truth even if it's not true now. It is a truth of you even if it's not true now. Swords, especially, have been part of your culture for thousands of years. You have far many more alternate expressions where swords were a real part of that expression than you have anything else, weapon-wise. You always had a knife. You always had a knife. Some of you still carry these little Swiss Army things. You always had a knife with you. Until the Industrial Revolution, you always had a knife with you. You always had a knife, some of you had swords, and then guns came along. Many of you carried guns all the time. You wouldn't leave the house without one. Just like now, you go everywhere with your cell phone. And it's normal. You leave the house, you take your phone. Well, not very long ago, you wouldn't have left the house without a gun. And that is true. That's true about you. That's true about you. And there's a place to make peace with that because it's true.

Now, most of you don't have guns now. Most of you aren't interested in having guns now. And most of you probably have some judgment and fear about guns. And you hear lots of stories about children hurting themselves because they find a gun in the closet and things like that, and those things are real and true as well. But that doesn't take away the fact that you have had a long-standing soul relationship with weaponry that you do not honor in this current lifetime. And it leaves holes. It leaves holes where you don't love yourself. And there are other things you don't love about yourself, but primarily this is the big one that is extraordinarily unconscious and unacknowledged in each of you. The place where anger, fear, frustration, survival, protection, defense, was all done in a very externalized way. You didn't call a lawyer. You got your gun. You got your knife. You got your sword. You got your buddies. You got your bow and arrow. You got your tomahawk. You got all kinds of things. If it was big and it was heavy and it could hurt somebody, you went and got that thing and you went and took care of business in a way that your body demanded you to, using the survival instinct. Which was, "The only way to be safe is to take out the person who makes me scared." That's how you lived. That's reality. And just because you don't live that way now doesn't mean that there isn't some healing that needs to be done about the fact that you did. And that's why we have come. All right?

Just making sure everybody knows. This is a night of making sure everybody knows where everybody stands because things are going to be—not increasing, expanding, getting bigger—but things are just going to go "poof." It's like a popcorn kernel. They're kind of neat by themselves and then they pop and they're more neat but that intense release of energy, just imagine, don't imagine with your brain, just allow yourself to recognize that each and every one of you is ready to pop. And there's plenty of room in the Council and with our breadth of information we can bring to you, to support that explosion. And that's another reason why the Council had to come. We had to come to pop, in essence pop Eloheim, before you guys were ready to pop yourselves, so that there would be enough for you. So there would be enough for you. And now there is an excess, so there is room for you.

Fred

We don't have a great deal to add to tonight's meeting other than to say that the opportunity to work with you all and to experience the physical form even just the little touch-in we do is a great honor and it's a great path for expansion for us. Our role at this time of course is to hold open the portal between you and your soul's perspective and we do this with a great deal of humility for being given the opportunity and we'll support you in this way as long as need be. What we do like you to know is that as we hold open the portal between you and your soul's perspective, it does not mean that we then create your soul's perspective integrating with you. That would be a violation of your free will. We simply make it energetically possible to stabilize the energetic difference between you and your soul's perspective once you reach a certain vibratory rate and as we hold that it's like the coupling between the airplane and the ramp that you walk on. We hold that place. We don't force you to walk on the ramp. We don't force you to exit the plane. We don't do anything other than hold that there so that there is a pathway, portal, opening, between the two. That's our current role. Once that portal is more comfortable to you and you start moving energy and information between the two and the intensity of the moment ramps up as was explained earlier, we will help to smooth the energy flow. But right now, there's not so much going back and forth so we don't have to do too much for you yet but eventually we'll help smooth the energy flow. Not unlike what the Guardians do on the body level, we will do on a vibratory level. Goodnight.

Matriarch

The Matriarch's section was not recorded.

August 25, 2010

Summary

Guardians: Emanation of the truth of you is the overall desire, is the overall path, is the overall journey.

Visionaries: Emanate the truth of you, and allow yourself to see the places where you feel you cannot love yourself. Where do you not love yourself? Allowing yourself awareness of your shadow places does not mean that you have to fix them, but will give you the gift of releasing the façade of "I can't love myself because…." A discussion of how Short, factual statements can be an excellent tool to work with shadow places.

Eloheim: The concept of home. Examining it as a first-chakra paradigm. Do you carry your stability, strength, security in your body, or do you expect your outside world to give it to you? Also, a short discussion of the difference between feelings and emotions.

The Girls: When you look at the idea of what you don't love about yourself and figure out whatever it is and then she sit with it, it changes. Sitting with it changes it. And it is absolutely not about you having to fix it.

Warrior: Continues the story of Eric, illustrating making choices and knowing that your creations are your own, and that nothing comes to you from outside of you.

Fred: The true nature of your infinite, and immortal self resides just a breath away in any moment, and it exists for you to access at any time.

Matriarch: When you find yourself triggered or confused, you just say, "It's possible there's more here."

Guardians

As the sound starts to fade, allow your attention to be drawn in, just as you would have to listen more carefully to hear the sound as it gets quieter and quieter. Allow yourself to bring your attention more deeply and deeply and deeply into the center of the circle—which is really the center of you, the center of your awareness, the center of your desire to know yourself more, the center of the desire for you to have the truth of you emanated into this world—the center of you and the reality of you as you experience the truth of you emanating. As we come together, every time there's always a little bit of a different thing that we have that we're focusing on. There's always a little bit of a different approach, but really, what we want to say tonight is that emanation of the truth of you is the overall desire, is the overall path, is the overall journey, emanating the truth of you and what does that mean, and this is what we will focus on tonight. So, let us just come in and look at your energy field and release what is being shaken loose by that idea, by that concept. Nicely done. We feel a lot of energy going out the bottoms of your feet tonight, so allow yourself just to be conscious of the bottoms of your feet a bit more than normal and acknowledging the energy that is releasing without having to understand, explain, reproduce, or any of that about it. Great. Excellent.

Visionaries

Emanating the truth of you. It's really your birthright. You really came here to experience the emanation of the truth of you. And because you come here with amnesia it's always a path back, almost a clawing back, to where you started from. And we know many of you have asked over the years: "Why in the world is it that we come here to do what we do if we don't come here?" And of course, because you come here to add the physical component to the whole situation. You come here to experience free will, to be in duality, to be isolated from each other, and to still bring the truth of you into the moment—which is that you are an immortal, infinite soul expressing. And as you express and you incorporate the physical form into that expression, it begins to be something new, and you as souls crave newness. You love it, you feed off of it, you enjoy it, you delight in it. So, as you come into this space and you come into it with the intention to be able to emanate the completeness of you while incorporating the physical form, you run into all kinds of barriers, you run into all kinds of hiccups, you run into all kinds of places where it can't work, it doesn't work, it hasn't worked. And what we've been doing over the past whatever amount of time, is looking at how to transform your relationship to the physical, transform your relationship to the survival instinct, to allow you to have the opportunity to have the experience of the completeness of you expressing in physical form.

One of the things about the completeness of you is that you're perfectly aware of the truth of you, which is that you're infinite and immortal, and the body will not believe that. Not for any length of time. Every once in a while, you might get the body to have a sense of it but getting the body to believe that you're infinite and immortal is very, very challenging, and one of the ways this is done in your society is by threat. If you don't do certain behaviors you won't get to be immortal. Well, there is no way to take away your immortality. There's no way to take away your birthright of living with the rest of the souls and experiencing the journey that continues. There's no such thing as going for punishment, for what you might term hell. None of that is actually real. All of that is in relationship to the survival instinct and a relationship to control that doesn't honor the free will that you actually have.

So, as you come in with the intention to emanate the truth of you and you ask yourself, "What is in the way of me emanating the truth of me?" a big chunk of it, of course, is your survival instinct and the belief that "it's not safe to emanate the truth of me, it's not allowed to emanate the truth of me, it won't be accepted," et cetera. The other thing that happens when you start to emanate the truth of you is: Can you handle it? Can you handle being the truth of you? That's a very, very good question. Can you handle the truth of you being emanated? And as the Girls love to help you understand, sometimes the answer to that is: "It's hard because I don't actually like all of me." And if you don't like all of you and you know it's being emanated out in the world, well, there's a tricky bit. And if you find yourself challenged by parts of yourself it can be very, very, very hard to feel love for yourself in your completeness.

Veronica had a deep exploration of this this week that she wrote about in the most recent newsletter that she sent out, where she asked herself: "What is the thing I don't love about myself? Where is the place that I don't love me?" And for her, it came around the idea of rejection and how she handles perceived or actual rejection. Your answer might be the same and it might be quite different, and you might have a long list but it is very important to contemplate: "Where it is in me that I don't love?" And not just in a bunnies-and-rainbows way: "Oh, where don't I love me?" but in a real, practical sense of: "What part of me am I so ashamed of or embarrassed of or regretful about that is actually holding me back from advancing spiritually and holding me back from connecting with people more deeply?" Because that's really what happens, is you're asking yourself to emanate the truth of you and asking yourself: "Where do I lie?" and asking yourself all these questions, and the barrier to the answer is often the places where you've said: "I am not lovable here. I maybe can be lovable for my parenting skills or I maybe can be lovable for my kindness or I maybe can be lovable for the work I do or I maybe can be lovable for the cooking I do," or whatever your version of it is. But the truth of the matter is, there are places in yourself where you don't feel you're lovable. And it's not just that you can't love yourself but you're not allowing others to love you completely because you're putting up barriers around parts of you so that people can't see the thing you're embarrassed about. And the thing that you're embarrassed about, unfortunately what that actually does, is keeps you from being loved deeply by others, keeps you from being understood and enveloped and embraced—and we don't even know what the other words are but we hope you get the sense of what we're trying to convey.

So, we're really coming down to it now that as we walk up that next set of stairs. We've said you have to be responsible for your reactions to your creations and where are you lying to yourself and what are you ashamed of, and it really comes down to what parts of yourself don't you think are actually lovable and as somebody who's not lovable, what is that doing in your life, how is that affecting the relationships that you have and that you want? Because we're clear that when we see places within you that you decide aren't lovable, it creates situations within you that prohibit people from embracing you deeply. And also, again, we like to point out to you if you switch between: "I can love and appreciate myself here but I can't here," the energetic, the vibrational shift between those two, is so drastic that you end up doing that boing, boing thing we've talked about so many different ways, and that is really hard on the body.

Now, the key here is that you do not have to fix this. This isn't something you say, "Oh, I've never loved x, y, z about myself and damn it, I better start loving me." Well, that's just crap. That's not how it works and you know that. The way it works is that you say, "This is true." Short, factual statements. "I don't love myself the way I react to rejection, period." And it's not: "period—oh God, I better change that because it's holding me back on my spiritual path, I missed the bus, oh my God, oh my God." It's: "That's just a fact." And shining the light of consciousness on something doesn't require you to act. What it asks of you is to be aware. Simply be aware: "I am aware that this is the thing that I don't love about myself," or "these are the things that I don't love about myself," without having to actually do anything about it, and watch as your interaction with that truth [and how it] can change because you're not hiding it from yourself anymore. You have done enough work and you've progressed enough spiritually that it's not about the doing to fix these things. It's about the becoming aware and sitting with the truth and the truth allows you, allows you, to release, to abandon, the façade of: "I can't love myself because…." There's a pre-programmed idea in you that that's true but since it's false when truth replaces it, which is simply the truth that that isn't true. "I don't love myself because, wow, have I actually ever thought about it or have I just always felt it?" Here we go with the emotions/feeling thing. "Do I actually feel that way or is it a habitual pattern that I can reevaluate?" And you reevaluate it by being in it and not going into the past or the future, just sitting with it and seeing how it changes. And it will change if you will sit with it and then when it comes up in another opportunity to look at it comes, sit with it some more until it loosens its hold on you.

Because the truth is, on a soul level everything you've ever done has been fascinating, interesting, wonderful, and has produced growth. So even if you don't like certain aspects of yourself, they have still benefited you. We would like to shift you from the: "I don't like it," to the: "This was a benefit to me." And the way you do that is to let go of: "I don't like it,: and watch it from the position of: "It happened and it benefited me. Even if all it did was teach me I don't want to do it again. It still benefited me. It still gave to me. And it still allowed me to come to this moment where I'm exploring the truth of me right now, and finding this place within myself that's a gift because it's showing me something that I'm ready to transform. It's allowing me to compare me to me in a very powerful way." If you find yourself with a part of you that you hate or can't love, and you shift your relationship to it, boy, is that a compare-you-to-you moment. And it's a true, true, true gift that you give yourself.

So, we're going to pass the baton on to Eloheim now, but we want to really, really, really impress upon you that the thing that you don't love about you, the thing that you don't love about you, is the doorway to the next levels of your spiritual growth, and you have a responsibility to explore that question. You have a responsibility to explore that question. And you owe it to yourself to be kind enough to not demand that you have an answer. Not demand that you fix it or change it but to allow yourself to sit in the revelation of the truth of you, which is that you have this aspect of you that you don't love, and see how sitting in the aspect of revelation allows for transformation.

Eloheim

Now that we have the lights on, it looks so different in here. We can see all of you much better and make eye contact with you much more easily. So, there you go. The Visionaries. Laying down the law, right? They love doing that. That's what they're good at, so we can't deny it.

You all, for many, many years, have come [here] wanting spiritual growth, wanting transformation, wanting it to change, change, change, push, push, push, all the time. You've all been like that and we tease you about it all the time, but it's true. That's how you are. You really want transformation, and at this time, one of the key things is what the Visionaries introduced and this is the idea that within you, you know that you don't love yourself completely. Within you, you know that you deny the truth of you, which is that you're an infinite, immortal soul having a physical experience. As much as we've taught you it and as much as you've thought about it and as much as you've played around with it, the truth is it's hard to believe when the kids are cranky or the bills aren't paid or the clients are driving you crazy or the car doesn't want to run. It's hard to believe: "Oh yeah, I'm an infinite, immortal soul and I'm an idiot, too, because if I'm putting up with this crap," right?

We get it. We get it. We know that's how you guys roll and we understand it. It's not something we actually are surprised by. But you come to a point where you have to say, "All right, my external world is a reflection of my internal journey." One of the things that Veronica posted on Facebook today was a reminder, and we want to give it to you tonight as well, is that your external world is a reflection of your internal journey and it doesn't mean you're always screwing up. It can also mean, wow, you've got things actually rolling pretty nicely internally when you experience the world showing you ease and grace and even bliss or serenity. So it's not always: "Let's look for the next thing that has to be fixed." Like we were talking to you guys about, you look around and the things you notice are the spider webs that need to be gotten or the vacuuming that needs to be done or the laundry that needs to be folded and, yeah, there's other stuff going on, too.

So, allowing yourself to see that complete picture. And we've talked about this in a lot of different ways with all the color crayons and all these different tools we've tried to come up with to convey the idea that there's more going on here than you're able to perceive because you've been trained to perceive less than what's going on in order to narrow the focus down to things you could actually handle. To experience the truth of you and emanate the completeness of you, you have to expand out of the little narrow box that you've been putting yourself in to keep safe. The danger is: "What happens on the other side? What happens if I allow myself to express the complete-ness of me? How are people going to react? How am I going to react? Can I actually love myself that much?" These are the little places, now, that we're refining. A while back, we were having a good time talking about the sculpture and the block of marble and the fact that you're in there and we're just chip-ping away. And really, we're getting down to the fine-tuning here, and part of that fine-tuning is: "What about me don't I love? What about me do I have a hard time admitting is true? And who have I kept that from purposefully and who have I kept it from unconsciously?"

We'd like to open the floor to anyone who would like to make a comment about that or of any nature. You can talk about the thing you don't love about yourself or you can talk about what that feels like to hear that information.

Question: I still want to drive my father up to Montana and yet I know that would wreak havoc with what I'm trying to do with my world.

Eloheim: Why do you want to drive your dad to Montana?

Response: So he can see his family again.

Eloheim: And has he asked you to do this?

Response: Yes.

Eloheim: And how does that wreak havoc in your life to spend some time doing that with him?

Response: Well, it would take probably three weeks, and it might not be good for him to be away from his home, and it definitely wouldn't be good for me.

Eloheim: Whoa. If it definitely wouldn't be good for you, then we wouldn't say that you need to do it. And again, it'll take three weeks and the idea that it has to take three weeks and can there be other arrangements made and can airplanes be involved and trains be involved instead of cars. And again, with you, it always comes back to—and this is good because you're working your main stuff—it's that service thing. And now it's even more complicated because now it's not some nameless, faceless.... Now, it's not clients. Now, it's not acquaintances. Now, it comes right down to it. It's Pops. And, "Oh God, he's old and he wants to see these people before he dies and he asked me to do it." And at this point, it would be service if you did it because you know it's not what you want to do and it wouldn't be right for you. And what's interesting is, we love how you tacked on: "and it might not be good for him, either." That's true.

However, on some level he's saying, "I want this," right? We've talked about this before. If he wants to eat dingdong's for breakfast, you're not going to stop him from eating dingdongs for breakfast because it's what's right for him in his mind. So, if he wants to go see the family in Montana you're not going to stop him if he really puts his mind to it. We've met the man. You're not going to stop him if he puts his mind to it. Now, you don't have to enable him, either, and you don't have to be in service yourself. So there's a sense of: Can those people go see him? Can there be some kind of one weekend where everybody gets together to shorten the amount of time for everyone? There's a sense of: "We don't have to do it in this big, grand, drawn-out way to make it very dramatic and service-y." It's, "OK, you want to see them and they want to see you. Let's do something that makes sense for everybody. Where's a hotel? We'll just meet at a hotel for a weekend or something." Shorten it. And the desire to do right by dad, to do right by the family, to be that female figure in your family and gather the chicks together under your wing—all those dynamics that you're very well aware of. That's why you're standing at the microphone because you're like, "I know what's going on and I don't want to do it." The easy thing to do is say, "No, that plan doesn't work, let's see if we can work out one that might make a little more sense." We can tell you want to give this gift to him and if it's a gift, in the sense of: "I'm giving you my time because I want to have this interaction with you," rather than: "I'm going to enable you to eat dingdong's for breakfast." You see the difference? That's a big difference.

Question: Just today, my daughter asked me when the webcast was because she wanted to ask you a question. And I realized it had something to do with me, too. She said that when she goes to bed at night, she feels afraid. I asked her about this. I told her that I thought she was afraid of the new changes that are on the horizon of what you just got through saying—what does this look like for me if I emanate the truth of me? And everything changes in a big way. And I'm thinking the same thing, too, but

I don't go to bed with it, I wake up with it. And I didn't realize it until the other day when I had a very intense talk with my husband, I realized that once I actually allowed myself to get angry and yell but be conscious at the same time, that I woke up the next morning after our discussion and realized: wow, I released. I didn't realize every morning when I wake up my solar plexus is tight until it wasn't there. But now, it's starting to creep back a little bit, so something on that would be great.

Eloheim: The first thing we want to say to all of you, because we know you're all facing this, life feels like it's changing a lot thing—wait, Veronica is like: "You are not going to sell them on this." So we're just going to take a moment to re-word what we were going to say because she's like: "I can tell already the direction you were trying to go with that, they're not going to believe you because I don't believe you." The thing here is this: You said, "the big changes that are coming in." And yes, you all feel big changes coming. But big changes come moment by moment by moment. So yes, big changes are imminent for lots of you, if not all of you. But if you sit in: "Oh God, I'm in the middle of big changes," you will be paralyzed. And that's what you and your daughter are experiencing, is paralysis because you're looking at the big picture and "I don't know how to do all of it," you're talking to the choir here. So the: "I don't know how to do it, I can't possibly figure it out, I don't have any help," whatever your version of it is, when you try to look at the whole picture you'll never get there, and that's why all these months we've been trying to help you with tools to stay in the moment, stay in the moment, stay in the moment, so you can be at high vibration and receive insight. Because the insight is going to help you move along the path of the illumination, illumination, illumination.

You tend to go big picture all the time, anyway. It's the big event, the big planning—all the details— "It's got to be perfect, it's got to be set in stone, it's got to be planned ahead, I don't want to try it unless I know exactly how it's going to turn out," basically, and that is old energy for you. That's an old pattern for you. And your daughter is in a position where it's all so new because she's so young that every big change—she has no track record with big change. Like most of you have lost a job or quit a job, lost a home, moved a home, lost a lover, got a lover. You've had all those experiences, so even though it's intense and painful and challenging you're like, "Well, I've done it before and it didn't kill me last time, so it probably won't kill me this time." While your daughter's 19 and she doesn't have enough life experience under her belt to approach big change with any sort of grace. So the gift you give to her is by saying, "Let's break it down, let's break it down. Let's talk about what is in this moment." If she's going to bed she's in the moment of going to bed, but we bet she's thinking. So if she's thinking, she's not in the moment and she's cutting herself off.

Response: I mentioned to her today to use the short, factual statements. Is that something she should use? Her imagination starts going with her short, factual statements, though.

Eloheim: Yeah, that's the thing about short, factual statements is if you make your short, factual statement and then you go into just thinking about it some more, what's the point? You need to go into short, factual statement followed by period to interrupt your brain that says, "and that is the end of that thought and now what else is going on as a result of that thought? Where am I tempted to go?"

We should reiterate: With the short, factual statements thing, you guys make a short, factual statement: "I'm afraid," the tendency is to go: "Think about fear now." You make the short, factual statement: "I'm afraid," and you stop and see where it wants you to go, and you observe where it wants you to go. So, "I am afraid," and then all of a sudden she's thinking about school or she's thinking about the boyfriend or she's thinking about moving out and having her own place and it's like, "Interesting. Here I am in this moment and the temptation is school, boyfriend, moving, but the truth is, it's time for sleep." And then she brings it back to: "Very interesting, but now I'm going to sleep." And if she doesn't go to sleep and she finds herself thinking—short, factual statement, observe where it wants you to go, and then make a statement about the moment again. You want to observe where you want to go because when you observe where you want to go, it's like what the Visionaries were talking about. Awareness of the unconscious temptations, habits, in your life. You don't have to fix them. You are aware of them, you watch them, and it's almost like: "I see you." Like your dog or your cat is sniffing around and doing something, sniffing around the table, thinking it's going to get something off the table and you say, "I see you." You notice them, they know they're busted, and they toddle off. It's the same thing with these temptations into habit. Noticing them diffuses them. It's when you refuse to notice them that they build.

Response: For me then, the big bee event, it was funny that I wasn't as attached as I have been in the past. I did have some moments, of course, but this time it felt like I delegated a lot better than I have in the past and I also released that expectation out there to others, as well. When you say that's old energy for me, is that because you're seeing that I'm going more into the moment or because it's old energies, so I have to stop thinking that and being in the moment?

Eloheim: Yeah, well, your old energy pattern would be plan, plan, plan ahead. And the truth of the moment is this moment is not about the outcome. This moment is about insight. So yeah, of course if you put on an event you want to plan ahead but you want to plan ahead in the moment. And so, in the past it might look like: "I wonder how many tickets we'll sell. I hope we sell this many tickets because if we don't sell this many tickets then we won't make money," blah, blah, blah. OK, short, factual statement. "I'm concerned about how many tickets we're going to sell, period." And then you see, "I'm concerned about how many tickets we're going to sell," and then you go into, "what will people think? I'm new to this organization, oh God, what if we don't make money," and you just watch where you want to go. It's like we've said, you see the jackets hanging on the coat rack, you don't have to put them all on but you know they're all there. So, there's the jacket that says, "I'm worried about the money and what people will think," et cetera. "Which one do I want to put on? Well, I want to put on the jacket of this moment, which is in this moment I've done everything I can do, I've followed all the insight I have, and I'm willing to receive insight about further aspects of this project."

Response: What I was seeing was other people behaving that way and I was able to kind of view it neutrally. Oh, look at that person doing what I would normally do.

Eloheim: That's comparing you to you, and that's a gift you gave yourself was you drew in script holders to show you what it's like to act the other way.

Response: What a pain. Glad I'm not there now.

Question: How do you tear a quarter in half?

Eloheim: A friend of a friend of Veronica's tore this quarter. Part of being able to do something like this is deciding that you can. The greatness of you. The greatness of you, "Am I able to do something that feels and seems impossible?" and we would say to you right now that every single one of you is doing something that seemed and felt impossible just a short while ago. It may not be externalized in such a fashion. In fact, it isn't. That's the perfect example of what the Warrior's been talking about with their whole story. Last week, they explained the whole thing—the externalization, the internalization. So here's an externalization. Why? Because it's fun. We knew it would make Veronica happy to have an externalization of the Warrior's energy and we thought you guys would dig it, too. How do you do it? You believe you can, one, and part of what happens there is the belief that you can do it is a creating your reality kind of a thing. The belief that you can do it and the desire to apply yourself toward that outcome. A lot of people don't want to apply themselves to their desired outcome with any consistency. This person just decided that would be a cool thing to be able to do and continued to work with their body and their belief system until the probability became an actuality. So it became in the physical.

We told you that martial-arts types can do a lot of things that seem impossible or are difficult to re-create in other circumstances because you're creating so powerfully. So, it's inspiration, we would hope, to see that impossible is a perspective. And proof is a fallacy. So it's: "What is your attitude? What is your philosophy? What is your focus?" And if something like that is important to you, you can do it, too. You have different things that are important to you and some of the things you can do that other person probably can't—and we don't just mean physically. It's just the physical things get all the attention. The external world—you're designed to look at things and experience them. It's when the internal world is happening and the internal world changes, we've said you don't get a diploma by not being triggered by your core emotion, but that's why you have to compare you to you, so that you give yourself a diploma because nobody else is giving it to you that we've seen.

So, you want to tear a quarter? We bet you could do it if you wanted to. Is that where you want to spend your energy? Probably not. Maybe, we don't know. Your creations are so varied and diverse as it is. It's just a journey. You're all on a journey and you're all creating, creating, creating, creating, all the time. And you see something that comes out of the blue moon, like you have this show, this talent show that's on TV, and you see the people do these amazing talents. Some of them can sing, some of them can dance, some of them can ride bicycles. Veronica hasn't been watching it but the commercial comes on every once in a while. And you look at that and say, "Wow!" Well, part of it is some people were born to do certain things. Certain people were born with extraordinary physical strength; some people were born to be creative; whatever it is. A lot of times, what's impressive to you are things that feel impossible to you. You look at that and you think, "I couldn't do that," and so it's exciting and interesting to see something so foreign. But the truth of the matter is, you're doing something as remarkable. There's just not a TV show for it to be shown on. But you are your own broadcast station. That's what we talk about—emanating the truth of you and offering an alternative to people. Just like seeing that quarter might inspire you to believe, "Wow, something's possible that I didn't think was possible," that's emanating a truth and giving you information about a part of life that you didn't know. And if you don't like the quarter, then seeing people on these dancing shows, you think, "Wow, I'm so inspired," or you hear a singer singing, you think, "Wow, that inspires me to see the world in a different way, it's bigger." Well, when you guys go out into the world emanating the truth of you, being high-vibrational, living consciously, taking responsibility for your reactions to your creations, asking yourself questions, you're doing the same thing. You're offering people an expanded sense of what's possible. It's just not in the physical form. It's in the energetic form, which is ordinarily powerful but not as recognizable yet.

Question: About the bees. Where did the bees go?

Eloheim: They flew until they couldn't fly anymore. They just flew until they couldn't fly anymore. Their ability to recognize home was distorted. They couldn't recognize what home was and so they flew looking for home until they perished. They're dispersed over a great amount of space. That's why you don't find them all in a pile. Because the idea that that was home but it's not home anymore, so home must be someplace else. And they went looking. Their ability to recognize home was destroyed, in essence, and part of what they're showing you is that: How do you recognize home? Emanating the truth of you might be a place to start. How do you recognize home? How do you know what home is? And you look at bees and they all live together and they have a community and some of you yearn for those days when you all lived as a community, and all of a sudden the bees can't figure out where home is. And part of that is because the flow of life isn't consistent for them anymore. The flow of life.

The way that they're—this is so much information, hold on—let's just back down a notch. We always like to bring it back to you guys. So, the idea that we don't know where home is, and most of you have a sense of the loss in a similar way because you came here with amnesia—"It doesn't make sense, I never belonged here, why did I come?" et cetera. Your relationship to the idea of home can be very distorted, especially once you get past the four walls you live in. You live in this building, that's your house. But a sense of home, of belonging, of comfort, of knowing, security—first chakra. So the "plight" of the bees is very, very, very illuminating about your sense of home. Well, as the movie indicated, there's some disruption in the flow of their lives because of pesticide use and because of that pesticide use, that new energetic interrupted their ability to sense home. They said in the movie, "Why would they abandon the baby bees?" Because they no longer saw the baby bees as home. They no longer saw that as a responsibility, as a place where they had a duty or a role. And they went seeking, they went seeking that answer. And it is sad in an emotional way. It's very sad that they're having to be that example for you guys. But what a gift. Billions and billions of bees saying: "We're confused." Worldwide.

Worldwide confusion about the sense of: "Where is home? What is home? What consists of home?" Safety in going out into the world and coming back home. What you bring back. The interaction you have with the outside world and your home. We always like to bring the sense of home back into the body and how are you interacting with your sense of home? How are you interacting with your sense of being? Like you talked about with your family. your daughter's this and your husband's that, how is your sense of home being reflected to you? And it would be interesting also for you guys who really resonated with that movie and resonated with the idea of the bees, the idea of: What do you feel like you're bringing into the house? Like they were bringing the pollen from the plants that this chemical had been used on into the home and it was disturbing the cycle of the home, so what are you bringing into the home that disturbs the cycle of the home? And what you're bringing into the home can be like the Visionaries talked about the places within yourself that you're embarrassed of or ashamed of or unwilling to talk about or look at. There's that, too. What are you bringing into the home and what are you bringing into the first chakra? What fears are you bringing into the first chakra?

Because, in essence, you guys go out into the world and then you bring that stuff into your body. Just like the bees bring that pollen home, what are you bringing into your first chakra? How are you relating to your first chakra and to the fears that you have around safety, security, money, stability, home? They're all very good questions and not everybody's resonating with the plight of the bees, but if you are, those are some of the things we think they're illuminating to you. Also the idea that some of the chemicals that have been approved for use, there is no long-term sustainability in that use, and there's sometimes the sense—it's the opposite of lack—it's like a greed state. Like, "If we don't get 300 bushels per acre then…." And a lot of times the company's predicated on the idea that they have to raise 300 bushels of whatever per acre in order to forestall starving and it's like, "People will starve if…." Well, the bees are starving because they can't properly nourish their young. They can't properly nourish themselves. So starving is still occurring. It's just occurring on a different level. And if you look at the land, the land is sometimes not nourished.

It's like: "Let's grow a bunch of food using these means in order to feed," but what are you actually feeding? You're feeding people but are you feeding them well? Are you feeding them things that help them grow? Are you feeding them things that nourish them? It's the opposite of lack. Sometimes, that can be a sense of lack. "We don't have, therefore we have to do..." and then you end up having the same result as you would have had and you also, a lot of times, leave long-term effects in the soil and in the life forms that are abiding on the planet. So, it's another place to look at yourself and say, "Where do I feel lack and where do I feel a sense of greed in the sense of I've got to gather, I've got to collect and hoard?" Because it's hoarding energy. It's the opposite of lack is like hoarding. But it's lack based. You're still in lack. You're just hoarding to deal with your sense of lack. And they'll say, "Well, we have to feed people." Sure, but you also really are trying to make money. You're trying to make money but you're saying it's because you want to feed people. OK, that's an interesting idea and if you really were only trying to feed people you wouldn't be selling, you'd be giving. So let's be clear. Let's all be conscious. It's not just about feeding people. It's about making money feeding people. So let's be clear.

So they're giving you a lot of interesting ideas. What we would suspect is that if you could go—one of your scientist types could probably calculate how far a bee could fly before it died—five miles in one trip. If you went five miles away from these big beehive places right after you have this colony collapse, we think you'd probably see a perimeter of where they are. They flew until they died. They also flew until their life force and their bodies just gave out because really they just flew until they couldn't fly any more. That's what we see happening. About five miles, maybe. Maybe sometimes eight, but depending on the wind we'd say about five miles away you would tend to find them. But you'd have to look right away because there's not that much to them. They're not like crows. They're just a little bee. You fly five miles totally confused and see what's left of you when you get done. That's what we see.

So, as you look at things like the oil spill, the bees, these things that come up, remember it's here to teach you. It's here for you to grow from. It's a gift for you to learn from, always. So look at it from that perspective. It's not: "Oh, the poor bees." It's: What have the bees shown me?" Always. And then you can feel emotion for the bees and you can feel feelings, but if you don't take the gift they're giving… we see that as a choice that you'd want to make. Just take the gift that they're giving first. Because it is a huge gift.

Question: The Pakistan floods. Veronica hasn't been reading much about that. Lots of water, 20 million people displaced. Also, the Indians that are committing suicide because of the Monsanto seed.

Eloheim: It's a very, very, very complex issue with many gifts and much challenge in both of these. People are flooded, people are displaced, people are earthquake'd, people are tsunami'd, people are tornado'd, and fired, and you name it. Your planet has many different ways of giving you sandpaper to work with. And again, the idea of home. If 20 million don't have a place to stay tonight, the idea of home is very loud in those of you who are following that and those of you who are drawn to be involved in it. So—what's the best way to say this—just a moment. Here in California, fires and earthquakes are pretty much the things that you guys have to trouble yourselves with, especially where you guys live you don't have to worry so much about flooding, but fires and earthquakes are on the list. Not very often you guys get tornadoes but fires and earthquakes are really real for you guys, and if there were a fire or an earthquake that displaced some or all of you, the first question we would ask you is: "What are you carrying with you still?"

So, we'll take it away from the people over there and we'll come back here because it's so much easier to talk about here and it's more real because it's more present to each of you. And you don't have to think, "Oh God, what if we did have an earthquake?" You can just say, "I'm going to the store, what do I carry with me? I don't have to be displaced in order to realize the truth or the lesson or the gift of it." And it really is a long exploration of: "What do I carry with me? How do I see myself as experiencing home?" And again, safety and security, first chakra, those two are so important to really be clear on because if your safety and security are externalized and you get in a flood or a tsunami or a fire or an earthquake, it's hard to come back from that emotionally. And it will bring your spiritual growth to a grinding halt because all of a sudden you've got to worry about water and food and there's no room for you to contemplate other things.

If instead you're carrying the truth of you with you and you're emanating the truth of you and all of a sudden you have an opportunity to emanate the truth of you in a tent instead of a house, you're going to have a much more graceful transition between those two. And if all of a sudden you emanate the truth of you in a mansion instead of a three-bedroom house, you have a much better opportunity to emanate the truth of you, too. It goes both ways. It's not just if you have loss. But sometimes people who have great gains have just as much struggle. They may have food but they have still internal strife about that change, as well. So, bringing it home. Bringing it home.

Now, you brought up people who were committing suicide because the land wasn't functioning properly. Again, we would imagine it's a sense of home because that seems to be the theme tonight, or we can tie it into a sense of home if you have made your life and you've lived on land and all of a sudden it functions differently, that can be very disturbing. Just like you changed jobs, your father lived with you, and he doesn't live with you. All of those things are ordinarily disruptive and it's likelier that you guys would look out of you at something like a tsunami or chakra thing. Do you carry your stability, strength, security, do you carry it in your body or do you expect your outside world to give it to you? The answer is everybody expects their outside world to give it to you until it doesn't, and then you see if you're carrying it in your body. How about instead of that, we start with: "How can I feel it in my body?" The way you can feel it in your body, part of the way, is the Warrior energy. Allow yourself to feel a sense of strength, a sense of power, a sense of, not invulnerability, but a sense of: "I take care of me first. I attend to me first. I walk in the love of me first." The Warrior has immense love for himself. He has immense love for himself because he puts himself first. He tells the king to piss off if he wants to. And why can he tell the king to piss off? Because he doesn't base his feelings about himself on the king and what the king thinks. He bases his feelings about himself on what he thinks, and if it's true for him to tell the king to piss off and if it's not true for him to do that, he doesn't. It all starts internally and then goes external. And you guys are all so empathic the temptation is to start externally and then have the external world tell you who you are. And we've had to work on that, haven't we? And for those of you who are very empathic, the work you've done on that has paid off in spades. But there's more. There's always another layer of it and the barrier to it now that we see is this loving you piece. The where you don't love yourself. Because that creates weakness in you. Whereas when you tell yourself the truth about that, it allows you to be vulnerable—vulnerability means opening up to a greater version of you. That's really, as the Visionaries pointed out, the real focus for tonight, is where do you not love yourself. And we've talked about it before but this is a big one, so we can have a little repeat, a little replay.

Now, we know we need to get on with it or else everybody else won't have a chance to talk, but we've been receiving a couple of e-mails about people who don't understand the emotions/feeling thing. Have we lost all of you as well? Then we'll ask you to indulge us while we give a little blurb here so those people who aren't getting it can get it more.

The example someone wanted us to use was our famous example of getting cut off on the freeway, so why not use our famous example of getting cut off on the freeway? It's been a couple of weeks since she sent this e-mail, but we remember it something like this. When someone cuts you off on the freeway and you're angry with them she was having a hard time discerning between emotions and feelings there. Perfect example because everyone knows what it feels like. When you get cut off on the freeway and you have an emotive response, we believe the Visionaries called it, to that experience the temptation is the big F.U. "How dare you? Don't you see you? Don't I count? You're an asshole. You're ignorant. You don't know how to drive." You pick—it's one of those. Those are all emotions or multiple versions of them. Those are all emotions. Those are all emotions because they're not reflective of the moment.

What is actually going on in your body in the moment if you don't attach to the habitual reaction to the stimulation? So, you're tempted to the emotion of blah, blah, blah and then you can say, "Wait, wait, wait. Right now, what's going on? There is a nice song on the radio. The guy didn't hit me. He's already a mile down the road. He's not even in my life anymore and I'm being all emotive about him. I'm feeling good…" or "I'm concerned about something," or whatever happens to be true for you. You were driving down the road in one condition. Let's assume you were in a feeling. Let's assume you were in the moment. Let's assume you were experiencing your car. Let's assume you were experiencing your body. Let's not assume you were in a different emotion. Let's give you the benefit of the doubt and say that you were experiencing a feeling. Someone came in, habitual emotions arose in you. The emotions attached typically to the past and the future or to judgment. Not preferences. Judgment. Past, future, or judgment. Are you going to go into the past, future, or judgment when you could be where you were before it even happened? Because the guy didn't hit you, there's no damage done, he's on his way, you're still with you. Are you going to keep him close to you energetically, be bitchy with him when he's down the road? Remember, he's a script holder and sandpaper. How you use it is your choice and how you decide to interact with it is your choice. So are you going to interact with it as an emotion, which is habitual, or are you going to react to it as a feeling which is actualized experience of what's really going on right now. That's the difference between feelings and emotions.

Response: So could it be accurate to say you're going down the road feeling good, this guy comes in, cuts you off, so you feel fear and then because you don't want to feel fear you go habitually to the emotive state of being angry, which prevents you from feeling the fear and acknowledging it? Is there a component of denial of the emotive moment?

Eloheim: Yeah, and that's a good point because people would say, "Well, the fear I felt was an emotion." No, the fear you felt was biological. It's adrenaline. It's fight-or-flight. So you say, "I felt fear." OK, are you going to stay in fear? Staying in fear would be the emotion path. Acknowledging "Wow, I felt fear there for a minute but there's nothing to be afraid of," go back to feeling. That's probably where people get confused is because the biologically emotive state is so strong a reaction they don't think it's a choice. But remember, everything is a choice and that's a big grown-up way of looking at it.

We'll tell you an example. This is a good one. You guys know that Veronica is not so much for big cities. It's not exactly the place where she likes to hang out and she found herself yesterday alone in San Francisco. Randy, who's known Veronica for a long time, just shook her head. And she was only going to be alone for a short period of time, but she immediately went into fear. She felt afraid. "I'm alone in San Francisco for 20 minutes. Oh, my God." Tsunami alert. And then she stopped herself. She said, "Wait." Literally, "Wait." And she looked all around, she was in the financial district for God's sake, she looked all around. All she sees is tall buildings, nicely dressed people, and shops. She thought, "There's nothing to be afraid of here." So then when she came into the feeling state of the emotion, it was curiosity and she said, "I'm going to go look in the store windows," because she likes to look in the windows and see what's going on. So, she strolled down the street looking in the windows for 20 minutes and it turned out to be a very nice experience. If she had stayed with the emotion, the one that came up, the answer that was obvious was to be in fear and Lord knows what kind of crazy stuff she could have created down there in San Francisco being in fear. She would've found the one person who wanted to be in fear with her in the financial district probably, because everyone else was just busy being in the sun. First sunny day in San Francisco in a really long time.

So, what we're saying to you is this: Yes, your body may react but it's a choice to stay with that emotion or to choose the feeling that's actually reflective of the moment you're experiencing. Not reflective of the habit you have assigned to stimulus, which, if you go into fear, there's all kinds of things like you said—anger and denial—that are attached to fear typically. And if you find yourself having a specific emotive response all the time, then it's really much easier to catch yourself and ask for the feeling. And again, the feeling can be facilitated by "What's my big toe doing? What's my left elbow doing? How do my feet feel in my shoes? What's the weather like right now?" Anything that brings you into the actual physical experience of the moment. It's going to be helpful to help you determine what your feeling is—and a lot of times it will be curiosity, fascination. Because you're very curious and fascinated beings when you're not afraid. That's why we said: Is it fear or fascination? You're very curious, fascinated beings when fear is not the predominant experience. And we could talk about that for another hour but we're not going to. Because if we don't move it along… technically, we have 16 minutes to get through everybody else.

The Girls

So, there was the big aha this week for Veronica when she looked at the idea of what she didn't love about herself, and then she figured it out, and then she sat with it and it changed—and this is the hope we want to give all of you, is that sitting with it changes it. You absolutely don't have to fix it. You don't have to fix it. And that's the beauty of high-vibrational experiences is you don't have to fix them. You don't have to change them. You don't have to do. You get to be. When you alert yourself to something you don't love about yourself the invitation is to then allow yourself, allow yourself, to sit with it, be kind to yourself through it. And love it as your creation, love it as your opportunity, love it as a way you have come to this moment. Not: "Oh God, why did I ever do that to myself? I suck," but: "I've come to this moment, this has been the path, this has given me the gift of being in this moment."

It's never that you have limited yourself. It's that you have allowed yourself to progress at the right pace. How's that? You've allowed yourself to progress at the right pace, and if you're ready for your pace to change then you can look at the things you've previously decided were limitations and have a new interaction with them. Not by changing them but by observing, "Wow, I have used x, y, z to limit things, to change the pace of things, and I'm ready to renovate how I react to these things. I'm ready to make some transformation in how I react to these things." And the kindness that you show yourself when you ask yourself for transformation without judging the previous state, the kindness that you show yourself when you ask yourself for transformation without judging the previous state, that makes sure you don't create any more of these places within yourself where you don't love you. Because if all of a sudden you decide you want to change something and you kind of hate the fact that it was the way it was, you see what happens? So, don't do that. You don't want to create more things that you have to sort out later. This is like internal fire-hosing. Don't do that to yourself.

Allow yourself to experience the transformed state and to come out of the state you were in in a very gentle way of appreciation. Appreciation for the journey you're on, appreciation for the way you set it up, and then move into the grace of "and I'm going to do it differently this time." Not from a judgment place, but from: "I just want it to be different this next time." That's all. "I just want it to be different. Before wasn't wrong, before was just different and I'm ready for it to be even different again." Again: "Before wasn't wrong. I'm just ready for it to be different. And as I move into different, I am not going to judge before." That's kindness. That's love for yourself, and we want you to do that. We're going to go so that the Warrior has a little space for their story. Remember that, OK, because that's a big one. We don't want to have to have the Guardians come in and do a bunch of scraping and all that stuff because you had to judge where you were in order to change into something new. Just make it easy on yourself and don't judge it. Acknowledge that it taught you something, acknowledge that it was a gift you gave to yourself, and get on with it. Beating yourself up about it is not going to help anybody. Now, we're really going.

Warrior

Let's see, we were at the point when Eric and his merry band weren't so merry with each other anymore, weren't we? Eric—was his band defecting? We can't remember exactly. Oh yes, because Eric decided not to tell the story correctly. Yes, yes, yes. We left a little time in between, as you perceive it, so we have to come back to the story.

What is Eric going to do now? His men have lost confidence in him. His men are confused. "Why are we tromping around in the woods with these strangers when we could be going home to our sweethearts? And why are we tromping around in the woods with these strangers who seem to know what they're doing so much better than the guy we're here with? What are we doing? Why are we here? What is going on?" These are questions you've asked yourselves many times, and just as the men look externally of themselves to Eric for the answers, we see you doing that, too. You look outside of yourselves, saying, "Why am I here?" You're asking the wrong person. It's not: "Why am I here with him?" It's: "Why am I here now? Who am I? Who am I and why am I having this experience? And do I want it to change and, if so, let's get on the business of changing."

Back to Eric. He's a bit young. We don't know if we ever told you that, but he's a bit young for his position. His men are more experienced. He's got some kind of royalty in his blood, we're sure of it. He's got some kind of: "I can be in charge because I'm the son of the King" kind of energy that he runs, and his men are like: "I am here because I've been here my whole life" kind of energy. And the men would like to be in a position where they can respect their leader. Their leader would like to be in a position where he's respected by the men. This is not what's happening currently.

Some of the men have come to us now. They've come to us and said, "OK, this is the deal. We are not happy. We either want to be with you or we want to go home. We don't want to be in this limbo-land you've got us stuck in." And we say, of course, "We don't have you stuck in any damn thing. Walk away if you wish." And then here it comes—and you all do this one—"but how would I? But what would happen? But what would be the consequences?" But, but, but, but, fucking but. Geez, if we need to hear that word one more time we think we have to stab someone. But, but, but, but, what? What is it that you want? What are you doing to bring that into your life? Are you willing to face the consequences of your desires being made manifest? Those desires may be that you get more money, that you have a better position, that you have a husband, a wife, a kid, whatever, but are you willing to deal with what happens to you when you do? And we don't just mean being on the 10-most-wanted list. We mean being happy for once. We mean stepping into the world in a way that allows you to know yourself. You see, we look at Eric's men and we say: What is in your way? And we look at you and we say: What is in your way? What is in your way of being the truth of you? Just like we look at them and say: What is in your way of being the truth of you? "Well, I've sworn allegiance to Eric." Well, then, why are you talking to us? Because if you've made the choice to swear allegiance to Eric, you're not being very allegient right now. So you're blowing it already. You may as well stop blowing it and get what you want instead. You're afraid to change but you're already sneaking around the outside of change in an unconscious and rather unattractive way. Change or don't change. "Well, I can't break my allegiance." This is the one we're going to stab. If the urge comes upon us and we can't hold back, we've already picked out the one we want. That one. That one that keeps repeating: "I've sworn allegiance. I can't leave him but I don't want to be with him." Sounds like some of your relationships. "But I'm married to him. We live in the same house. I love him." Yeah, you love him, but why are you talking to us again?

Back to Eric. His men are all in a various stage of disruption. You've got grizzled veterans that are like, "This is the one that's going to get me killed," and you've got the younger ones that are like, "This isn't nearly as much fun as I thought it was going to be." You've got the other ones who are like, "Can I just go home now?" And then there's Eric. So now, Eric has come to us. God, he's pissed. Shit. Maybe we should stab him, instead. He's mad at us because he thinks we're trying to steal his men. Yeah, we want the one that's sworn allegiance to you but is backstabbing you. That's the one we want. Please give him to us. Yeah, right. We're tempted to stab him. Stand close, we'll get both of you with one go.

So, we're just listening. And you have to remember that we've been as a little band here for a very long time, and so the men, our men, are starting to realize where things are headed. What's really interesting about the guys that have been around with us for a while is they'll do very interesting things. Like all of a sudden in this conversation, everyone needs to sharpen their knife at the same time. You see, sharpening your knife gives you a very, very good reason to have your knife out. Do you understand? Because as fast as we are, it's always very nice for it to start in your hand. So, all of a sudden, everyone just feels the urge to sharpen something. It makes a nice soundtrack for the conversation with Eric. Eric is mad because he thinks we're trying to steal his men. And we say: Eric, you can leave anytime you want. This is the other thing you guys do. You get into a path and you forget you have choice. You do this at your jobs a lot. You start to want to buck the system and you start to resent the system and you start to resent your coworkers and you start to resent the environment you're in, and all the while we're going: Quit, quit, quit. Just leave. If it's that bad, why are you still there? Why have you decided that you have to fight in that environment? Why can't you just walk away? So we say to old Eric: Just leave. "No, no, no. I don't want to leave." Why don't you want to leave? "Because I still think there's more for me to learn here." Yes, learning that you can leave is probably at the top of the list. Any of you resonate with this one? Learning that you can leave.

So, we tell Eric: Look Eric, this is the deal. We don't want your men. We're not trying to steal them. We brought you along because you wanted to come, you bitch about what's actually happening, and you have every opportunity to leave at any time. The conversation's over. See, we don't have to justify our position. Do you justify your position? Yup. Remember, "No" is a complete statement. You might want to put a period on there just for fun but " 'N' 'O' period" is complete sentence. You don't have to justify the decisions you make. We are not going to beg Eric to stick around. We are not going to diffuse his anxiety about the fact that we're stealing his men. We're not going to puff him up to try to make him feel better about himself. The bottom line: Eric, make your choice. You came here to learn or you came here to leave. Do what you want to do. We don't care. And that's one of the hardest things for you to hear: I don't care what you do. But the truth is if you care about you first, you don't need other people to care about you, for you to know who you are. Eric doesn't know who he is and he thought tromping around with us would teach it to him. And the bottom line, what he's learning, is he doesn't like who he is, but he hasn't yet gotten to the point where he knows how to handle that.

So, unfortunately, Eric is not leaving and we're not stabbing him. But there's more to the Eric tale and we will share it next time we tell our story, which most likely will be next week, but since we skipped a week we won't assume. Eric decides to stay. Eric decides to stay and we are going to do mad-scientist on Eric. We are going to take the fact that we know Eric and we know his men and we are going to mix up the dynamic a little bit. Because since Eric decided to stay, it's no longer Eric in charge of his boys and we're in charge of our boys. It's we're in charge of all of it. Suck it up, Eric. Let's see what Eric thinks next time. Because we always reserve the right to stab him. We keep a special sword just for the ones who are really annoying. We have hope for old Eric, just like we have hope for all of you. Eric, unfortunately, isn't as advanced as your left toe, so we'll hopefully be able to boost him up a little without having to go into service, but he might not like what we're going to do next. We think he's got some time of not liking it coming. But sometimes you learn to like things you didn't like at first.

Fred

Frankly, we don't understand. We're very, very confused by the idea that you don't love yourselves completely. This is extraordinarily confusing to us. Part of the reason this is extraordinarily confusing to us is that we see you as your complete, whole selves even though you're in the physical form. We know that's odd but that's how we see you. And if you could see yourself as the glory of the infinite, immortal soul that you are, the idea that you don't love yourself is unpalatable. We are confused by the conversation tonight, we will admit that freely. But what we're not confused about is this: The true nature of your infinite, and immortal self resides just a breath away in any moment, and it exists for you to access at any time. And we exist to hold that access portal open, and we constantly support you in making the choice to choose for that. Just as they explained earlier, you can choose between emotions and feelings, you can choose between emotions and feelings, you can choose between experiencing yourself as your infinite, immortal true nature and the amnesiac that you pretend to be. Step out of the limitation that you've existed in and move into the truth of you. We were the last to come to the Council for a reason. We're the least like you in your physical form and it is confusing to us, but we are growing, too, and we will do our best to mitigate our confusion and allow it to become clarity for all of us. But know that you are not the only one that is confused by this issue and we're learning just as well as you are. At some point, we'll get to the point where we're very, very skilled. At this point we can't even make the hand point but we'll get better. That's all we have.

Matriarch

Ahhh. Let's all have a deep breath. After all this talk of love, of appreciation, of feelings, emotions, of the way you interact with the world in that way, just allow your attention to settle into your heart chakra, into your chest, just for a moment let's all contemplate not the if's and the and's and the what's and the were's. None of that. None of that. Just allow yourself to contemplate the "is," the is of this moment, the is of your body, the is of the community you've created here, the is of the truth of you. Just allow yourself to experience the is of the truth of you. And you don't have to have it figured out. You don't have to have it perfect. You don't have to have everything from your past erased. You don't have to have it all transformed. In this moment, you're making a choice to be the is of you. That's all.

Just be the is of you present, present and experiencing the truth of you. And the invitation is, of course, to allow it just to be possible. Just open a door to it being possible, just possible, not even probable, just possible, that there's even more of you for you, and that it's possible for you to access it. That's all. Just that. It's possible for me to access the more of me for me. More deep breaths. That's all.

So when you find yourself in a conundrum, when you find yourself triggered or confused, you just say, "It's possible. It's possible there's more here. It's possible. It's possible there's more here." And allow the possibilities to become actuality in their own natural flow. We love being with you. The entire Council expresses the love of being with you. And we will come again next week to love being with you even more. And we say, for now, goodnight, and enjoy the rest of your time together here.

Tools

Big toe, left elbow

This is a great tool for bringing you into the moment. When you find yourself pulled into the past or the future, ask yourself, "What is my left knee doing? What is my big toe doing? How does my tongue feel? If I touch my teeth what does that feel like?" Asking what your body is feeling short-circuits the temptation into thinking about the past and future. The key is once you've thought about your elbow and short-circuited the temptation into the past or future, to then let go of thinking about the elbow and allow yourself to stay in the moment. Then, open to insight from your soul by saying, "What's really going on here?" If you find yourself getting tempted away from the moment, repeat the tool, "What's my left elbow doing? What's my big toe doing?"

When you use this tool, be sure to use a body part that you don't normally think about. This will make it even easier to avoid habitual thoughts.

Veronica writes:

I love the tools that make me smile when I use them. The inquiries, "How does the back of my knee feel?" or "What is my right eyebrow doing?" make me feel light and joyful, which I'm sure helps me sink even more deeply into the moment. This fun tool is easy to remember and quick to apply.

***

Focusing on my big toe reminds me that I can point my feet in any direction I choose.

—Denise

Choose and choose again

The transition from the fear-based operating system to the consciousness-based operating system is not done in a straight line. You must choose and choose again for transformation. Habit is very strong, the survival instinct runs very deep, cultural and DNA pressures are intense—your choice to grow spiritually requires spiritual discipline and persistence. It is an act of committing and re-committing to the journey.

Remember: Fear is a choice, not a mandate.

***

Veronica writes:

A reminder tool. Sort of like a condiment. Use frequently. Use liberally. Always have it around.

Color with all the crayons

This is a fun way to talk about the idea that there are multiple perspectives on any situation and that, in the past, you have limited your perspective to the crayons (perspectives) you're used to. We are trying to open your eyes to the idea that there are more crayons in the box and, "Wouldn't it be fun to color with new crayons?" In order to do that, you have to be willing to look past your habits.

If you had been coloring with only 3 crayons, but realized there were 61 more in a box of 64, wouldn't you like to color with the other crayons?

Don't limit yourself to just what the mind has to show you, but allow yourself to experience the "unseen color crayons" as well. Don't limit yourself to, "my experience is only what I can see or prove."

Invite the unseen crayons and the infinite possibilities of your soul's perspective to give you a new opportunity for experience.

***

Veronica writes:

This tool helps me get out of the "black or white" mentality by realizing there are so many more options (colors) available!

***

I've realized what a control freak I am and that I have only used a few crayons in the past. I realized how much certainty I expected in all aspects of my life. This tool has allowed me to expand further. I am now encouraging myself to look for a new perspective in every aspect of my life. I am encouraging the unknown.

—Mike Imbach

Don't be mean to yourself (Four-year-old child)

If there's something you genuinely want to change about your-self, you don't have to be mean to yourself in order to change it. Take a moment and let that sink in. You don't have to be mean to yourself to change.

You don't berate at a child about learning to walk, or talk, or write. You say, "Hey, it's OK, let's try it again."

Yet, you will be extremely critical of yourself at nearly any opportunity.

How do you know if you are being mean to yourself? If you're talking to yourself in a voice that you wouldn't use with a four-year-old child, especially somebody else's four-year-old child, you're being mean to yourself.

When you find yourself being hard on you, simply ask yourself, "Would I say this to a pre-schooler?"

No, you would not.

It's OK to have a new plan or to desire something different for the future or to reevaluate how you handled a situation, that's all growth. But beating yourself up is so contrary to everything we teach that we have made it our only rule: You don't get to be mean to yourself.

Oh, and be aware that someday soon we are going to evolve this tool. Someday soon, we are going to lower the age. It will be, "You can't say anything to yourself that you wouldn't say to a toddler or an infant." Since you can be fascinated by EVERYTHING an infant does (Oh look, it's a poo poo!), you can, eventually, be fascinated by anything YOU do, as well. Imagine that!

***

Veronica writes:

When Eloheim says, "We only have one rule: You don't get to be mean to yourself," they really mean it! The seriousness and attention they pay to this concept is above any other.

***

I have found that this tool of "don't be mean to yourself" represents a lot of change for me! It means letting go of a lot of people who, if I am truthful with myself, no longer fit in my life. Being nice to myself, ultimately, means being willing to be available for new people entirely, by being willing to be alone first. It's somewhat sad but also liberating to be in my truth in this way.

—Anne Marie

***

Just last night, I was talking with my friend—he was sitting on the edge of my big overstuffed brown couch. I was on the opposite sofa looking past him for a way out of a conversation that was spiraling down into argument-land. "Don't be mean to me" popped in and in that instant, we softened our stance. Our outcome also magically changed.

Experiencing the words "don't be mean to me" feels like folding my legs and falling into soft ground with my arms around the neck of a lovely, beautiful beast.

"Don't be mean to me" is my "fallback" tool. It wins every argument. It connects with everyone's heart, so everyone gets it.

—Denise

***

I used to berate myself internally all the time until I started practicing this tool. I would catch myself as soon as I started to hear the negative chatter, and have been able to transform that nasty voice into a loving, supportive, helpful voice for me now!

—Randy Sue Collins

Equal signs

2+2=4. That's not what we mean by equal signs.

What we mean when we say you are using equal signs is that you believe a fact is tied to a specific outcome. In our book, facts and outcomes don't get tied together. Facts stand by themselves, all alone. A fact is a fact. "I have $20 in my checking account." That is a fact. That fact does not equate to a certain outcome. It is simply a fact.

One of the main ways you tie facts to outcomes is to say, "I only have $20 therefore I can't pay the rent." The rent may not be due for two weeks, but you've already decided you can't pay it. When facts are equated with preconceived outcomes, it makes it very difficult to shift the energy of a situation.

HERE IS A COMMON PATTERN: You determine your truth and then use your hamster-wheel mind to determine the outcome, which is typically a shitty outcome! You don't say, "Fact is, I look glorious therefore I'm going to have seven lovers by the end of the weekend." You say, "Fact is, I look glorious and no one gives a shit."

But, you don't stop there. You make it even more challenging. You say, "I have a fact, which I am equating to a sad outcome; that means facts are dangerous, facts are frightening, facts are not safe." And what does that do? It makes discovering "what is true now" terrifying. See this icky thing you do?

Instead, take the fact of: "I have $20 in my bank account," and the fact of: "Rent is due in two weeks," and do not put equal signs between them. Look for, "What is true now? I just have a truth." You sit with the truth and ask for insight about your facts. You determine your truth and then you look for insight about it. Don't have preconceived notions about the outcome of your discovered facts.

Facts live on their own. This is the beauty. What is a fact? A fact is an outcome of consciousness. It's awareness of your truth.

What is true now? What are your facts? "My facts are I have $20 in my bank account. My facts are: Rent is due in 14 days. My facts are: I'm afraid of that. My facts are: I'm tempted to go into an outcome, a disaster scenario. I'm tempted to feel like I will end up dead in the gutter."

Now, be careful "fact" doesn't get co-opted to mean thinking. This is not hamster-wheel thinking. This is evaluation of the truth of you including your boundaries and preferences.

"What is true now? What is true now is I have $20 in my checking account. What insight do I have about that? Damn, that really tempts me to be afraid. Hmm… well, what is true now about the temptation to be afraid?" Use the Short, factual statements tool to describe your facts. The point of short, factual statements is to stay in the moment and see what's really going on. When you think, "Oh God, am I making an equal sign?" a way to know is, "Am I in scary outcome prediction or am I in "what is true now" insight?" If something is going on in your life, the strong temptation is to believe that the perceived outcome is your reality. You are not the perceived outcome! That is make believe. That isn't real. You are not the perceived outcome of your problems. You are the person experiencing a truth and choosing whether or not to use the habit of equal signs to process that truth or to open to something new: insight about that truth.

Question: Would it be helpful at all to imagine a better outcome?

Eloheim: That's like vision boards and intentions and all that stuff, which is all well and good but useless if you're still projecting into the future and not attending to what's true now, because if you think you suck it doesn't matter how many vision boards you make. Until you get rid of "I think I suck," you're generating your vision board from "I suck." So, it's all well and good to have a vision board. We're not saying that's not a good tool. But we're saying if you have a vision board that says, "I want a Maserati," but inside you're saying, "I suck," it's much harder to make the Maserati come into your life—and if it does you'll probably crash it because you think you suck. Attend to the fact of "I think I suck," first. That is the fact that needs your attention and needs transformation.

AN EXAMPLE: You know you need to talk to someone and you are anxious about it. "Oh God, I need to have that conversation," and you get worked up in your mind. "What's she going to say, how is he going to react?" You work yourself up so much that you project disaster outcomes: "Oh, I'm going to be in the gutter, homeless in the gutter with no money, no food, and a broken arm." If you just said, "I need to set a boundary with this person," and just keep going back to "what is true now, what is true now, what is true now? What is my truth?" and reinforce what your truth is, when you set that boundary you will be more centered in your truth. When you're more centered in your truth, you give yourself the opportunity to receive more and more insight. Plus, you're in the moment, so you're higher-vibrational.

We know this can feel like a big change. Remember, the choice for consciousness is challenging, but habitual response is suffering. Challenges help you grow. You experience challenges all the time. You do something hard every single day. You're used to challenges. Now, you're challenging yourself to let go of habitual suffering. Habits are strong but they make you suffer and they don't go away. You can suffer the same way you're suffering today for the rest of your life or you can buck up a little, face some discomfort, recognize that you do hard things all the time, and make this change.

Note: We have created a wonderful video about this tool, Equal signs. You can watch it by visiting this page: http://eloheim. com/5525/equal-signs-the-tool-powerpoint-video/.

***

Veronica writes:

There is a distinct physical sensation I experience when I find myself making equal signs. It feels as though I am being stretched. It is not comfortable! I realized that it stems from trying to be both in the moment and in the future at the same time. If I am out of the moment, an equal sign is often the reason and it's also the path back to my center. Discovering the equal sign that drew me into outcome (the future) helps me find clarity about the trigger. Clarity about the trigger shows me just where I need to apply my attention to get transformation.

***

It is perilously easy to fall into the trap of equal sign mentality. Our society fosters the concept that if "x" is true, "y" must follow, as the day follows the night. Accepting that false assumption causes me to put my problem in a box, wrap it in pseudo-certainty, and slam the lid closed. Result: paralysis and fear. It precludes my tapping into the infinite field of possibilities where a different solution can come into being. In effect, I have made a judgment and have sentenced myself to an unwelcome outcome. How absurd! What sneaky things they are, those equal signs!

—*Janice*

***

Equal signs represent the duality of this physical reality. When I replay over and over the same scenario always getting the same results, I am in the past or in the future instead of "Now." It's a great reminder to stay in the present and fully appreciate the state of calmness that ensues.

—Mike

***

To me, the tool Equal signs is a major step toward living consciously, as these tend to sneak in whenever I'm not aware and actively engaging in the here and now. When you start seeing them it's nothing short of a revelation. One small step for woman—one giant leap for consciousness!

—Liz

***

When I think of equal signs I think of my automatic reaction to something, which may not be true. A simple example would be, if it is cloudy and damp outside then it is going to rain. But it might not rain! So equal signs warn me that there are more possibilities than I might be thinking at the moment.

—Rosie

***

Eloheim told me one time that I had the granddaddy of all equal signs. They said the equal sign was between capitulation to whatever is going on and safety. I have to be quiet to be safe. My belief was quietness, swallowing what I was feeling, keeping small, would keep me safe. I can only show this much of me because if I show any more it's going to rock the boat too hard, and if I rock the boat I won't be safe, and if I'm not safe I'll be in the gutter and then I'll die after suffering a lot more. When in reality my awareness of what I really want in life, my awareness of how I feel about things, my awareness of the truth of me expressed will bring peace. I am at the point where my pursuit of safety has taken second place to my desire for a transformed life. I am at the point where I have realized that the only true safety is to abandon the quest for safety and instead quest for peace, because safety requires certainty and there is no such thing as certainty. The option is to seek instead for peace, which is knowing myself and knowing whatever is going on I am still me.

—Marilyn

***

I was equating my worth as a healer with my ability to manage the logistics of getting my email list and class notices in active flow. When I relaxed the tension around this perceived "failure," I found that I was invited to give my classes by others who, by the way, had a system of sending out email announcements. Equal signs are everywhere in my thinking and I can usually spot them when I notice tension. Am I equating my safety with whether or not I find my lost purse? Does health equal pills? The antidote for me is to "breathe and breathe again," then trust that my life takes on a unique, precious quality each time I'm willing to experience it as it is.

—Margy

***

The equal sign tool always made sense to me whenever Eloheim would explain it, but somehow I never internalized it and used it on my own. It was one of the tools I kept in the drawer, so to speak. At one of the recent weekly talks Eloheim was speaking about the creative power of our thoughts. I asked about the creative power of negative thoughts and how best to "cancel" some unwanted scenario that pops into my mind.

"Give us an example," Eloheim said. "OK, suppose I'm walking down a grassy hillside and it occurs to me I should be more mindful so I don't step in a badger hole and twist my ankle. That's not an experience I want to create."

"Look at those equal signs!" Eloheim said. "Not being mindful as you walk equals stepping in a badger hole and that equals twisting your ankle." They went on to tell me that the best way to "cancel" the negative creation is simply to acknowledge that my mind had jumped into territory I don't want to visit and to redirect my atten-

tion. Change channels intentionally, as I like to call it. That was the gate-latch for me that night, not the point about equal signs.

This afternoon I was hiking and found myself thinking about a situation in my life and what I could do if such-and-such happened, ways to respond, things to say. More of my attention was on this conjecture than on the beautiful landscape around me. Suddenly it hit me like a ton of bricks that I was spinning a web of equal signs! A = B = C = D = E = F = G and so on. Not planning, mind you, but worrying, to be blunt. "A" hadn't even happened and I was already getting reactive about "G."

What is true now? I'm walking along this lovely trail and there's nothing I can do RIGHT NOW about any of those conjectural outcomes. They're not even particularly likely and they're certainly not where I want to put my attention right now.

It's very helpful to see that the equal sign tool is a much broader sword of discernment than I had thought. What is true now? And what is the equal sign here that takes me out of what is true now?

—Richard

Feelings are not emotions

There is a difference between emotions and feelings. It's important for you to recognize that there are two different things occurring and it's important for you to see that very, very frequently, they're all mixed up together like one of these ice creams where the chocolate and the vanilla are swirled together.

We recognize that you have emotive responses to situations. We want to help you recognize when that emotive response is a habit, and when it's actually a reflection of the truth of the moment.

The issue at hand is that emotions are typically habit-based, culturally based, past- and future-based. They are not the same as what we identify as feelings. Feelings are based on what is actually going on in the moment.

Emotions often draw you out of the moment; feelings are going to deepen your experience of the moment. An emotion tells you that you need to be jealous or fearful or envious or depressed or confused—lots of those kinds of generalized emotions. A feeling gives you the opportunity to be completely present and reflect upon what's going on.

Typically, your emotional states are patterns. Something occurs and you already have an emotion that is pre-programmed to be assigned to that situation. If it's not assigned to you by your culture, it's assigned to you by your family of origin or your role, or it's assigned to you by habit or things that have happened in the past or projections of things that could happen in the future.

As you have an experience, the kindest thing you can do for yourself is to ask, "Why am I feeling this way?" Acknowledge that the feeling you're having may not actually be representative of what's going on in the moment. This is going to offer you an incredible amount of freedom.

AN EXAMPLE:

You've seen these cowboy shows where the barn's on fire and they open the doors and the horses run and run and run, and it's, "We don't care where they go, we've just got to get them out of here." In essence, that's the energetic similarity behind what happens when you allow your emotions to take over, because the next thing you know, you're three ranches over, pissed off, tired, angry, broke, whatever. And think, "What the hell just happened?" How many times has this occurred—and it's probably a huge number—that you get yourself back to the barn and you say, "Oh God, I had a strong reaction to that," and the other person says, "I don't even know why you were mad, I was trying to give you a compliment," or "I was just trying to explain." If your emotions take over, you're three farms down. If your feelings take over, you can be vulnerable.

AN EXAMPLE:

Veronica was able to see that when she was in emotion she was very, very disturbed and when she was in feeling, it felt very, very profound; but it was as though she was constantly switching between the two during the conversation. So, parts of the conversation were like, "Holy shit, this is really amazing, to have this conversation, to feel closer to this person and have this happen," and then on the other hand her heart was beating and she was sweating and she was nervous and her stomach was roiling and she was thinking, "Why do I feel good one minute and the next I feel bad and then I feel good and then I feel bad?"

After we explained the difference between feelings and emotions she was able to say, "Oh my God, all of that confusion was because I was not in the moment," even though she knew she was focusing on being in the moment—her emotional system wasn't. Her attention was in the moment but her emotional system wasn't.

She was able to say, "Oh my goodness, when I was in this side of it I was in the feeling of the moment, which was, 'Wow, this person is really telling me something deep and profound about themselves which was an opening and a friendship.' " On the other side it was, "Oh my God, what does that mean about me, what does that mean about the past or what does that mean about the future?"

Emotions are like climbing up a wall and whenever you grab, it just crumbles away from you. It's not real because it's not based in the moment. A feeling is a strong handhold that you can put some weight on. What will be interesting is when you default to feeling and the feeling is a sense of bliss, serenity, what some people like to call love, and fascination. That's the default feeling that you will get to as you work this process. But now you're still discerning between emotions and feelings and probably needing to take a pretty strong stand with yourself about not following the temptation of emotions into habit.

The opportunity is for you to have wide, varied experience of feelings, and that experience feeds you in a new way; leave behind the narrowness of emotion and wallow in the experience of feeling. Not only does it make the moment more pleasurable, it also gives you the opportunity to experience an ever-expanding palette of experiences. When you get into the feeling state, instead of it being just blue or green, it gets to be sky blue or royal blue or you-name-it blue. It starts to become these nuances; these nuances of feelings are available to you. We expect that you'll start finding yourself being able to discern between the nuances of feelings you find yourself in just like you can discern between different shades of blue.

You have the ability to discern between emotions and feelings in this way and we invite you to play with it and enjoy it so that you can emanate more accurately the absolute authenticity of you. Because that's really what's going on here, you're emanating accurately the authenticity of you, shared with your soul, so that you might combine your ability to be physical with your soul's ability to comprehend the universe. Can you imagine what that must be like? Well, that's what you're doing, combining those two things, the ability to be in density and the ability to be in expansiveness at the same time.

***

Veronica writes:

This tool falls into the category of "when I remember to use it, it knocks my socks off." I need this tool when I am in a triggered state; however, it's hard to remember that when I am upset! I'm committed to practicing with this tool. I know it will make a tremendous difference in my life.

***

As I use this tool I realize that emotions disturb my brain and that feelings open my heart!

—Donna

***

On the morning of the eclipse, I had a disturbing dream. I dreamt I was being rejected for something that I said, which is a recurring theme in my life. As I tried to review the dream, it was a jumble of emotion and feelings. The feeling was dominant, but I couldn't seem to hold onto it. I didn't recognize it and I wrestled with trying to keep the mind out of my evaluation. The feeling was so intense that I found myself getting distracted by a variety of fears. For the first time, I was aware of my mind quickly jumping from one fear to another.

The survival instinct won this round and the feeling slipped away.

Later, insight suggested that it was a feeling of separation, as in, the Homo sapiens illusion of separation from the One.

　　—Mary T.

***

Emotions muddle my thoughts. They jerk me around. They certainly are not in the now. They represent the past, past, past. Feelings are in the now, they are honest and true. Feelings help keep me centered and emotions do not.

　　—Mike

***

Feelings in the moment are very strong and often confusing. This morning I saw a squirrel out the window, and it saw me, too. It jumped onto the fence top and started to come toward me. It showed no fear of me at all and it was so young and endearing in its innocence that I just loved it. I welled up in tears so much that my mascara was starting to run. I thought "What the heck is going on?" I realized that I was feeling emotional that it might be caught and killed by my cat who has been a good hunter of squirrels in the past, and that emotion had overtaken my pure "joy of the moment" feeling. The past history of experiences had intervened to detract from my feelings of the moment, which were originally pure, sweet joy.

　　—Rosie

***

I was at the dentist today and I was told some concerning news about my gums. I took in the information and as the afternoon progressed, I shifted myself into a fearful, emotional cascade of stories on all matter of subjects, not just my gums. I have an old pattern of projecting fears into my future—my gums are needing more care, my bank account is depleting, what kind of job am I going to be doing 10 years from now, will I meet the love of my life, I'm getting old, etc.

So funny, really! I'm catching myself on this and notice the habit of taking an emotional trigger and then proceeding to set off a whole stream of "what-if" scenarios that are unnecessarily scary.

The truth is that the feeling I had today at the dentist was a sense of powerlessness with the involvement of an authority figure, my dentist, and not feeling in control. I don't know if anything I'm doing is really going to make my gums perfect when I'm 75, or if I'll even be alive then, but the dentist was just informing me of things I can do to take good action. I have the power to act on his advice or not. I was triggered, and it feels good to catch this, and honor myself in observing this pattern/habit of creating an emotional storm that takes me out of my "center." I can hit my "reset" button and get back into my power. YAY!

—*Anne Marie*

***

All my life I have had a "bad" temper. I realized early on that the emotion of anger was a brilliant disguise for my true feelings. Most of the time, anger has been a default position—a place that I felt comfortable in and one that I could depend on. I knew how to use anger. I have used anger to power through intense situations like death, illness, abuse, abandonment, and betrayal. I used it to make art. And I have also used it to simply get my way. Anger was my survival tool. It was my energy and the way that I moved in the world. It made me fierce and unstoppable. It was a huge habit.

I have always known that beneath the anger I had feelings of deep sadness and a lack of love. But over time, the habit of anger supplanted those real feelings, making them difficult to access. After surviving cancer in 2001, I returned to my studio to make some paintings and realized that for all those years I had been making my work from a well of anger, resentment, and separation. I looked into the place in myself that made paintings and found that the well was dry. I was filled with such love and appreciation for life that I was completely unable to tap into my habitual painting place. It was shocking! But it was true. So I didn't paint. That was the first clue.

Recently, I have had occasion to understand this habitual response in relation to my workplace. I am so much more conscious now. I catch myself using anger as a response to triggering situations. I see it so clearly now. I am almost embarrassed. But, as Eloheim says, I am grateful for the triggers because I get the opportunity to practice!

I am losing the habit of anger. I am finding growth in the truth of sadness and love in the moment.

—Rene

Feet under shoulders

A quick way to ask yourself if you are coming from a balanced and centered place. "Are my feet under my shoulders?" A very important tool for those that are working to heal service mentality. Also powerful when you find yourself trying to convince someone you are right. Are you leaning forward to make your point or are you centered within yourself?

✳✳✳

Veronica writes:

I love that this tool has such a strong visual component. It is quick to use and very easy to remember.

Go to the bathroom

On the spiritual journey, you may find yourself in situations that feel low-vibrational. Sometimes it is very difficult to know how to remove yourself from these situations in a way that feels graceful. This can be especially difficult if you are in a public setting. Fortunately, you have a built-in way of getting out of almost any low-vibrational situation.

Just excuse yourself to the bathroom. It's a free pass!

The vast majority of people won't balk at you leaving a conversation to use the bathroom, and you can stay in the bathroom a really long time if need be. If the situation warrants, flush the toilet a bunch of times and spray the deodorizing spray. If you still aren't ready to reengage the conversation, do it some more! Read the magazines, count the little flowers on the wallpaper, flush, spray, turn the water on, flush, spray, turn the water on. And in the meantime, OK, yes, you've used up some clean, potentially drinkable water, we recognize that, but in the meantime you've kept your vibration high, you've entertained yourself, and you haven't matched energy with a low-vibrational situation.

Be nice to yourself! You can easily remove yourself from a triggering environment—be willing to step out of it to regain your center.

IMPORTANT: This isn't a pass to be unconscious. This is a way to take a break from a triggering environment without requiring you to explain or make excuses for your need for some alone time to regain your center.

∗∗∗

Veronica writes:

This tool is a fabulous alternative to just "going with the flow" and tolerating situations that really don't serve me. It's surprisingly easy to use.

∗∗∗

The first time I tried the "going to the bathroom" tool I felt like I was running away. While in the bathroom I used several more tools to "get myself together." Over the months, I've found that taking a trip to the bathroom makes a quick getaway from anything I'd rather not participate in. It honors my sensitivity to my surroundings while equally honoring the opinions and expressions of others.

    —Denise

∗∗∗

Today I had an encounter with a vendor at the hardware store who was complaining at length about another vendor. I listen politely for a long period of time and decided to set a boundary with her. I gave her some good advice for solving her problem and excused myself to other duties. It felt really good.

    —Mike

∗∗∗

I was shocked and surprised when I realized that I have been using this tool for as long as I can remember. My wonderful father taught it to me when I was very young. I was having difficulty with my verbal skills and had a controlling mother and later a controlling husband. As I grew older I started to believe that if I used the tool I was weak by avoiding what I needed to face. So I dropped the tool and started remaining in the negative energy, trying to get my thoughts out and listened to. This only dragged me down as I fought and fought thinking that somehow I was getting stron-

ger. I developed physical issues. A huge shift occurred in me when Eloheim presented this tool. I am once again using it, but this time with consciousness. It is now so much easier to stay high-vibrational. P.S. The bathroom isn't always available, be creative for there are unlimited ways to exit!

—*Donna*

How ridiculous does it have it get?

How ridiculous does it have to get before you are willing to change a habit? How much suffering must you experience? How many times do you have to experience the same patterns?

How ridiculous does it have to get? The answer? Usually, pretty damned ridiculous.

You're constantly putting up barrier after barrier after barrier to taking responsibility for your creation because the habit of victimhood is so strong in you. Sure, the choice for consciousness is challenging, but suffering is painful and repetitive. Owning "I did this" might be hard, but what is the alternative?

Don't require it to become ridiculous before you are willing to transform it. If it has become ridiculous, then transform it immediately!

***

Veronica writes:

When it gets ridiculous, I KNOW whatever it is must move to the top of my to-do list. I must stop and become as conscious as possible about what is going on and what I am experiencing. When it is ridiculous, I bust out all the tools until it isn't ridiculous anymore!

***

I remember this tool when I notice things building to a frenzy and chaos begins to reign. It reminds me to get conscious quick—and often leads to a bout of laughter!

—*Randy Sue Collins*

***

How ridiculous does it have to get? This tool is actually somewhat soothing for me. Living in a foreign country with a busy schedule and acclimating to new standards and rules, many interesting and exasperating scenarios pop up daily. At one point, I was writing them all down because I didn't know what to do with them and all the emotional responses that were getting triggered. With this tool, I can be amused. I can laugh more. And it helps me focus on what I get to look at—on why this is happening FOR me, or what is the VELCRO here, who is answering the door, why this is in my lap—it is a personal inner adventure more than an external chronicle of events.

—*Anna R., Mexico*

Mad scientist

If you are in a situation that you are unhappy with, rather than leave the situation, experiment within the situation. Let's say you are in a job you do not like. Rather than find a new job, consider staying in the present situation but approaching it in a brand new way.

Then when you start to make changes, you're the only thing that is changing. This makes it much easier for you to see the dynamic play out.

Become the mad scientist and start experimenting, and by experimenting we mean changing what you think the outcome of *you* being in *your* integrity is. You think you can't be in your integrity because you'll get fired or because they won't like you or because, because, because. You have all these projections, all these fears about what being in your integrity means. Change your energetic and see how it plays out. You don't like where you are now so it's worth taking a chance that it could get better, and you will learn a lot about yourself in the process. Make what you are not happy with your little factory for experimentation.

Show up at work, sit down, and instead of saying, "God, look at all this work, look at all these voicemails, and oh, the boss is already bitching at me," try this, "OK, I'm a mad scientist today and this is my factory. What do I want to create? How do I want to be in this space? I don't mind the work. I mind the attitudes. So, how are those attitudes true about me? How is my bitchy boss just a voice in my head that's really loud when it comes out of somebody else's mouth?" You are able to look at things in a new way because you are not requiring the situation stay the same in order for you to feel safe. You use the process of experimentation to create a reality with less suffering and more self-awareness.

Experiment!

***

Veronica writes:

I love the mad scientist tool. It's nice to have such permission to experiment in a difficult situation. Oftentimes, a painful dynamic is really just a specific thing or person and there is actually a lot more about the situation that I like than I don't like. The mad scientist tool lets me keep the parts I enjoy while I attempt to transform the parts I don't. It can be a lot of fun!

***

This is a fun tool. When I become a mad scientist I really see how different a situation can become just by my changing the perception of it. That's really all it takes. It's amazing how quickly a trigger can get diffused by using the mad scientist tool.

—Randy Sue Collins

***

We think of a mad scientist as trying many different combinations of things to come up with the magic jackpot. When there is a problem, I look first at what I can do—which usually hasn't worked—then I think, "A mad scientist would try many different approaches to try and solve the issue."

An example jumps to my mind. I returned my phone equipment as instructed to a local UPS store. This took about 40 minutes even though there were only two people ahead of me. Since I had so much time and I was practicing being sincerely in the moment, I heard and retained the stories and intentions of the customers ahead of me. I knew where their packages were going and what they were shipping. When it came to my turn, all went smoothly. The service person apologized for the wait. I remained in the moment and happy.

Upon returning to my car, I jotted a note in my date book that I had sent the package and that I had a receipt. Weeks later I received a notice from the phone company that I was being charged $150 on my credit card because I didn't return the equipment on time. I searched for my paperwork. I had part of it, but no receipt. I looked and looked everywhere, old receipt files, new ones, high and low, every place I might have put it, and it was nowhere to be found.

Then I thought, "Maybe I didn't get one." I looked at my datebook and confirmed that I did get a receipt. I checked in with the mad scientist, "How else can I prove this, what else can I do?" I remembered the details about the other people and the time of their transactions. I got excited that being in the moment had rewarded me with the knowledge of where UPS would have record of my transaction. Just then I looked down at a bag tucked behind the couch and went, "Whoa!" A quick look inside revealed my original receipt.

Problem resolved. This tool reminds us there are many ways to look at and solve problems. It reminds me to try everything I can think of.

—Rosie

Money mantra

"I am in financial flow and money comes to me in infinite ways."
Whenever you feel triggered by your financial situation, use the money mantra to shift your perspective. You can say it multiple times in a row to help you stay grounded in the moment and resist the temptation to jump to the past or the future.

The word infinite in the money mantra is incredibly important because what the money mantra is doing is teaching your system—your brain, your body, your neural pathways, your energetic system—it's teaching your system that limitation is not the answer to this question. It's teaching your system that infinity is the answer to this question and that is an incredible gift to give yourself.

A fun way to use the money mantra is to make a list of all of the ways money comes to you. Be sure to stretch beyond the obvious income sources. Go ahead and list fun things like, finding money on the sidewalk, discovering change in the washing machine, nearly vacuuming up a coin under the sofa cushions, et cetera. The point of the money mantra is to rewrite your preconceived notions about how money comes into your life. It comes to you in infinite ways!

***

Veronica writes:

The money mantra has been very helpful to me. It really changes my perspective of a situation. If I find myself feeling lack, I repeat the mantra until I become more centered. This tool breaks habits; it's a tool you can really lean into.

***

I use this tool all the time. I wrote it on Post-it notes and stuck them to my computer and refrigerator. It makes me feel good to know that money does come in infinite ways. It's fun to recognize when money appears in unusual ways.

—Randy Sue

***

I am an expert explorer with this tool. What could be more fun than looking for abundance in infinite ways? I say this mantra and remember that there are many solutions present. Then I work in a linear fashion. I write down all of my wishes. I then zone in on one thing that I would consider "big," like a complete life change, or two or three "little" things, like a new car, vacation, or health. I explore what it would feel like to be living this abundance. At some point, I meet resistance to "me now" and "abundant feeling me" which brings to mind another set of tools! What has to change in my life to allow this abundance? I envision who I am and what needs to change inside of my life to be the "abundant me." I accept that I may just have to change. This willingness cracks the door to abundance. Then I appreciate what comes. I treasure the free rubber bands, the dollar bills I step on to get to coffee, the free lunches with friends, coupons for pastries, job offers, masterpieces I paint for my house, love and laughs with my friends, and the insights from my superhuman self. In this way, I pick up the scent of my wish on the trail of my everyday life. I intentionally practice this mantra package for 30 minutes to an hour a couple of days a month. One hundred percent of the time, the "thing" or the "essence" of my wish comes... and I have money in the bank to prove it!

—Denise

***

I do love the money mantra, because I have always used it without knowing it. The "infinite ways" that might be under-appreciated are little things, like discounts on what you want, or sale prices on what you are going to the store for. These are all money in your pocket. I love it when the cashier at the store says you have saved almost as much money as you spent (buying on sale or coupon or specials). If I know a big expense is coming, I will start telling myself, "Money comes in infinite ways, now let's see how it shows up!" It is really fun. It is trusting in the universe and it comes with a request for curiosity or excitement of discovery and can't be requested in panic or worry. A long time ago I figured out that since we don't make enough to cover our expenses, I would have to spend every dollar twice. And that is what I have worked at doing. It is because money shows up in unexpected ways, that all has worked out for me (us).

—Rosie

***

I love this! As I move forward with my astrology practice and leave the wine business behind, I continue to remind myself that "I am in financial flow and money comes to me in infinite ways." This works! Chanting the mantra while I drive seems to work best. I am very relaxed and focused when I drive. Inevitably, after chanting a few rounds off and on, I will be contacted by a new client or an old client I haven't heard from in a while. Some other interesting manifestations have been people who want to trade services. I have traded for body work, yoga, and pet portraits. Hey, it's just as good as money! I find it useful to chant silently while doing my breathing before bed, as well. I know that I am in financial flow and that money can and will come to me in infinite ways.

—Rene

Money does indeed come to me in many ways. I proved that to myself when I made my list of income sources. I complained at the time that it still wasn't enough. Clearly, the list was finite and I needed to stretch my expectations. When I am tempted to think of ways to earn money, I remind myself of the limitations of my brain and repeat and repeat: I am in financial flow and money comes to me in infinite ways!

—*Mary T.*

***

I love to use this Mantra when I am not feeling lack. This produces a light, airy energy in me. It is similar to singing a nursery rhythm like, "Row, row, row your boat, gently down the stream." Sounds silly, but it works!

—*Donna*

***

I was triggered about money when I received the email from Veronica about this tool. I repeated the mantra over several times and could feel my body and my mind relax. I could almost feel new pathways opening up in my brain and a more expansive feeling came over me.

—*Joy*

***

The money mantra has help me become so centered in my thoughts that it has cleared the pathways for instant manifestation. Unable to pay my rent for a few months, I was pushed to the wall; it was either pay or I was on the street. Mentally reciting the money mantra, I went into a deep meditation where the only thing that resonated in my being was, "I am in financial flow and money comes to me in infinite ways." As I came out of my meditation, I was guided to read my emails. An email had arrived from a client in South America who I had not heard from in two months. She had been laid up for two months and had just sent a wire for her order. So the rent was paid.

—*Anthony*

Neutral observation

A tool that says, "I'm not going to take my habitual response as the mandated action." It means, "I'm going to stop and ask what is actually going on here in this moment."

Neutral observation is like carving out a little space that says, "In this moment, instead of all the habitual ways I could react, I'm going to open to hearing a new way, open to insight from my soul, and ask, 'What is this teaching me?' and, 'What am I learning?' to carve out a space where my reaction can be something new rather than habitual."

Neutrality doesn't have duality in it. Neutrality doesn't have judgments in it. Neutrality doesn't have all these places within you that you have habitually gone with situations. That's one of the reasons that it's hard to go into neutral observation, because you have all these little niches in you where your habits runs. Habit takes you here, habit takes you there, and you're just thinking, "How can I be neutral in this moment?" Well, it takes a little practice. You're literally rewiring your neural pathways in order for this to work.

So, let's say you have insecurity about a project, "Oh, I have this project and I don't know how it's going to turn out." If you're in the fear, then it's "I don't know what's going to happen," and you start hamster-wheel thinking, "I should do this, maybe I should do this, maybe I shouldn't have started this." Everybody knows what that feels like. If we take that up into a higher-vibration space, it's "Wow, there's that feeling in my chest again, interesting, it's showing up again. There's that feeling of 'there's potential for failure here.' Wow, failure is a judgment. The truth is, everything's a learning experience. If I can look at this neutrally, then the outcome isn't what drives this experience. This fear is based on a need for a certain outcome. These feelings in my body are being elicited by a need for a certain outcome. If I can see this neutrally and just say 'Wow, there's that fear, there's that habit popping up again, I can feel it in my chest, I see it in my life, but I'm not attached to the outcome that that fear is trying to get me to attach to'."

The fear is saying, "The shit's hitting the fan." Neutral observation says, "Everything's interesting." When you can stay neutral, you can feel the fear but say, "I'm just going to see it. I'm not going to let the feeling of the fear tell me what to do next, I'm going to let neutral observation and insight from my soul reveal what's going to happen next, and every time that fear stirs up in me, I'm going to make another choice for insight. I'm going to make another choice just to watch it rather than let it drive the experience I'm in." And that, of course, takes a little bit of practice but those neural pathways will lay down very quickly because it's a high-vibrational activity and because it actually leads to so much relief of the body's tension.

When you can sit in neutral observation and say, "I see the body reacting but that's not the choice I'm making", the body starts to calm. You "calm" into a higher vibration rather than "stir up" in a lower vibration. And that's really the cusp of this whole thing. Watch the fear, knowing it's an option and not a mandate. Choose again and again to see it, rather than be it. Even if you feel it, still say, "I see you, fear. I feel you trying to show up in my life and run the show but I'm not going on that path. I'm not attached to the outcome you're trying to scare me about. I'm going to sit here and I'm going to be as neutral as possible and point you out to myself," and the fears will dissipate. They have to. Because when you take something that's low-vibration and infuse it with high-vibration, it can't last. It's like putting an ice cube in a microwave. It can't last. Biologically incompatible. It can't last in that environment.

Neutral observation is not numb. Neutral observation is being extremely aware of what is going on and choosing to have as neutral as possible experience of it.

Neutral observation doesn't make you a doormat. In fact, neutral observation only works when you set boundaries.

***

Eloheim: Neutral observation stops in the moment, collects what the moment is offering, sets boundaries, and then moves into, "Where's the aha, where's the learning, where's the next step here?" and then into action, which leads to a new moment, which leads to an opportunity for neutral observation.

Response: Which is so hard.

Eloheim: We understand. But we also see very clearly that when you live in habitual response, it's painful. Neutral observation is challenging but habitual response is painful.

Response: Where's the switch to turn it on and off?

Eloheim: It's really spiritual choice. It's that choice that says, "I know I'm in habit. I know I'm in a coping mechanism. I know I'm using fear. I know I'm bringing the past or the future into this moment." It's just catching yourself and then saying to yourself, "I know where this leads." It's like when you have a bad breakup and you're listening to a sad song on the radio and you have your hand on the phone and you're gonna call. You're gonna call that person that just broke up with you and you know, you have your hand on the phone and you know, what's going to happen when you dial that phone. You know it's going to be ugly. You know they don't want to hear from you. You know that you're going to hear stuff that you don't want to hear; even if you get the answering machine, you don't want to hear the answering machine, you don't even know what you want from the person, you just know that that's what you think is your coping mechanism. That pain on the other side of the phone.

Now, to let go of the phone, to be conscious—to sit with that is very challenging and it can be emotional, but you know what happens if you pick up the phone, so you have a choice. And the choice is to be disciplined enough to say that the habit of picking up the phone is less attractive than the challenge of becoming conscious in this moment.

Neutral observation doesn't mean numb. Neutral observation means, "I don't know everything, therefore I'm going to open to my soul helping me see all that I can so that I choose, state preferences, and set boundaries in order to operate from the most grace, ease, and bliss possible in this dynamic." And that can be applied to every single moment.

***

Veronica writes:

Oh yes, Neutral observation, my old friend. This was one of the first tools Eloheim ever gave us. It feels like putting on a comfortable pair of jeans or my favorite boots. Relaxing into an alternative to the hamster-wheel mind and the requirement to know everything.

***

To me, Neutral observation is one of the most important and useful tools of all. When I am in neutral observation, I immediately go into the present moment and I become aware, at a gut level, that my thinking mind holds a gentle tyranny over me. If I'm not very aware, it runs my life through habitual patterns and knee-jerk reactions. This practice has also made me aware that there is room for very little or no spontaneous action on my part when the habitual mind is in control. I live much more cleanly and peacefully when I can remember to stay in Neutral observation.

—*Janice Imbach*

***

This tool helps me step back and not take things so damn seriously. Allows the bigger picture to be seen.

—*Randy Sue Collins*

***

Neutral observation stops me from becoming overly emotional when I am triggered. I find myself in a space where time seems to stand still and provides an opportunity for me to view my situation and its many options.

—*Donna Price*

"No" is a complete sentence / Say "no" first

This tool allows you to set a boundary or state a preference without feeling the need to justify or make excuses for your position. You are not responsible for others' reactions to your choices. Stating a preference is an act of free will.

A fascinating way to learn about boundaries, preferences, and "What is true now?" is to say "no" first. Just give it a try! Someone calls you up and asks you to go out. Say "no" first.

If you are habitually saying "yes" to keep other people happy, try saying "no" and seeing how it makes you feel. The result we have seen is that being able to just say no is incredibly liberating. Importantly, it gives you the time to actually find out how you feel. When you say no first, you can then consider your feelings on the matter without the pressure of having the question hanging over your head.

If you decide that you actually do want to participate——because YOU want to, not just to make another happy—you can always call back and say you changed your mind.

And "No, period" is a complete sentence. You don't have to explain. There is no need for a lie, an excuse, or even other plans. If you are asked, "Why?" you can just say, "It's just not right for me."

If they don't respect that, well, that is something very good to know about them, isn't it?

***

Veronica writes:

Oh yeah, NO... who knew? When I started saying NO first and then giving myself time to check in about how I felt, my life changed. What else is there to add?

Point fingers

You can't point fingers anymore, meaning you no longer have the option of saying that someone else or something else creates in your life. Nothing else can create in your life, and every time you point your finger and decide how it's going to be, and decide and decide and decide, you're turning over the only power you have in this life, which is the power to create your reality using your free will. You can go right along living the victim mentality quite nicely, but if you actually want to experience the magnificence that's possible with the Homo sapiens moving into Homo spiritus paradigm you have to stop looking at other people and other things as creating in your reality and start to recognize and acknowledge that you are the one. You are the one who put it there.

It can be hard when you realize, "Oh my God, I point fingers every second of every day." However, this realization allows you to access the wow of responsibility, the wow of creatorship, the wow of: "Yes, I did that. Yes, I did that. I did it for me. I did it for me so that I could have the experience that that scenario offers me."

The idea that you can't point fingers at anybody anymore is a radical concept. It says, "Everybody in my life, everything in my life, is my creation. And as my creation I take 100 percent responsibility for it being there and I take 100 percent responsibility for how I choose to interact with it." When you stop pointing fingers, it's not: "Why the hell is this in my life?" It's: "Wow, this is in my life!" And that's a big shift. That's a big shift. It was a big shift to get into 100 percent responsibility, even if taking 100 percent responsibility meant "I'm taking responsibility even though I don't like it." Now it's: "I'm taking responsibility, I know there's something here for me, I don't have to figure it out as much as I have to allow myself to experience it without throwing barrier after barrier after barrier up between me and the experience."

***

Veronica writes:

I remember quite clearly the night that The Council talked with us about no more pointing fingers. I was struck with the power of this idea. It really is quite a shift to go from seeing yourself as a victim to realizing you are a creator. Then, to start realizing that you created everything (even the shitty bits!), well, that's a doozy. To further realize that you can't pin it on anyone else, even when they "did" it… it's a lot of responsibility. However, it's my responsibility to work with my creations and my reactions to them. This puts the ball in my court, which suits me just fine.

***

The part I remember about "pointing fingers" is that when I point my finger at someone else, one finger is pointing away from me and the other three fingers are pointing back at me. Just a little reminder that I created this situation to show me something about myself. I created it to have a learning experience, which is liberating. Taking responsibility for my creations instead of spinning and suffering in victimhood is quite a relief.

—Mary T

***

It is really easy to point fingers at any person and say "This is happening because you did this." That is pointing fingers at someone else instead of saying that I have created this to learn from it. I am taking the power of creating what happens to (for) me instead of simply going along for the ride. It gives a person a sense of confidence that you have a hand in what is going on.

—Rosie

Preferences/Judgments

Judgment is not the same as preference. Judgment is the belief that you have to have a position *against* something in order to have a position *preferring* something. So, all of a sudden the choice between chocolate and vanilla must become, "Chocolate is a good flavor and vanilla is a bad flavor, so I am going with chocolate because that's the good flavor," instead of just saying, "I have a preference for chocolate."

You're an immortal, infinite soul that chooses to have every experience you can manage. If you set out a lot of judgments and you start saying that vanilla's wrong, then when it comes around time to experience vanilla you have to deal with the baggage of already assigning it as "wrong." It's always nice to not put extra baggage on things that you'll probably get around to wanting to experience someday. It's also quite helpful to limit the amount of baggage (static) about anything you are experiencing.

Most of the time, we see that you had to make one thing wrong—sometimes VERY wrong—in order to set a preference because you weren't feeling strong enough to just say "No" is a complete sentence.

When you are new to boundaries and preferences you will

sometimes believe that you have to get really worked up in order to use them. Actually, when you discover "What is true now?," you can set boundaries and state preferences from a very calm place.

Keep in mind that there is a damned good reason for having a preference, which is: You're a soul experiencing the physical form in a free-will zone. So, if you don't have some preferences, what the heck is the point of being here in the first place? Not very much that we can see. Having preferences is the one of the main events!

Someone once said to us, "Well, if we are infinite and immortal, aren't we going to do everything?" And we said yes, but you do them in an order. There's an order to it. In a linear sense, there's an order to it. Where today you decided to eat chocolate, tomorrow you're going to decide to eat vanilla. So, even if you're immortal and infinite, you're still deciding right now to be here instead of being someplace else. Preference. Choice. Free will. You don't need to have something be wrong in order to have something else be what you want to do.

Coming from judgment is low-vibrational. It takes a lot of energy to stay invested in a judgment. It can be difficult to change your mind because you are so invested energetically in the judgment. Sometimes your identity can even be wrapped up in a judgment, which makes it that much harder to change. Judgments don't serve you, on so many levels.

***

Veronica writes:

Another tool to help you realize that you get to choose. This one helps me clarifies when I am actually choosing and when I am running an unconscious habit, which shows up as a judgment. I like vanilla and chocolate ice cream so this example is perfect for me. It really is expressing a preference in the moment rather than deciding on a right/wrong.

***

This tool has whittled down my list of people, situations, and things that I have judgments around and helps me realize how many judgments came through societal conditioning. Preferences allow for choice through fascination and true passion of my life's purpose. It brings me closer to the relaxed feeling of contentment and fulfillment.

—Deb

Re-queue

When a problem, a situation, a challenge, a trigger, arises and you say, "I can't deal with it"—either unconsciously or consciously—when you say, "I can't deal with it," you are re-queuing that dynamic. It will come up again.

When it comes up again, there can be a feeling of: "I couldn't fix this before; I probably can't fix it now. I couldn't handle this before; I bet I can't handle it now. Oh my God, it's still scary. It's still scary." If you re-queue the same dynamic multiple times, this tension can build up to a level that makes it feel impossible to resolve.

This is where the idea of the "current version of you" is extremely important. You are not any of the other versions of you who re-queued this dynamic. You have learned and grown so much since you last re-queued this dynamic. The current version of you has the best chance you have ever had to transform this situation.

Here is a good example using baseball: You are the batter, and the 90-mile-per-hour fastball being pitched at you is the trigger:

You're five years old and you step up to the plate in a big-league ball park to try to hit a pitch from a major-league pitcher. There isn't really a chance you're going to hit that ball, and if you do it's not going to go very far.

Five years later—now, you're 10. You step up, take your swing, and once again you can't connect.

Now you're 15. You probably have a chance at 15—maybe, maybe. The best chance you've had so far. You can swing well and you can hold a regular-size bat. There's something to be said for that. But it's still the big-league pitcher pitching the 90-mile-per-hour fastball at you and you've never been able to hit it before, and you've watched people on TV and they hardly ever hit it. Combine that with your knowledge that you have never hit the ball in the past and a lot of self-doubt can creep in. You swing, you miss.

Now let's say you're 20. You have every chance in hell of hitting that ball, if you bring the 20-year-old version of you to the ballpark. If you bring the guy who played baseball in high school and played baseball in college and who's already been hitting 90-mile-per-hour fastballs, he has every chance if, in that moment, the 20-year-old version of him stands at the plate.

OK, that's true. But, you know what else is true? You know all about this situation. Your previous attempts gave you all sorts of information you can use to support a different outcome.

Continuing our example: When you stood at the plate before, you were little and you didn't feel like you could handle it, but the truth is you now know what it feels like to stand in the ballpark. You know what it feels like to look at the guy and go, "Oh shit, a 90-mile-per-hour fastball is coming my way." You know what it feels like to have the catcher right behind you. You know what it smells like. Use all of this as an advantage. Don't only connect to the "I didn't hit the ball in the past," connect to, "I've been here before." It's not completely new. The hitting the ball would be new, but all the rest of it isn't new. Recognizing this is such a kindness to you.

Another way to think about re-queuing is to do what we call conscious re-queuing. Conscious re-queuing can be a huge kindness. Let's say you're having a problem with your birth family. You could say, "We have too many triggers, we have too much history, we have this, that, and the other thing together. It's just too hard to heal this aspect of myself in the context of these relationships." Conscious re-queuing states, "When it comes up again, in a different context, I'll work on it again."

It is very important to keep two things in mind when doing conscious re-queuing: 1. You are acknowledging that you want something to change. 2. You are acknowledging that it is your relationship to yourself (and your triggers) that is the focus of this change; it is not an attempt to change another person.

When the dynamic reappears you may still feel, "Oh yeah, this feels extra scary because I tried it so many times and it did not 'work out'." But, remind yourself, "I'm a different person than I was before. I have different people around me. This interaction is on a different level. I don't have to feel the cumulative fear." Make sure that any anxiety you feel is only the anxiety that's present because it's a triggering event, not the cumulative trigger for all the other times you have worked with this dynamic.

***

Veronica writes:

I have re-queued many things in my life. Initially, I thought this meant I failed. I felt like I somehow should be able to work out anything with anyone. Now, I know that re-queuing is setting boundaries and using free will to create in my life. It's also choosing to be kind to myself. I know that when I focus on "I want healing above all else," I create situations that help transform residual triggers in a more gentle way. It blows my mind when something that completely threw me out of balance a few years back comes up again and I am able to transform it without leaving my center. It is one of the major celebrations of my spiritual life.

***

Speaking in public has always been my greatest fear. As a child I just didn't speak in class. In college I had to memorize my speeches and practice so that my teachers wouldn't catch on. My occupation required short public speaking. I would wake up early, memorize and then be thankful when it was all over. I just knew I couldn't do it another way! As my current version of myself has changed, I find that I can speak in public without preparation and panic. It may not be my choice of a "good time," but I am no longer uncomfortable.

—*Donna*

***

When my family relationship issues come up again I say to myself, "Oh, I must have re-queued this!" It feels good to know, "I put this here on purpose." Then I do a quick check to see how I'm feeling this time. I love to give myself credit for growth. I see re-queue issues as a time to stop and do a spiritual checkup.

—*Denise*

Script holding/Script-holders

You are the only thing that is going on. Everything else—all of the physical structures you see, the plants, the animals, the people, the houses, you name it—all things in your life are just actors in *your* play.

They act in your play in order to give you opportunities to grow. We call them script-holders. Imagine that everyone is walking around carrying a really, really big script. When you do something—you respond to a trigger, repeat a habit, feel fear, act consciously—all the actors in your play are then give a cue to turn to a certain page in your script.

As an example, a guy pulls in front of you on the freeway. This triggers you into a habitual and unconscious revisiting of other experiences when you felt like you weren't seen. You then start to relive the pain of those past experiences. You are completely disconnected from the moment you are in. Your choice to be unconscious directs the driver to turn to page 500 and it instructs him to flip you off. This is likely to further upset you and may result in additional unpleasant interactions with the driver.

If your response was, "Wow, check that out, that guy just pulled in front of me. I'm going to stay in the moment with my reaction. I'm going to be conscious about what comes up for me. I'm going to recognize the temptation to go into the past, but I'm committed to staying with how I actually feel right now." The next thing you know, the driver has sped away and he's gone out of your life. Your choice to respond consciously directed him to turn to page 750 which says: "Just speed away. You've done your part."

As you become more conscious and you start directing your play—creating your reality is another way to say it—then you have people turning to the pages in the script where they respond to your emanation of consciousness. You make conscious choices, you emanate consciousness, and they turn to the pages that are all about consciousness. This is how your emanation moves out into the world and affects your manifestations. In effect, you're telling all your script-holders to reflect the consciousness you're emanating. If you do encounter script holders that react in an unconscious manner, you set a boundary by saying, "Oh no, no, I'm on page 500 because it's my job to reflect consciousness back even though you're giving me unconsciousness."

Your perspective shifts to, "Everything in my play is my responsibility and my creation," because you're putting it there through your choices. Your choices of what to think, how to handle habits, how to manage triggers, how to process interactions you have with people, how to deal with the temptation to live in the past or the future. "What's the next act going to be? Well, the next act is going to be an act of consciousness and I'm going to emanate consciousness into the world so that everyone around me has the opportunity to turn to a new page."

Another way to say this is: Your internal world generates your external experience. That's why you can change internally, never speak a word to the other person, and the dynamic between you can shift. Why? Because you're saying: "I want page 500 out of you instead of page 300." Energetically you are emanating a different connection to them and they are responding with a different response, turning to a different page.

You will find it fascinating to view your world as full of script holders. We love to hear stories like, "I know that guy's script-holding for me because he just said the exact words that my mom used to say to me and he has on the same shirt that my dad used to wear! God, talk about good script-holding."

There is one aspect of script-holding that we want you to be very, very clear about. Let's say you have a little tête à tête with somebody—you don't get to say, "Well, I must be holding script for you." No. It doesn't work that way. No, no, no. That's missing the point. If you have a little tête à tête—stay in you. What is it that you're experiencing about their interaction with you? It's not, "This is awkward so I must be holding script for you." It's, "This is awkward and you are holding script for me to see what I can learn here."

Recognize the truth that you're all here to facilitate each other's growth. In all interactions that you're experiencing, look around, see the other parties as actors in your play, and recognize how they are acting is affecting your growth and your journey. When you can see other people as actors in your play, it can oftentimes take away the intensity or the trigger of the dynamic, and instead help you to see what's going on as neutrally as possible.

Another important aspect of script-holding is this: Everyone is an actor in your play and you're an actor in everyone else's play. It's all happening at the same time. You are having simultaneous experiences of being the script-holder and the center of the play. This is a great thing! There's room for everybody to be center-stage and for everyone to be a script holder as well. It's beautiful.

You've all agreed to participate in this dynamic with each other. It's really cool. You've all said: "Hey, let's play make-believe. Let's play make-believe; I'll help you and you help me."

***

Veronica writes:

It's very powerful to see the world as "holding script" for you. I find it especially helpful to do this when I am strongly triggered by something. It puts a bit of distance between the event and my emotional state, which helps me get a new perspective.

***

I use this tool all the time and also find myself reminding my teens to use it, too. Knowing that I assigned everyone in my play (my life) helps to remind me that I truly am the creator of my experiences. It's a great way to feel empowered immediately.

—Randy Sue Collins

***

I know that script holders are a direct reflection of me. When someone causes me discomfort, I thank them for showing me a habit or baggage that must be dealt with. It works quickly and dramatically changes the dynamics of the situation.

—Mike

***

Someone called me a bully yesterday (which I still am finding fascinating…). He could have said nothing, since I wasn't even talking to him or he could have said that the person I was verbally sparring with had a weaker argument—compounded by the fact that he was louder, upset, and wouldn't stop defending his position—but no, he told me very clearly to stop bullying my classmate. I had been playfully telling the vice-president of the class that it was his obligation to let all of us know about the free tickets the school was giving away to the soccer game this weekend (of which he scored 4)…mind you, I already had plans for Friday night. Bully? How ridiculous does it have to get? This guy was really holding script for me. I can't control what other people think of me. I can't control others' projections onto me. Do I not say anything anymore? That would turn me to a page I know I don't need to go to again. I'll just thank this guy for helping me move on in my algorithm of consciousness.

—Anna R.

Short, factual statements

Your brain is accustomed to thinking a certain way and it tends to continue to think the same way unless you intervene. Spiritual growth and other types of transformation require that you think in new ways. We often refer to this as rewriting the neural pathways. One of the ways we've found to help you rewrite your neural pathways is to use the tool we call "short, factual statements."

Here is how it works: identify something that you wish to change in your life and make a short, factual statement about it that ends with a period. Don't follow your statement with a "but" or a "because," and remember, we aren't doing short, factual paragraphs!

Make sure that the short, factual statement is grounded in the moment. Your statement should be about how you're feeling and what you're experiencing now.

Always end the short, factual statement with the word PERIOD. Adding the word "period" at the end let's your brain know that you aren't just thinking the same thoughts you have always thought, but that you are doing something new.

Immediately after making your short, factual statement (followed by the word "period"), observe what you are tempted to think about next. Our experience is that you will start thinking about the past or the future, or both.

It is extremely important that you catch yourself here and observe the temptation to leave the moment rather than just start to rethink your habitual thought patterns. Make a short, factual statement about the thought you are tempted to have. Now observe where your thought patterns want to take you. Continue making short, factual statements in this manner.

You are not making a short, factual statement to get an answer to a problem; you are making a short, factual statement in order reveal habitual thought patterns. You are using short, factual statements to identify the static that is clogging up the moment. Once the static is cleared, you will be able to access the moment and your soul's insight about the situation.

AN EXAMPLE:

Eloheim: What is something going on that you would like to change?

Response: My back hurts.

Eloheim: Your habitual thinking pattern would be something like this: "Oh, my back hurts, oh God, it's going to be so hard to go to work tomorrow. Oh, I don't think I'm going to sleep well, oh, I wonder if it's because the bed is no good. Oh, I wonder if it's because I'm stressed out. Oh, my back has hurt for so many years, oh, it's probably going to hurt for so many more."

A short, factual statement is: "My back hurts." Short, factual statements are stated in the present tense. This is an incredibly important part of this tool. You have to say it in the present tense. It's not: "God, I've really been bummed out in the past because my back hurt." That's not what we're shooting for. You want to ground the tool in the moment. "My back hurts."—first step. Then, important, but funny, step. We always try to throw in a little humor wherever it fits. "My back hurts. Period." And say the period out loud. The reason you say the period out loud is because that is actually what makes your brain get on notice something new is happening. If you just say, "My back hurts,"—you've said that a million times. "My back hurts, period," gives your brain an exclamation point. It says to your brain, "Something new is going on here. Something is happening. My back hurts, period." And if you can do this out loud, or at least under your breath, that helps, too, because then it's not just more mind chatter. It's literally being put into your reality. So, "My back hurts, period."

What happens within you after you make that short, factual statement?

Response: Just memories of weeks on end of pain and not being able to do what I wanted to, and having money issues because I couldn't go to work.

Eloheim: Perfect. This is what we were trying to get at. So, all those fears and memories and "Oh, my Gods" come up and you are tempted to obsessively think about them again. Once you have spent some time in the past, you will typically start thinking about the future. Your habitual thinking patterns don't give you access to the moment and the moment is the only place anything actually transforms. Using short, factual statements will help you stay in the moment and actually change your experience.

Going back to our example: "My back hurts, period." Say your short, factual statement and then just wait and see where you go. Continuing with your example, you went into, "Oh my God, I might not make enough money because I can't work."

The key here is to hold yourself in the moment by making short, factual statements about what's true right now. So, you say, "My back hurts, period." And then you watch. "Wow, I'm tempted to go into the past, period." And then you watch, "Wow, there I go off into the future, period." Then, eventually, what happens is that the past and the future cannot hold you because you've made short, factual statements about them rather reuse the old neural pathways and habitually think about the past and the future.

That's the magic in this, when you acknowledge the temptations that seek to pull you out of the moment, the temptations lose their power. So, it's not: "Oh, God, I'm such an idiot, I thought about the past and the future again." We don't play that game, ever. It's short, factual statement about what's currently going on, and then short, factual statements about what comes up when you acknowledge that. Remember to keep your short, factual statements focused on what is actually occurring now. What ends up happening is you experience the moment in a new way and you can attend to what's happening from the current-moment version of you.

KEEP IN MIND:

When you realize you have something you want to change and you make a short, factual statement about it, be really, really careful that you don't expect the short, factual statement to give you the answer to the "problem." That is not the role of the short, factual statement. The role of the short, factual statement is to reveal the habitual thinking that is blocking insight coming to you about the "problem."

The temptation is to say, "My back hurts," and expect the short, factual statement to make your back stop hurting. The role of the short, factual statement in this example is to illuminate what you are actually thinking about when you experience back pain. When you become clear about that, you will be able to actually address the back pain without the baggage of the habitual thoughts getting in your way.

ANOTHER EXAMPLE:

Question: My weakness in computer repair is working on Windows 2000 servers. I don't get a lot of practice. So, I got a lucrative contract with an attorney. I did all the easy things first and then today, I had to deal with the server. So, I'm trying to research and I can't find a solution, so I start to panic. I get that feeling like, "I'm no good; I'm an inadequate technician."

Eloheim: So, a short, factual statement would be: "I can't find this answer, period."

On some level what you've been telling yourself is you have to have the answer or you suck. And by using a short, factual statement of what is really true—"I don't know the answer, period,"—what it does is takes away all of that sort of sticky, oohy-gooey stuff that's saying: "If you don't know this answer something's wrong with you." It just brings you to the truth of the matter. "I don't know this answer, period."

So, when we say that to you, what happens inside you?

Response: I'm not exactly sure what happens. What happens is that I…

Eloheim: Wait, don't think about this. If you say, "I don't know the answer, period," what happens inside you?

Response: Well, when I looked at the question I wanted to go backwards into, "You don't know and you're going to look like an idiot, and when they find out that you don't know they're going to lose respect for you." Totally into the past!

Eloheim: This is what we were saying. Typically, you go to the past first. Maybe not every time, but this is what we're seeing. You immediately thought 3, 4, 5 things. See how fast there are so many things there? The key here is not to run with any of those but instead to say, "Wow, I'm tempted to feel very insecure right now, period." And if you say that, what happens next?

Response: Um.

Eloheim: Are you thinking about it, by chance?

Response: I'm trying to feel what's going on in my body!

Eloheim: Let's not think quite that hard. What comes immediately to mind when you say, "Wow, I'm tempted to go into the past," or "I'm tempted to be insecure?"

Response: Just feeling the feeling in the gut.

Eloheim: We're picking up that it's something like, "Well, yeah, I'm tempted to be insecure because I should be." It's like, "Well, of course I feel insecure, I should feel insecure." And that's the point we're trying to make. The "Yeah, I should feel insecure," how helpful is that? Not very helpful. That's not going to get you to the answer. Abiding in insecurity is not going to get you to the answer. But abiding in "I don't know," abiding in the question of the situation, opens you to insight. Abiding in insecurity—all it does is get you more insecurity and then spirals you down. And that's why with the short, factual statement tool you're constantly saying, "Wow, I'm still tempted to be insecure, I'm still tempted to be insecure," until at some point the charge of that temptation to be insecure, it kind of gets boring, so you stop going there. Chances are, you'll eventually go to, "God, these people are going to really think I suck." You're going to go into the future. And it's like, "Wow, I still don't know the answer and they're going to have a judgment about me." Which doesn't bring you any sort of solution, either. See, that is what we're trying to alert you guys to. None of that is solution material. All of that is distraction material. All of that is taking you out of the place where you can connect with insight. Because it's lowering your vibration, it's putting you in the past or the future, where nothing happens.

A thing to also say would be: "I am ready to receive insight, period." Short, factual statement, and see what comes. We suspect you might go to, "There's no insight, there's no way, I'm not going to get it." Just rephrase that to, "Wow, I'm tempted to think there's no such thing as insight, period." You just keep bringing it back to acknowledging the truth of what you're doing. Acknowledging the truth of what you're experiencing. Short, factual statements based in the now followed by the word period. Remember, it's not about: "Oh, God, I've yet to figure out the solution." It's: "I'm training myself to live in the moment and open to insight and not be distracted by the past and the future, not be distracted by insecurities and low vibration, not be distracted by fears and lack and judgment, but to stay in the moment and to train myself and to train my brain that this is the place where answers come from."

Response: Yes, I agree.

Eloheim: We're so glad you agree.

Response: I can't hear the answers until I get to that space where I'm not afraid. It wasn't until I just lightened up on myself about it and thought about two things: So what if they do think I'm incompetent? And maybe it wouldn't be so bad if I just told them I don't have a lot of experience with Windows server but I think I can do it.

Eloheim: Or, "Maybe I need help. Maybe for this one little part of this job I could ask for help." Maybe it's OK that you don't know everything. Because at some point when you say, "I don't know anything," it means "I don't know everything." And "I don't know anything and I don't know everything means I can let myself off the hook." And it also means that it's OK to open to insight because if you think you know anything and everything then at some point you're like, "I know everything, I know enough, I'm smart, I've got it, I've got this handled, I don't need any help," that whole thing. Now, you're going, "Wow, it would be interesting to know more when I need more." And that's really what we're also looking at in this.

And it's not short, factual solutions. Don't get all heady about this. Something like, "I am in a state of insecurity but I will be moving out of it immediately," or some woo-woo talk like that. No. Tell the truth about your body. Tell the truth about what you're doing. Tell the truth about the experience you're having. And this is where the shadow thing really comes into play, too, because sometimes, what you're going to make a short, factual statement about is something that you never would've admitted to yourself six months ago.

You were pretty honest about how you felt really insecure, but another thing that you could've said is: "and I feel like I'm cheating the guy," or "I feel like I'm a liar because I said I could do the job and I can't." You could go into more shadow and that's OK, too, because what you're doing is you're making short, factual statements about it, not living it. You're taking the high-vibrational aspects of the temptations to the past and the future to illuminate what you're really doing now. What you're really doing now is acknowledging that you don't have to know everything and feeling OK doing the part that you know how to do, asking for help—whether it's from your soul or from some other technical person or Google—to do the parts that you have left and seeing if you deserve a lucrative contract when you don't actually know every single thing.

***

Veronica writes:

I can't begin to count the number of times I have used this tool. This one is like an icebreaker ship! It breaks through to the heart of the matter. When Eloheim first explained it, they said it was the most powerful tool they had given us to date. They turn to it time and time again during our meetings. I turn to it time and time again as well. This is one powerful tool, PERIOD!

***

Every time I use this tool it grounds me in the moment with the truth of what is going on with me at that time. It's a great tool for getting to the meat of the current issue and it quickly brings consciousness into play. It also stops the hamster-wheel mind from taking off and going down a path that's not helpful or healthy.

—Randy Sue

***

When I am really in any kind of jam or fighting with a friend, Short, factual statements gets me straight out of the messy drama.

It breaks down the issue into manageable little pieces. Working with this tool for only a few minutes, or a half an hour, I come to the "truth" of me through insight. Minimal effort with maximum results.

—Denise

***

Short, factual statements help me most when I feel fear from an unknown location. A simple example would be going outside at night across my property, which is a few hundred feet. I have occasionally felt uncomfortable like someone or something was watching to do me harm—too much television when young. Having the Short, factual statement tool really helps neutralize that, as I say, "I feel a little afraid of something, period." Then, "Is there a saber-toothed tiger within pouncing range, period?" I answer, "No, I don't believe so, and I don't have much to fear, period." That usually works just fine. I don't really feel very vulnerable these days, but if I happen to, I say, "What the heck am I worried about? I create my own reality and I create a safe place to reside, period."

—Rosie

***

This allows me to cut through the crap of habit; habitual response. It allows me to act in the present instead of the past or future.

—Mike

***

I find that when I am faced with situations and people that trigger me, Short, factual statements becomes my best friend. If I am angry, instead of flying off the handle, losing my temper and allowing myself to indulge in potentially hurtful behavior, I will use a short, factual statement like: "I am really angry about _____." Then I don't say anything else—I let the other person respond. In many instances, the other person is spoiling for a fight and is relying on me to lose my temper so that we can really have at it. Well, the 2011 version of me doesn't do that, she responds with short, factual statements. I let the other person rant until they demand an answer or interaction from me and then I respond with another short, factual statement. This can go on for a while but not as long as an actual fight, and certainly with much less wear and tear on me!

The first time I tried it, I was totally afraid of what the outcome might be. I was not sure that I could hold to short, factual statements alone without indulging in argument and screaming. I had never not responded in kind during one of these engagements. I was petrified that I would be beaten down with words, which had always been my secret weapon, but never yielded a satisfactory result. I knew I had to try using this great tool. I was actually shaking inside. But it didn't turn out that way—the other party exhausted their verbal anger rather quickly (to my surprise). I couldn't believe it!

The entire time I had to notice my habitual responses to the other person's anger and baiting words. I was shocked at how often I had to reframe my responses and quiet my mind to a non-reactive state. I had to be one hundred percent present in her anger and my own. I had to take complete responsibility for my creation in the moment. I was completely amazed as I realized that a recurring pattern that had been in place for almost 40 years had been broken simply by using short, factual statements. This has been a superpowerful friend and ally ever since.

—Rene

***

I'm not very good at remembering this tool, which is a shame because Eloheim said it would "change your lives." When I have remembered to make short, factual statements about what I am experiencing, it immediately brings me out of the habit of thinking about the past or future and into what is happening right now. I can handle the present; I can't do anything about the past or future. It's a big relief!

—Mary T.

***

This tool is phenomenal, especially for an obsessive like me! When I say that "period" at the end, I stop. There is no thought for a moment. It's like my brain doesn't know what to do with this. The thoughts that come next are usually just, "Wow, this is really interesting. I can feel it all over my body." It does interrupt the obsession with the past or the future, at least for several moments, and I can feel my brain jump to a new pathway with a more conscious thought that I choose.

—Joy

***

Having been on the spiritual path for the last 25 years or so, I was guided to contact Veronica and Eloheim through a radio interview I heard. I wanted to know why, with all my hard work, etc., nothing was really changing in my life. I was focusing on nothing; the fact that nothing was changing and expecting the change to come from outside not from within. Now one could say, "No wonder you're in status quo."

During my session with Veronica and Eloheim in November of 2010, Eloheim advised me to watch all of my thoughts and when I found myself habitually thinking make a statement regarding those thought patterns and end the statement with a period. Watching every thought for three days, I started to feel my entire consciousness shift. My entire being opened up to more experience and being more in the moment. The part that is so amazing and so unbelievable is that it is very hard to describe, for that past part of me seems so distant and so far away. I cannot imagine myself habitually thinking or feeling my life is so limited. My life is more and more in the moment and more and more opening up to all that is there for me.

—Anthony

Velcro

Velcro has two different sides, a loop side and a hook side, and it only works if you have both sides. We want you to not have Velcro for the judgments of others. Don't have Velcro on your side. Just don't have it.

You have silver hair. If we said to you: "Wow, you have ugly black hair." Your response would be, "I don't have black hair." You have no Velcro for that judgment.

If, however, we said, "Wow, you have ugly silver hair," it might be more challenging to not have Velcro for our judgment. But, it's still your choice. Use your free will to decide.

Another important place to look for Velcro is in your judgments about yourself. When you stop having inner Velcro for your judgment about yourself, it makes it much easier to not have Velcro for the judgments of others.

This tool is very important. Ask yourself, "Do I have Velcro—even empathically—do I have Velcro for it?" And you do. But you don't need to. Now that you're alerted to that, you can re-evaluate whether or not you want to have Velcro on any subject.

***

Veronica writes:

As a sensitive, psychic, empathic, channel, etc., I was a walking Velcro strip. Not only in the ways that Eloheim describes here, but with the feelings of others. I really got this tool and have used it countless times. When I realize I am picking up on others' energy I can say, "Don't have Velcro for that." And then shift to What is true now? to check in with what I am actually experiencing.

***

Velcro is a nifty tool. I use it to bring awareness of issues that need my immediate attention. It's fun to see where issues that once had Velcro no longer do.

—*Murster*

Vulnerability vs. weakness

Weakness is when you're in a position where you don't feel secure, you don't feel strong, you don't have certainty, you don't feel completely safe, and you try to hide it or you lie about it. Vulnerability is when you're in the exact same position and you tell your truth about it. When you're in a position of vulnerability it's actually the ultimate strength because there's nothing hidden, you're not pretending, there's nothing fake, there is no way to topple you. You may crumble but you can't be toppled. You may crumble because you feel like, "Oh my God, this is the hardest thing I've ever had to deal with." Yeah, OK. You kind of crumble and then you use some tools and you perk yourself back up. But you don't get knocked off your center. Telling your truth keeps you centered.

Weakness is very low-vibrational because you are hiding the truth of you. Vulnerability is a high-vibrational position; your strength is revealed when you're willing to tell your truth. Weakness is very concerned about other people's actions: "What do they think? How will they react? How can I avoid them being upset with me?" Vulnerability doesn't require action from other people. Vulnerability says, "This is my truth." From that position, it is much easier to set clear and healthy boundaries.

An example: You're in a relationship and you feel you've fallen in love and you want to tell the person you've fallen in love with them. That's a big moment, right? Weakness would be: "God, I'm in love with this person but what if they don't love me back? How's it going to affect me? Oh God, oh God, oh God." Vulnerability is: "The truth is the truth and I'm in love with this person." Weakness would be: "I really respect this person, I enjoy their company, I like spending time with them, and I want to tell them that, but how are they going to receive that or then maybe once they know I like them so much they'll use that to manipulate my feelings or manipulate my actions or try to get stuff out of me." Vulnerability is: "I really like your company and I can still set boundaries even if I admit that. I like your company and if you start acting like an idiot I'm not going to like your company anymore and I'm going to move on from there."

If the word "vulnerability" is very triggering, you can use the word "open" or "openness." But we would encourage you to stick with "vulnerability." We use the word vulnerability because it's been misused for so long and we want to reclaim it. Most of the misused words we give up on, but this one we want to reclaim. The energy of vulnerability is so much like the rose opening. It's so much like the butterfly coming out of the cocoon. It's so much that point of: "Anything could happen." And what you most often think is: "Anything bad could happen." But in vulnerability there's: "Anything could happen, period."

***

Veronica writes:

A lot of the Council's tools are intellectual; this one is very emotional. For me, there is an intense feeling associated with being vulnerable and strong at the same time. Truth and openness can be strong? What a relief!

***

I learned from Eloheim that if I am living and expressing the truth of me, there is nothing to fear. Weakness seems fearful, like I'm being a victim; being vulnerable feels courageous. If it's the truth, then I can wear it proudly and come what may, I'm true to myself. I don't have to waste my time or energy trying to cover up, keep myself safe, hide, or tweak anything about my truth. I may be vulnerable because I am more exposed, but what is the point of riding a roller coaster gripping the sidebar, eyes clenched shut, huddled in a ball?

—*Anna*

***

I use this tool strategically to get from war to peace. I know that by relaxing into vulnerability I will win, and that is not weak!

—*Denise*

What is, IS

When you encounter something difficult, the temptation is to try to change it or ignore it. We suggest that you go first to, "This is happening. What is, IS." Accepting that it is happening doesn't mean that you desire for the situation to continue, accepting that it is happening simply means that you ground your experience in the truth; the truth that "what is, IS."

Change can't happen when you are reliving the past or speculating about the future. Change only happens when you are in the moment. If you're experiencing something you wish to change, saying yes to "what is, IS" puts you where you can actually transform your experience; it brings you into the moment.

Once you are in the moment and acknowledging the truth of "what is, IS," you are perfectly poised to ask for insight and experience the learning and transformation you desire.

***

Veronica writes:

Three little words and three little paragraphs. Writing about this tool evoked so much emotion and awareness in me, it took several writing sessions to finish it. Yep, it's that powerful.

***

For me, this is the simplest expression of: What is true now? What's true now is that I am responsible for my creations. The truth of my situation reflects the truth of me. What is true now simply is. The past is gone and the future is nowhere near this moment. The present holds infinite possibility. What is, IS.

—Rene

***

There's been a temptation for me to use this tool for glossing over whatever's going and not really looking at what there is to learn from the situation. But the more I use it, the more I recognize when my mind starts to take that path again. When I really look at what's on the table, I can recognize it as something to explore and also accept. What is, IS, helps me keep in the moment, understanding that whatever it is, it's MY creation.

—Randy Sue

***

This little phrase saves so much energy! It brings the hamster-wheel mind to a complete stop so that I can assess, realistically, what I can do or want to do. It cuts through any drama or judgment so that I deal with fact-based energy rather than with illusory thinking. I can then move forward responsibly. If habitual thought wants to drag me from my calm center to a place of fear, What is, IS stabilizes me. Often it clarifies what is NOT mine to do. What is, IS. How beautiful!

—Janice

***

When I remember to say, "What is, IS," I stop reaching and relax. Acceptance of the moment without all the anxiety saves my body lots of stress. From this more relaxed place I really feel much better.

—Denise

***

The only thing that matters is now. Stay in the now, the moment is the truth, and what happens is fascination.

—Mike

***

The statement "What is, IS" has always meant stuck or permanent to me. Now, this very powerful tool enables me to experience the unpleasant moment, accept it, and realize that the next moment is an opportunity for transformation. I follow my intuition and move on with conscious change.

—Donna

What is true now?

Asking yourself "What is true now?" is a way of staying connected to the moment and your soul's insight about the moment.

It's fairly easy to remember to say "What is true now," but it's also very easy to be habitual about the answer you allow yourself to experience. What is true now is not answered by the mind. What is true now is answered by an "aha" from the soul, so by asking yourself what is true now constantly, you're creating a very strong connection between you and your soul, which is a fine thing to do if you're interested in transforming your life. The truth of you must be experienced consciously.

If what is true now is answered by a sentence of, say, more than say 10 words, it's your mind. An "aha" from the soul is going to be shorter than that. It doesn't need to be lengthy because it's not processed by the mind. It's an energetic truth expressed briefly in order to really sink in. If what is true now starts to have a lengthy explanation, suspect that the mind is encroaching on the soul's turf and ask the mind to shut up.

When used with consistency and consciousness, what is true now can be used to uncover unconscious coping mechanisms and lies that you tell yourself.

Veronica writes:

Another tool to keep very close to you. I use this one a lot to help sort out when I am acting from my current preferences and when I am acting habitually or out of patterns from the past.

***

I like "what is true now." I find the greatest challenge is being aware when the chatter-y monkey-mind starts with its unsuspectingly clever maneuvering to make me feel uncomfortable or irritated or going around and around on the same conversation. Old news, stuff that is past its expiry date, as they say. When I realize it, I immediately go to "what is true now." What is usually "true now" is that I was enjoying whatever I was doing before the sneaky bits got into my conscious thoughts. It seems never-ending.

—Rosie

What's in your lap?

When you are tempted to get into somebody else's business or find yourself judging people and/or events, ask yourself "What's in my lap? What is going on in me? How does this reflect something in me?" You can't tell anybody else what they need to see or what they are seeing; you need to deal with what's in your lap.

Are you in this moment? What static are you aware of? Where are you lying to yourself? What are you afraid of?

Need we go on? There is PLENTY for you to focus on right there in your lap.

***

Veronica writes:

I love this, "Need we go on?" Eloheim specifically told me to put that in there.

***

I use this tool a lot when I'm triggered by my birth family. We have a lot of issues around lack that we've been working out with each other from the time we were children. So now, when one of my siblings calls to complain about not having enough money, I look at what it brings up in me, what's in my lap, and it helps me to not go into "savior" mode. When I am conscious about this, it amazes me how much the conversation can change.

—Claire

Where am I lying to myself?

What things do you have a hard time admitting to yourself? What are the things you don't want anyone else to know? What are the things you have kept hidden?

In order to realize your authentic expression, you can't be lying to yourself. "Where are the holdout places where I'm telling myself stories about who I am?" They're typically going to be around one of these areas: sex, money, relationships, job, health, and housing.

"Where am I lying to myself about my marriage?" The word lying is such a triggering word but we are using it on purpose, because in essence you're lying to yourself if you know your marriage isn't working for you and you don't say that to yourself. Don't fall into the belief that you have to act on this awareness, simply allow yourself to be conscious of what your truth is. This one step is powerfully transformative.

What is the truth that you haven't told yourself or you've hidden from other people? What's the thing you're embarrassed people will know about you? What is the thing you're trying not to think about all the time? "What is true now?" reveals the things that *can serve you*, "Where am I lying to myself?" reveals the things that you wish *you could ignore*.

Where you lie to yourself generates static in your life.

***

Veronica writes:

At first, I thought this was going to be the same as What is true now?, but it is quite different. What is true now? helps me come back to the moment. Where am I lying to myself? helps me see why I don't want to be in the moment in the first place. Make sure to be nice to yourself when you discover where you are lying to yourself. It is easy to slip into judgment.

Who answers the door? The current version of you

A PRACTICAL EXAMPLE:

The ex-boyfriend is banging on the front door, you go to answer it but you don't want to talk to him—ask yourself, "Who answers the door?"

Does the four-year-old who's looking for her daddy's approval answer the door? Does the 20-year-old who just wants a boyfriend because she doesn't want to be alone answer the door? Does the 40-year-old who doesn't want to be divorced answer the door? Or does the you of the now that knows that guy shouldn't be in your life answer the door? Who answers the door? You decide that.

This tool is empowering because you say, "OK, I'm not bringing the 4-, 20-, or 40-year-old into this. The current version of me knows that I no longer want this guy in my life. The current version of me can say, 'No'." The four-year-old probably wouldn't be able to say no because the 4-year-old's still looking for daddy to make it right, and the 20-year-old still feels like she did something wrong, so she's going to have a hard time saying no, the 40-year-old's feeling like he might be her last chance at love, so she's not turning him away.

But in the moment where you bring your high-vibrational

self together and you look at that person and you say, "In this moment, with who I am right now, this situation is not OK, and you need to leave. Off you go. The door's getting locked behind you." And then you turn the ringer off on the phone and you just sit with the fact that you actually made a decision based on who you are today. That's where you give yourself the gift of being who you are today and living your life from who you are today, rather than allowing all baggage from the past or projecting into the future.

USING THIS TOOL WITH FAMILY MEMBERS:

A lot of times, when you're working with biological relatives, the stuff that you're learning about is the stuff from when you were five. However, now you're 40 and you're still doing your five-year-old shit, often from a five-year-old's perspective. Work on the issue when you're 40 as a forty-year-old, rather than, "I'm 40 but I'm acting like I'm five, which I've been doing for 35 years with my mom." This gives you a better chance of success, or a different chance of success, of actually learning and growing and becoming more of who you are.

Yes, you can say, "There's something for me to learn here, but my God, me as a 40-year-old trying to act like an eight-year-old with my mom who is now 70, is not working." It's not working and you have the right to say, "I want to learn this some other way."

This is loving yourself, giving yourself permission to set boundaries across your life. Set the boundaries you need to set in order to give yourself the best chance at learning what it is you desire to learn.

***

Veronica writes:

I remember so clearly the first time Eloheim talked about this tool. I was channeling in a living room facing the front door, so it was very visceral imagining the ex-boyfriend on the other side. I have used this tool time and time again in almost every sort of situation. Definitely one of my favorites.

***

I have used this tool, especially with my birth family members, where it was easy to slip into being a 10-year-old again. I no longer do that. I now respond and create from the person I am in the moment.

—Randy Sue Collins

Why, why, why?

This tool is designed to help you get to the heart of the matter.

When you find yourself stuck, ask yourself, "Why? Why do I feel this way? Why is this going on?" Use the answer you discover to ask yourself again, "Why?" Take the answer to that question and ask yourself again, "Why?"

Each answer to the question, "Why?" reveals more and more about you.

Although we call the tool "Why, why, why?" you can expand the inquiry to include questions like: "What am I getting? What am I loosing? What would be ideal? What would be the highest version of this?"

The purpose of this tool is the exploration of the layers present in any experience.

Keep in mind that you are not looking for a final answer to, "Why?" It's more of an acceptance of: "I am here to learn who I am." This learning process is a permanent state of exploration.

Your soul asks a question and the exploration of the question—not the answer but the exploration of the question—is you.

Be careful that you are not using the "Why, why, why" hammer!

This isn't a tool to beat yourself up with, this is a tool for revelation. You are asking the question and asking it again in order to reveal things you have hidden from.

***

Veronica writes:

I have to be really careful not to turn this tool into an intellectual exercise, but to keep it in the realm of insight and revelation. Using this tool to rethink the same thoughts isn't the point. It's, "Why, why, why, show me more about this, show me something new."

"Wow!", not "why?"

When you look at your creations, you typically say, "Why is this here?" This is not the question to ask. It is not: "Why is this here?" It's: "Wow, this is here. Wow, I am an amazing creator. Wow, I have generated something really, really complex, complicated, fascinating," whatever word you like, whatever word applies. But it's not: "Why?" It's: "Wow!" You have to shift out of the idea that you have to understand why it's here and instead say: "It is here."

An example is this: When you go to Disneyland and you ride around on the rides, you don't say, "Why are there pirates in the Pirates of the Caribbean?" You say, "Wow, I am transported into a completely new world here. What does this give me? What does this generate in me? What feelings am I having? Am I a little scared? Is it a little shocking? Is it a little surprising? Is it a little funny? Am I getting wet? Am I cold? What am I doing here? What is the experience I'm having in this wow?" You might get a bit brainiac and say, "Why did they choose that color paint?" or something like that, but don't take the example so far that it ruins it. Stay with the truth of it, which is when you find yourself in an experience it's not: "Why is this here?" It's: "Wow, look at my creation. And I'm going to acknowledge my creation."

You know you'll go to a movie theater and watch a very complex movie that's been created for you for your entertainment but you don't experience your own creations from that perspective. Like, "Wow, look at this fabulously detailed creation I have presented for myself, that I can explore, that I can roll around in, that I can feel wow about." So we'd like you to start experiencing your creations from that perspective where instead of a "why" you let yourself have a "wow." And that doesn't mean that it's not painful, but what it means is that when you're in it, you're not feeling pain because you feel like you're a victim, you're not feeling pain because you feel like you have no choices, you're not feeling pain because you feel stepped on. What you're feeling is: "Wow, this is just mind-blowing. This is just mind-blowing how detailed and in-depth and powerful it is that I've created this environment to explore. This is here for me to grow from. This is here for me to have an experience with and it's amazing."

***

Veronica writes:

Such a good reminder and such an easy one to remember! When I find myself saying, "Why?" I can just change it to "Wow!" What a shift of energy! It puts the focus on the fact that I created this and takes it off of the temptation to feel like I am a victim of my creation.

***

Since I'm a brainiac who comes from a long line of brainiacs, "Why?" has been my default method of operation. Breaking the victim habit hasn't been easy, but Wow! is a quick link to, "This is my awesome creation." It shifts the energy from dark and dank to light and cheery where insight is possible. Ha, I see the light!

—Mary T

***

When I get stuck in the repetitive circle of, "Why?" I don't feel good and realize that I am spinning my wheels in victimhood. When I say, "Wow... I created this," I feel more empowered and open to insight. I can feel my energy lift from "poor me" to "powerful me."

—*Paula T*

***

This tool changes my perspective on a dime. Often when a shift happens, I want to go into "Why?" "Why didn't he hear me?" "Why did she respond to me in that way?" and this can lead me into a big waste of time in which I am trying to figure out what part I have in other folks' responses to me. Other times, my "Why's" leads me into interminable ruminations of cause and effect that keep me in my head and out of the moment. The result is fatigue and low vibration and a perpetuated belief that I have control. Wow! is in the moment. Wow! is acknowledging that it is all so fascinating and unknown and fun. Wow! is an exhilarating way to live.

—*Anna R.*

***

This is a handy-dandy all-purpose tool! In my experience, "Wow!" is useful and appropriate in almost any situation that isn't calm and peaceful. It enables me to shift gears in an instant from whatever trigger might be presenting itself and to ground myself in the "is-ness" of the moment with awareness and appreciation for what I or someone else has created. For me, what follows is: "wow and allow," which shifts me into neutral observation.

—*Janice*

You can't have change without change

"I don't like my job!"

"Why don't you look for a new one?"

"Oh, I couldn't do that!"

This pattern is so common. Your desire for transformation and your fear of change pull you in different directions. The result is suffering and the tendency to live from habit.

To experience change, you have to know what to do with fear and evolve your relationship to the survival instinct. This is a core requirement on the path of ascension.

You cannot experience transformation unless something transforms. You cannot alter your paradigm unless there is an alteration of your perspective.

***

Veronica writes:

Short, sweet, and to the point. It's amazing how many times people have come to Eloheim for advice and it has sounded like the example above. Do you want change? Then something has to be allowed to change within you!

***

This is one of my favorite tools. It allows me to open the door and dare to dream—BIG! It takes the stale and stagnant out of life for me.

—Randy Sue Collins

***

Here is a physical lesson to make this tool clear. Our yard was surrounded with a thick group of trees creating a lush and contained, secure-feeling environment. One crashed down, with the fence, too. We were first devastated as the loss of our beautiful 20-ft-high natural wall. Then we looked farther and realized we could see many more stars, like we had long ago before they grew so tall and wide. Also, we could see a few miles to the mountains and the sunrise. All hidden before. Now changed. Then we lost another huge tree and a second tree's healthy limb, which left a very wide swath of nothing, no greenery, no strength, no buffer from the world. The old guard was gone. And we can see far now, our view expanded to the near hill. We set up new boundaries to this new world, and built a fence just high enough, but not so high as to block out the other parts of the world that we are just newly able to see.

—Rosie

You to you (compare)

Stop and pat yourself on the back every once in a while, won't you? Your inner truth is externalized through your life, and a lot of times it's the crappy bits that you notice. But we want you to start paying attention to the bits that reflect an internal journey that's actually moving toward bliss, that's actually on a transformational path. Because that's the truth of it. The truth of it is that you're on a transformational path and things are changing and it's easy to get lost in the changes if they're challenging. But the truth is, comparing you to you, you are transforming. And you need to be patting yourself on the back, giving yourself credit, and mentioning to your friends the things that are transforming in you in order to give them the kind of publicity within you that the shitty bits get. Publicize your transformation. Or at least notice it, at a minimum.

You are constantly in a pattern of transformation. If you don't do compare you to you, you're likely to feel like you are in one never-ending problem. When you compare you to you, you stop for a moment to realize, "Well, this is a different thing I'm dealing with now. That other issue shifted, so maybe I can try those tools with this new trigger."

***

Veronica writes:

This tool has such a loving feeling to it. You are making prog-ress. You are transforming. You are changing. It is happening. Stop and allow yourself to see it. Love yourself for the progress you have made. Be fascinated by the journey yet to come.

***

I'm so focused on moving forward all the time, I sometimes forget to do this. But when I remember this tool, I love myself for who I am—again.

—*Randy Sue Collins*

***

Compare you to you allows me to step out of an old situation and instantly reevaluate it with a fresh outlook.

—*Mike*

***

Comparing me to me in stressful situations has been both fascinat-ing and encouraging. There is always a gem of progress to be seen and felt that keeps my heart light and gives me courage to keep on keeping on.

—*Deb*

***

I find this tool extremely helpful in measuring my progress over time. How would a similar issue have affected me in the past? "Compare you to you" is a perfect measuring stick for gauging per-sonal growth.

—*Murster*

***

Compare U2U is such an affirming tool. It is so great to feel the progress I'm making. It is so sweet and so fair to leave everyone else out of the picture and just relish how far I've come. Nothing inspires like success, right?

—*Anna R., Mexico*

Terms

2012

The year 2012 is a shifting point on your calendar, a place of attention in order to help you focus. This is not a deadline, but a focal point to help facilitate your desire for consciousness and your desire for transformation. It is not a fixed point in time. The "place" of 2012 is a potential for dramatic transformation. That "place" is meeting you where you are; from there, you create the transformation that you desire both as a human and as a soul.

3D

Shorthand term for expressing the soul incarnate in the physical form, experiencing duality, density, and running the fear-based operating system. 3D is the status quo human condition prior to the shift to Homo spiritus.

4 billion

There are at least 4 billion people on the planet who won't agree with you, won't like you, or will never meet you. This number is likely underestimated. When we say, "Oh, you have found one of the 4 billion," it is not to dismiss or diminish their views, but to comfort you that this is a common phenomenon and put it into a perspective that hopefully helps you manage any triggers that come up. The energetics of this idea are similar to saying, "There are other fish in the sea."

5D
Shorthand term for expressing the soul experiencing the human form with a consciousness-based operating system. 5D is the experience of Homo spiritus, where the body is lived from an ensouled perspective.

Abundance
Abundance and "your abundant nature" are terms to describe the energetics reflecting the dynamic scope of possibility offered at this time, a concept meant to reflect the infinite possibilities (of all types) that exist in your physical world.

Our favorite way to illustrate the concept of true abundance is to have people look at how much nature surrounds them, for example: grass, trees, air, sky, and clouds. When one finds oneself lacking abundance, it is important to remember that abundance always exists in nature, and that is the place to start. You can also look at people smiling, hair on people's heads, or how many people have shoes. The point is to find a way to look into the world and see that there is much abundance.

The term abundance has also been corrupted to mean great sums of money or hoarding. Abundance, as an expanded definition, requires that one breaks the cycle or releases the belief that abundance only reflects how much money one has or how many houses one owns, to instead reflect any place where there is plenty or plentiful-ness. One simply needs to shift one's perspective about what plenty or abundance is.

Aha
A moment of clarity and insight that comes from accessing the soul's perspective; contrast this with the repetitive hamster-wheel-mind habit of thinking.

Ahas are commonly experienced while in the shower or doing other tasks that don't require full attention. The path of ascension and the choice for consciousness facilitate experiencing a steady stream of ahas.

Akashic Record

The galactic Internet.

A term that reflects the totality of: all of the lifetimes of those who have experienced Earth, all of the time that one has spent between lifetimes, all of the time spent in other incarnational opportunities, and all the time spent as a soul doing whatever the soul wanted to do. Think of a giant library where you each have your own section or file containing everything that has ever been recorded regarding what you've done, how you've lived, and what you've encountered. This isn't kept in anything that would resemble a library but it is helpful to think of it in this way conceptually.

Your Akashic Record is a reservoir of information that makes up the body of your soul. The energy that reflects that reservoir of information is what would be correlated to the physicality of the soul, if the soul had physicality.

When you are not in body and encounter another soul, your section of the Akashic Records is the information presented to the other soul. Your Akashic Record is the information that your soul presents to other souls at first glance.

Alternate expressions

Your "past and future" lives. Since time is not linear, these so-called "past and future" lives are all happening simultaneously; therefore your "other" lives can be referred to as alternate expressions of you.

Amnesia

The term we use to describe the "clean slate" of forgetfulness that a human experiences to facilitate living in physical form. It is a necessary state of being to incarnate into the physical body. Amnesia allows you to focus on the present moment in the present lifetime, without distractions from other lifetimes.

362 | Terms Veronica Torres

If you did not have amnesia about previous Earth experiences and incarnations it would be virtually impossible to stay in the moment because you'd be too busy wanting to go finish, redo, or undo things that have happened in alternate expressions.

Appreciation brings you into the moment

The high-vibrational space of love, appreciation, and fascination stops the thinking and clears the way for your soul's insight to drop in.

By appreciating yourself, you bring yourself into the space where you love yourself well. Appreciation is a very high-vibrational state. It's quite magnetic; it attracts other high-vibrational states.

Ascension

Ascension is a gradual, albeit drastic, transformation from a fear-based operating system into a consciousness-based operating system. Ascension requires evolution in the physical form and a radical shift in the way you respond to the biological messages the body offers.

Ascension is the term assigned to the energetic of the evolutionary leap into Homo spiritus. The Homo spiritus energetic allows for a life to be lived from the soul's perspective, and for a transformed way of interacting with physical matter.

Ascension does not mean you're leaving the body or the planet. Ascension means you're experiencing being in-body on Earth in a brand-new way that is a higher-vibrational, conscious way of living from your soul's perspective in which a spiritual partnership is formed between the soul, physical form, and personality self.

Audience or opinion

Sometimes, people just want an audience for their ramblings/ complaining and aren't actually looking for connection. Be cautious about matching energy and lowering your vibration in these situations.

Aura

A way of describing the energy field that surrounds objects, people, animals, and even places. Another way of describing the emanation of individuality; the emanation of the truth of you.

A person's aura is most easily perceivable 4-8 feet from the body; however, auras extend out infinitely.

Baggage

The past, future, cultural pressures, DNA pressures, habits, triggers, and other static that get in the way of you experiencing the moment.

Being a question mark

Each of you has a question that you have incarnated to explore. The broad way of stating this question is, "Who am I?"

You're a question. Your soul asks a question and the exploration of the question—not the answer, but the exploration of the question—is you and your purpose of being in the body at this time.

"What is the question I am answering by the current way I am living? What is the question I'm exploring by my expression?" consciously knowing you are in a questioning state is very important. Nothing is actually certain. When you make peace with certainty being a fallacy, you then say, "Well, what am I experiencing instead?"

You're in the question of you as you anticipate clarity coming in, not to answer the question but to give you the next step on the road of exploring the question that you are living. Clarity is not a stopping point. It is not a substitute for what you hoped certainty would be. It is simply an "aha" on the road of exploring the question of you that your soul is asking.

The question "Who am I?" does not go away simply because you have an aha about it in this moment. The question continues to exist. The questioning state is a permanent condition of your soul's nature.

"Who am I?" "Aha" and, "Who am I?" That's the path of consciousness. "Why am I here? Why am I doing this? Why, why, why, why?" The why doesn't need an answer. It is not about an outcome. Exploration of the why is a way to access the ever-unfolding truth of you. Your state of being is: "I am in why."

Bliss

The state of living in a spiritual partnership with your soul as a high-vibrational, conscious being. The state resulting from having tools for conscious living, being in neutral observation, and knowing that an experience previously judged as wrong (or right) is actually an opportunity for learning and growth. Living in a state of bliss is the result of living in the consciousness-based operating system as Homo spiritus.

Boundaries

Using your ability as a creator while living in a free-will zone to choose what you are interested in experiencing; directing the incarnation.

Boundaries with consequences

In order to leave fear, victimhood, and low-vibrational states behind, you set boundaries in the moment—boundaries with consequences. Boundaries without consequences are just hot air coming out of your mouth. For example, you might say, "You can't speak to me that way," and then the person speaks to you that way. If you don't then act (enact the consequences), all you're doing is blowing hot air. So, boundaries should have consequences attached for the person you're setting the boundary with: "This is what's acceptable in my life and if that doesn't work for you, then you're not in my life."

Is it hard to say to someone, "I'm setting a boundary with you and there are consequences attached"? Of course it is. Is it hard to continue the relationship without boundaries and feel like a victim all the time? We think that's harder.

Brain

Your brain is the biological functioning unit for thinking and it runs the body's processes. The brain also allows you to experience insight.

Bunnies and rainbows

You don't always have to put a smiley face on everything in order to be liked, loved, appreciated, understood, companioned. The way we like to say this is: It doesn't all have to be bunnies and rainbows.

EXAMPLES OF HOW THIS TERM IS USED:

You have to know what the truth of heart chakra energy is, and it's not bunnies and rainbows. It's not just love, love, love. It's loving yourself first.

***

The high-vibrational aspect of this situation isn't necessarily bunnies and rainbows. It's not, "I only want the bunnies and rainbows kind of thing out of that alternate expression." It's, "I want what's going to make me higher-vibrational, more conscious, in the now." So if you find yourself unable to love aspects of yourself, well, welcome to the shadowland. Welcome to an aspect of knowing what you need to work with. Why don't you love it? How can you say, "I love you" to that aspect of you? We are not going to fall for any, "I love you because you are bright and shiny and bunnies and rainbows." If you don't love something about yourself it is more conscious to say, "I don't love me" than it is to say, "Well I'm going to love me" or "I have to say I love me."

***

It's not as much that you have to say "I need to love it" or "I need it to have light" or any of those things. It's not, "OK, yes, my knee hurts; let's get the bunnies and rainbows out." It's, "Yes, my knee hurts and it's teaching me." So, say yes to what it is and then work with it, but continue to remind yourself of that "yes" to what it is.

***

The moment isn't a bunnies-and-rainbows spot, and a lot of times in some of the literature that's out there they say, "Oh, just be in the moment and all will be well." Well, that's crap. Be in the moment and you will start to experience the intensity that's available to you as a Homo spiritus individual. It is intense and it does ask a lot of you, but that's why you have lots and lots of tools to support your journey. The moment isn't necessarily going to be silence. It's not meditation. It's an opening to an enormous amount of insight, an enormous amount of information, and an enormous amount of opportunity to live differently in the *next* moment, to create differently for the *next* moment, to move differently into the *next* moment.

***

"Perfect" doesn't mean "feels good." Perfect is not bunnies and rainbows. Perfect is not easy. What is perfect? Precisely what is needed to give you the handhold on the climbing wall of ascension that you need right now.

***

Healing is an interesting word. By healing we don't necessarily mean: "Is it happy, happy, joy, joy, bunnies and rainbows?" No. By healing we mean: "Do I grow? Do I transform? Do I like myself more? Do I feel like I'm a better person? Am I becoming more of the truth of me?"

But and because

We use "but and because" as a red flag to alert you that you may be slipping into victim mentality. If you find yourself using those words, you may be leaving the realm of "I created it" and entering into the position of "it was done to me." Listen to conversation around you and begin to notice how frequently you hear "because this" and "but that."

At times, you may feel like you need to include a "but" or a "because" to feel like you have conveyed your entire story. That may be the case. We are not saying that you should remove them from your language completely. We are suggesting that you become conscious of how you use "but" and "because." We believe it will help uncover places where you are habituating to victimhood.

AN EXAMPLE FROM A CONVERSATION ABOUT INCOME STREAMS:

You said, "Yeah, I have 35 different ways money comes to me, *but* I still can't pay my bills." Instead say, "I have 35 ways money comes to me. Period."

"But and because" take away your high-vibrational state, they lower your energetic, make it more difficult to reach insight from your soul, and cause you to slip back into thinking, thinking, thinking. Remember, if thinking could have solved it, it would've solved it long ago, because you sure have thought about it enough. We aren't looking to think more, we are seeking insight.

AN EXAMPLE FROM A CONVERSATION ABOUT TRYING NEW THINGS:

You are tempted to say: "Oh, but I couldn't; oh, but I don't; oh, but that's silly; oh, but, oh, but." Right? It does not serve you to "but-and-because" away a fascination. A fascination is present for a reason. The exploration of the fascination is the gift, the gift you give yourself. What exactly do you think your soul's perspective is going to feel like? Souls are very curious. They want to learn and grow and do new things. Is it surprising that the soul's perspective comes in as fascination and curiosity?

Certainty

When you are operating from the fear-based operating system, change feels extremely risky. The survival instinct is constantly pressuring you to stay the same, because "the same" has kept you alive. Any changes to "the same" require certainty about the outcome in order to quiet the fears the survival instinct produces. As certainty is a fallacy—you can't be truly certain of anything in the diverse, vast world you find yourself in—you find yourself in a no-win situation: Change requires certainty, certainty is unattainable, and paralysis (fear) is the result.

Evolving your relationship to the survival instinct and certainty is a major aspect of the ascension process.

Chakra

Energy centers in the body. Traditionally, there are seven major chakras: Root (1st), Sexuality (2nd), Power (3rd), Heart (4th), Throat (5th), Third eye (6th), and Crown (7th). We use the idea of chakras as a handy reference tool. It's a shortcut that allows us to talk about different aspects of your body and energetic system without having to go into a long explanation each time. It is not required that you believe in chakras to follow the conversation.

Change

The recognition of an altered condition in the incarnation, which, if processed habitually, often triggers fear. When processed consciously, change becomes the mechanism for growth.

Channel

An incarnated soul experiencing the human form that allows non-physical guides to communicate through him or her in order to present helpful information in a palatable form. If out-of-body or non-corporal guides showed up as a burning bush, beam of light, or in a light body of some fashion, they would be far more likely to create fear than comfort. Channeling and channels allow a more human-to-human type of transmission of information, commonly less triggering than other types of transmissions.

Channeled message

Information that comes through a channel from guides that are not in physical form, but have perspective on the physical journey or the human experiment.

Checking things off your list

You incarnated into this lifetime with what we call a "list" of things that you hoped to do. The list includes experiences you wanted to have, things that you were interested in doing, unfinished business, experiences that you wanted to try again, or plans you made with other souls. You and your soul started this list before you ever incarnated into the physical form and it has carried over throughout all the incarnations you have experienced here on Earth.

What tends to happen is that as things on your list "come up," you check off the things that are less triggering, less challenging, and less difficult first. The items that are more difficult are often passed over to be dealt with another time. As you get closer and closer to the last few items on your list, they can feel very difficult. They feel more difficult because every time you said, "Oh no! I'm not ready to do that item right now, I'm going to do something else!" the item acquired a charge of impossibility. If you have re-queued the same issue many times, the charge of impossibility can feel quite large.

A lot of you have several things that have been on your list over many lifetimes of which you are very energetically frightened. Every time they've come up, you haven't been able to handle them. Now that you're at a higher-vibrational level than you've ever been with more awareness and tools, these things don't need to be anywhere near as scary as they used to be. In fact, you are more prepared to handle them than you have ever been before. In essence, you were clever by procrastinating! How often do you get to hear that?

The tricky part is that although you are now energetically prepared to experience these last few things on your list, the habit of fright is so deep that it can get in the way of looking at it from today's perspective and being able to say, "What's really going on here?" It's easy to lose sight of the fact that you have more tools and ability to handle them than ever before, but once you wade into them, they usually are much easier to deal with than you had imagined. It's just about being courageous enough to experience them after so many lifetimes of being so fearful.

Choose your reactions to your creations

"I am 100 percent responsible for my reactions to my creations." That's one of the most conscious things you can say. We strongly recommend that you write that down and stick it on your bathroom mirror.

"I am a creator; I created it all. It's all here *for* me, and I choose how I react to my creations as well." When something occurs, don't look for it to be different. Don't say, "I wish it were some other way." Say, "What is here right now is here on purpose. It's here because it needs to be here to facilitate my growth." Then, take it further; take your acknowledgment of the truth of you as a creator to the point where you can also say, "I am choosing the reaction I have to every single experience in my life. All of it."

It is your responsibility to set boundaries, state preferences, tell the truth about your creations, and to make sure that your creations bring out the authenticity of you, which you can then share. That's the gift of creating and choosing your reactions to your creations; it lets you share the truth of you. Consistently emanate the truth of you regardless of the circumstances you find yourself in by choosing your reactions based on your high-vibrational, conscious experiences of yourself.

Compassion

The traditional use of this word is very low-vibrational, as it tends toward victimization. Every experience is here to teach you something. Every experience is here as an opportunity for growth. When you feel compassion for someone, be very cautious that you are not casting them as a victim of their circumstances. You can say, "Wow, that seems like a tough way to learn, can I support you as you experience it?" But it is low-vibrational to say, "I feel sorry for you," or any other comment that implies the situation wasn't chosen.

This isn't a very romantic way to express what has been termed compassion, and may even feel harsh. However, you are either a victim or a creator. You can't be both. Exploring your creations (even if you have no conception of why you would have created them) is the path of consciousness and ascension.

Complex vs. complicated

Complex is fine. Complex is interesting. Complex is plenty of stuff going on and your brain likes it and your body likes it and your soul, of course, likes it.

Complicated is static. Complicated is low vibration. Complicated is unconscious. Complicated is, "Oh God, I have to make sure this person is happy," and "Oh God, I have to look after that person," and "Oh God..." this, that and the other thing. Complicated doesn't serve you.

Complex fascinates you. Complicated confuses you.

Complicated feels like there are no answers. Complex feels like "Oh, I get to put this puzzle together." Complicated feels like "All the puzzle pieces are the same color and someone's screaming at me while I'm trying to build it."

So, use "complicated" as a red flag. When it's complicated, look closely; it's an opportunity to become more conscious!

Conscious/Consciousness

Knowing why you do what you do. Choosing your reactions. Not being driven by habit. Experiencing the world as a creator rather than as a victim.

The world, as you experience it, has been programmed through habits, fears, and your biology. Through attention (consciousness), you can live the bigger picture that includes your personality's paradigm shifting and the embracing of your soul's perspective, as well.

Consciousness-based operating system (CBOS)

The consciousness-based operating system is the 5D or Homo spiritus way of experiencing the world that allows for conscious interactions with experiences rather than fear-based, habitually driven interaction with experiences.

Core Emotion (CE)

Your core emotion is a theme present in every thought, action, feeling, dream, hope, experience, and desire. It is present in all moments of your life. Your core emotion is unique to you and unique to this lifetime. Discovering your core emotion often answers long-standing questions such as: "Why does this keep happening?" "Why do all my relationships follow the same pattern?" "Why can't I get past this blockage in my path?"

Most people experience their core emotion from an unconscious or unhealed perspective. Learning to work with your core emotion from a healed or conscious perspective is often described as "life-changing." Since the core emotion is present in all aspects of your life, bringing consciousness to the core emotion brings consciousness to all aspects of your life.

NOTE: The exploration of your core emotion is one of our specialties. We have a specific process for revealing your core emotion and helping you move from an unhealed to a healed relationship with it. Because of the intensely personal nature of this exploration and the time required to fully explore it, we only offer this process through private sessions. For more information, see Contact, page 421.

Courage

Awareness of the temptation to fear and other types of static, but making the choice to act from consciousness instead.

Courageous enough

Are you courageous enough to think about now instead of running habit with the hamster-wheel mind? Are you courageous enough to think about this moment rather than skipping over it?

Creating your reality

"Create your own reality" is one of those terms that's overused and under-understood. Creating your reality is often believed to be a way to *control* your reality. It is thought to be a path to certainty and safety. Creating your reality is actually an outcome of your vibrational self, your vibrational nature, your emanation of a higher-vibrational choice.

Creating your reality works very much like a fountain. The fountain shoots up the water and it sprays out all over the place. No one knows where every drop's going to land. Who would want to? It would be tedious in the extreme. The uncertainty creates the beauty.

Similarly, creating your reality isn't about the outcome (where the drops land), it is about the experience (the beauty of the water in the air.)

In our fountain example, the water represents the truth of you (your soul's perspective and your personality), the water pressure represents your free-will choices and the fountain mechanism represents your preferences and boundaries.

Creating your reality starts with setting boundaries in association with your preferences. You then align your free-will to choose conscious reactions to your experiences (which often has the result of clearing static), and then you and your soul emanate together.

You initiate your creation, you choose how you react to your creation, and you remain open to insight from your soul.

Creator, The

If you believe that this world is created, then there must be a Creator. Therefore, the Creator is the one who created all. It helps to recognize that the Creator is not conceivable in its entirety while experiencing duality because of the inherent limitations of the human mind and the infinite scope of the Creator. However, the Creator can be sensed through insight from your soul and through experiencing creation.

Creator/creatorship

As a creator, you are aware that you are in a free-will zone and that you have the ability to choose your reactions to your experiences. When creations seem to be in opposition to what you "want," creators recognize that there are levels of creation and that everything is happening *for* me, rather than falling into victimhood.

Cultural pressures

Cultural pressures include: family beliefs, societal norms, and customs. Often, cultural pressures present as, "It's what everyone else is doing" and are used to justify forgoing transformation.

Habits and DNA pressures combine with cultural pressures to make a potent combination for habitual response to triggers.

Density

Experiencing the free-will zone in a body. Souls do not have physical form in the same way humans do. Incarnating on Earth provides for the unique experience of density, duality, and free will.

Digging a ditch

If you've been digging a ditch for fifty years, it's pretty easy to dig it deeper. You already have the walls there, you already have the guidelines and the exact dimensions of the ditch, and you have a plan.

If you decide that you're going to dig a ditch in a new area, it requires a different kind of attention. You start off by marking the lines where you want the ditch to be. Then you need to figure out where you're going to take the dirt you remove, etc. The new project requires many new actions and perhaps even some new tools.

It's the same with changing habitual responses.

Instead of repeating old patterns, you're starting a whole new journey. That changeover requires some consistency. Sure, you can always go back to the "comfortable" old ditch, but we're pretty sure you have learned all you need to learn about that. Use spiritual discipline to focus on new, healthy patterns to get out of the old rut and open up your life.

DNA pressures

Your DNA is the blueprint for your body. You and your soul collaborated to create the unique incarnation you are experiencing.

We use the term "DNA pressures" to refer to the interaction habits and consciousness have with your physicality.

As an example: Tall people habitually put things on high shelves while shorter people will habitually put things on lower shelves. Both are examples of people acting based on DNA (and convenience).

DNA pressures combine with cultural pressures to make a potent combination for habitual response to triggers.

Don't bring your baggage to the moment

Your ability to neutrally observe your life without bringing anything to the moment. You don't gather things up from your past. You don't pull things in from the future. You don't allow your fears to be involved. You say, "What is this moment? I am experiencing only *this* moment."

Duality

The idea that there are only two options, typically experienced as either, "what I think is right and what I think is wrong," or "what they think is right and what they think is wrong." A very limited way to experience Earth and the human form. The fear-based operating system loves duality because it gives a false sense of certainty. (I am RIGHT). The consciousness-based operating system leaves duality behind as it explores the truth of, "Everything that happens, happens for me and is teaching me something."

Earth

The planet Earth is designated as a free-will zone and was developed to provide opportunities for incarnating souls to experience density and duality. Earth, at this time, is engaged in an ascension process and will reflect a changed environment for ascended beings to explore. What that changed environment will actually look like is unknown, and highly anticipated for that very reason.

Ease

Living in the human form while utilizing tools for conscious living.

Ease not easy

We never said it would be easy to ensoul your physical form and evolve your body. We never promised "easy," but we did commit to you that you could start living in ease.

Easy

Please, please, please, give up on the idea that "easy" means you're right or that "easy" means it's working. It's not about easy, meaning: no effort. It's about realization, moving through, handling and processing triggers, recognizing transformation, and allowing change in.

Allowing change in is almost always the final step because things start to shake out inside of you, you start to create in your external world, and then all of a sudden something has to change. Your relationship to your world starts to shift. And if you're not willing to take that final step and shift your relationship to your world, then you've done all that work and you're not actually enjoying it or experiencing it.

Part of what happens is you think, "Well, if it's not easy, it's not worth doing," or "It's not easy, so I don't want to," or "It's not easy, so I'm on the wrong path." It's not about easy. It's about looking at your world and saying, "I'm triggered and I want to transform it," or "this habit that I'm not happy with, I want to make it different," and then paying attention to it, which allows you to shift it and transform it into something else. That's the freedom here—paying attention to the thing that you become aware of and then sticking with it enough that you allow your life to shift around the change you've made.

What we really see happen is that you do a ton of internal work and then when it starts to appear in your world, asking you for something new, you resist the external change. There is the temptation to stay small even though the work has been done. The temptation to stay small has to be dealt with. That means taking the internal work and experiencing it externally, walking it, emanating it. Don't drop the ball on the last step. Because that's really where the rubber meets the road. Until then, it's all personal, but when you take it into the world, there can be that last little hurdle. At some point you have to stick your neck out in order to experience your changed life.

Eloheim

We, the Eloheim, are a collaboration of souls presenting with a singular voice, channeled through the body of Veronica Torres with her explicit approval, willingness, and allowance. It is our great privilege to offer our support to you at this very exciting time on Earth to facilitate the transformation of Homo sapiens to Homo spiritus; moving from the fear-based operating system to the consciousness-based operating system. It is a grand experiment that many beings in the universe are watching with great interest, awe, and fascination.

Emanating (the truth of you)

As you live consciously, you emanate consciousness into your world. Your job is just to contribute, your job is not to try to dictate or control where your contribution to high-vibrational living ends up. It's not your business where it goes or how it shows up in the world.

Energetics

The way that souls communicate through nonverbal knowing.

Because your physical forms cannot yet communicate on the level that souls do, nonverbal knowing or "energetics" need to be translated into your language to facilitate understanding and communication.

Since it is always less accurate to use language than it is to communicate energetically, it is our hope and desire that your progress will eventually include the ability to communicate energetically without the need for language.

Energetic communication is happening all the time. Living consciously means that you are emanating a conscious energetic. It really does matter how you handle triggers and other upsets. Not just because it determines how you will experience the triggers, but it also determines how your emanation will go out to others. When we work with you, we are reading your energetics far more than we are listening to your words. Your energetics often show us visuals, which we can use to facilitate deeper understanding of the situations you are experiencing.

Ensoulment

The process by which soul energy is more deeply experienced by the personality incarnated in the physical form as the perspective is shifted from one of a survival instinct to a soul's perspective—from a fear-based operating system to a consciousness-based operating system.

Ensoulment, or living from the soul's perspective, is a collaboration between the personality self (you incarnate as a human) and your soul's wisdom. Don't misunderstand this to be that your soul "takes you over." This is not the case.

As an example, let's say you take a calculus class. The you at the end of the class hasn't 'taken over' the you from the beginning of the class. You have become a being that has the additional experience of the wisdom you gained in your studies.

Ensoulment is you realizing the wisdom and insight your soul already has; the completeness of you.

Fear

Fear is a biological reaction to change or the idea of change that typically creates the "fight or flight" response in the body, which is an adrenaline-based response to, "What do I do next?" Typically, the answer is that you run habit.

Consciously experiencing fear presents opportunities for extreme growth because it gives you the opportunity to break habitual patterns—to experience the moment rather than experiencing habit, which often involves projection of the future or bringing a memory of the past into the moment.

Fear can also be defined as the biological component of duality. It is the biological response to the belief in duality that is enacted regardless of which side of duality you're on. If you're on the side of duality that says, "This is wrong," then there's fear for survival. If you're on the side that says, "This is right," there's fear that it won't continue.

Fear and the survival instinct work together to keep you small.

Fear-based

Actions based on fear rather than conscious choice, a habitual, unconscious mentality (operating system) based on fear.

Fear-based operating system (FBOS)

You are a fear-based being. It is not something you can argue. It is a fact. Period. Full stop. End of sentence. You cannot argue with the fact that you are a fear-based being because you have been built to operate from fear in order to continue surviving. You've been built to startle at loud noises. You've been built to have the fight-or-flight response trigger in you. You've been built to be wary and aware of your surroundings. All of this can be summarized or reduced to fear. There is no need to be ashamed of admitting the fears that you find yourself experiencing because it is a core aspect of being human. You were brought into this incarnation running the fear-based operating system, meaning you're constantly experiencing the world based on fear.

The survival instinct is continuously asking you to be wary. The survival instinct is continuously trying to keep you small and it has extreme measures it can go to in order to keep you from sticking your neck out, from standing out in the crowd, from being noticed. The survival instinct flares up in you and requires your habitual responses to stimulus and triggers.

As consciousness is applied to the fear-based operating system, and as you break out of habitual response patterns, you're able to experience what is going on in your life from a new perspective and shift into a consciousness-based operating system.

Fear is a choice not a mandate

A high-vibrational reaction to a fear. Watch fear occur in your life. Watch it, watch it, choose and choose again to see it a different way, to see it rather than feel it.

Your reaction to an experience is a choice and not an inevitability. Fear is a choice, and so is fascination.

Fire hose

We use this term to refer to situations where strong emotions are acted out in unconscious ways. When you "fire hose," it's as though you are "spraying" your emotions onto those around you.

We frequently see this pattern with people who are learning to set boundaries. They find themselves in a situation they want to change, but are hesitant to act. They wait to act, which causes the feelings to build to a breaking point. When they finally do set a boundary, it is often accompanied by shouting, anger, throwing things, or other intense behaviors. A boundary was set, but it was done from a low-vibrational place.

Healthy, high-vibrational, boundary setting is an extremely important part of the spiritual journey. To do this, live consciously, know the truth of you in this moment, and act upon it quickly.

Free will

Free will is the opportunity to be in amnesia about the truth of you: the truth of your infinite, immortal nature.

Free will allows you to experience Earth as YOU see fit. No one can interfere with your chosen experience—not your soul, and not even The Creator.

Note, we said your chosen experience. You choose how you experience everything. Your free will gives you this ability. Now, we are not saying that everything that happens in your life feels like something you have chosen on a personality level; however, your chosen reaction to everything that happens in your life is within your purview.

Free will gives you the option to break out of the fear-based operating system, to break habits, exercise change and choose consciousness.

Free-will zone

An experiment that was initiated by The Eloheim after being invited by The Creator to come up with something new for souls to experience. It is an opportunity for souls to incarnate in a completely amnesic state and live a lifetime through their own direction, without influence from external forces, to grow as a soul. The free-will zone is inclusive of the solar system that holds Earth.

Fulfillment

Grace, ease, and bliss; living in the physical form and running the consciousness-based operating system, while having a spiritual partnership with the soul.

Gate latch

The sound that happens when a gate swings shut and the latch hooks. When we speak with you and you come to understand a concept, we hear a gate latch sound. Sometimes, we feel the change in you and then we hear the sound.

God

A word used to describe the concept of an all-knowing Creator, but can be interpreted to mean anything. God is a word defined by the individual according to his or her experience. There is not one definition for everyone. To say the word "God" and expect others to understand what you intend to mean by that word is too open to misinterpretation. To avoid this, we recommend using at least 10 words to convey complex spiritual concepts such as "God."

Going to see the king

We use this phrase to describe your interactions with authority figures.

AN EXAMPLE:

You want to speak to your boss about a promotion. How do you approach "going to see the king"? It is essential that when you "go to see the king," or anyone else for that matter, that you bring your high-vibrational, conscious self to the encounter. Keep "What is true now?" as your focus. Remember, when you encounter an authority figure, don't let their response to you tell you who you are. Emanate the truth of you, focus on this moment, state preferences, set boundaries, and remember that it is all happening *for* you.

When you go to see the king, whomever the king is in your world, if you show up authentically you've done your part to contribute to a conscious conversation. If you encounter people who know who they are and present themselves authentically—whether it's a king or a boss or a baker—you can trust the exchange to be high-vibrational or at least conscious or at a minimum not generating more static. If they don't do their half, well, that's something very, very important to know about them, isn't it?

Going with the flow

Comment: "I'm going to go with the flow; I'll just deal with things as they come up."

Response: Be cautious about this idea. "The flow" is often a "path of least resistance," a low-vibrational energetic.

Comment: What I meant is, "I'm going to be conscious about whatever comes up."

Response: Great, say that instead. It makes a big difference. There is an energetic pattern in the idea of "going with the flow" that is a mismatch with who you are now. Saying, "I'll attend to what arises," OK, that's fine. Saying, "I'll be conscious about what shows up," OK, that's good. Saying, "I'll go with the flow." Nope. Why?

Too frequently, "going with the flow" results in you forgetting to set boundaries because the idea is, "Well, whatever happens I'll just flow with it!" This is not a recommended activity.

We are not suggesting you become rigid; we love for you to explore uncertainty! What we are recommending is that you continue to be conscious as you explore flexibility. Even if you are experiencing someone else's plans, you can still stand with the intention of observing and making choices, setting boundaries, stating preferences, and using your free will to explore your reactions to your creations.

Grace

Grace is living your life knowing that everything that is happening is happening for your growth. "I gracefully recognize this experience is here to teach me. I don't have to approach this as a victim. I can approach this as a creator." That's being in a state of grace.

Growth

Consciousness infusing the incarnation, resulting in transformation.

Guides

A generic or general term used for beings that are not currently in physical form that are available to assist those who are in physical form, through a variety of means—through channels, through coincidence, through synchronicities, through dreams, and many other ways.

Habit/Habitual response

Habit is tied into the fear of getting dead and the survival instinct. Since the body is programmed to stay alive, it will say, "Well, this hasn't killed me yet, so let's continue." Change makes the body feel like there's a potential to get killed. Change means new factors to manage, new things to deal with, and new situations to juggle. It is easier on the body if it already knows the threats that are involved in your day-to-day life and has already established that none of them are threatening enough to get you dead. The body is going to want to keep repeating that pattern. If you know that a food is poisonous to you, you don't eat it again—making that a healthy habit. But the survival instinct, as translated into 21st-century Earth, ends up looking like, "I can't quit this job that I hate because I'm too afraid of getting dead. I'm too engrained in this habit to try something else."

Hamster-wheel thinking

The habitual mind repetitiously trying to think its way out of "problems." Repetitious thinking about past and/or future experiences misses the experience of the moment.

Healing

Consciousness-infused biological responses and choices which create growth and a transformed experience of the body.

Heart–power chakra combination

From a soul's perspective, your heart chakra (4th) and power chakra (3rd) are combining. We see the energy flow as a figure-8 pattern, or an infinity symbol.

There's no longer a difference between acting from your heart chakra and acting from your power chakra. This means that you no longer go out into the world expecting to gain if others are going to lose from your actions. You no longer go out in the world knowing that you could be powerful at the expense of others. The idea of climbing over someone else to get to what you want becomes as distasteful as murder, or rape, or arson, or anything that you personally have a big problem with. You are not able to function in the world in a way that is not within your own integrity. You can't cheat a little on the side. You can't sneak down and operate from your power chakra, ignoring your heart chakra for a few hours and then expect to jump back to the heart chakra and ignore the power chakra. You can't play that game anymore. Consciousness illuminates the truth of them working in teamwork and it says there's no way you can be in the world without being from your integrity, being from your authenticity, and being from your wholeness.

Heart chakra energy has often times been out of balance—either "I serve, I love, I give," especially women, "I give, give, give,"—or your heart's closed down. There's been a lot of out-of-balance heart chakra energy on this planet.

When the power chakra gets out of balance it tends to be either "I'm going to go take care of business," with a corporate-raider kind of energy, or you have no boundaries and you're a victim.

The merging of the heart and power chakras addresses this imbalance. When you bring in the density of the power chakra and combine it with the etheric nature of the heart chakra, together they operate from a more balanced state. That's really the beauty of it.

The combined chakra can be called the ensouled chakra or the ensoulment chakra. It's the chakra where the energetic center of the body emanates out into the world.

High-vibrational

High-vibrational refers to actions, thoughts, ideas, and relationships which are based on consciousness and conscious choices. It is not a judgmental term; rather it is descriptive of the fact that your body is actually vibrating at a different rate than it did before you infused consciousness into your life.

Your soul vibrates at a very high rate. Raising your vibration by living consciously is a very important step in living from your soul's perspective and walking the path of ascension.

Hoarding

One of the most low-vibrational states you experience. "I'm going to look out for me and I don't care what happens to other people." Hoarders are constantly in lack and looking for how they can get more. They are obsessed by the question, "How can I get what I don't have?" They never feel like they have enough of what they need.

Homo spiritus

A name for a state of being that is possible when you live in collaboration with your soul incorporating your soul's perspective; a transformed, expanded experience of the physical form and a shifted paradigm of how one is on Earth.

Living from the consciousness-based operating system, pursuing the path of ascension.

Insight

Information received directly from your soul.

The challenge when explaining the word "insight" is that it is a process that uses the brain but must not be confused with "thinking."

There are a few characteristics that illuminate the differences between the two: the mind is limited and will often present limiting messages. The mind's messages are repetitive and often negative. Insight will present ideas and options you've never considered before, which are always positive and constructive in their nature. Insight will never demean you; it will never be negative and it will always be supportive of your growth and transformation.

Jackets on the coat rack

Imagine that you have a row of jackets hanging on pegs by the front door. Each of these jackets represents an emotion. Just as you can choose which jacket you want to wear when you head out into the weather, you can choose which emotion you wish to experience.

Of course, this requires practice and spiritual discipline, but it is true: Every emotion is a choice.

What jacket will you wear today?

Joy

Joy is when you experience happiness without feeling like the other shoe is going to drop. You're just happy. And as you think, "Oh, but…" you don't let the "Oh, but…" have any airtime. Uncertainty makes joy possible. When you're comfortable with uncertainty, it is possible to be in joy. When you're comfortable with uncertainty, joy is possible because you don't require the situation to be a certain way in order for you to experience happiness, and prolonged happiness is joy.

Karma

The word "karma" had a strong definition coming out of Eastern religious beliefs. When it came to the West, the term became somewhat bastardized to mean, "If you're not good, something bad is going to happen to you."

Karma had a big duality perspective in it but if you take the duality out of it, it becomes, "Everything teaches me," instead of, "I'm waiting to get punished for any mistakes or slip-ups I make."

Lack

The idea that there is not enough. Lack is a fallacy; you live in an abundant universe. Lack is a sense of, "I should have more. Something is wrong or broken here." This is experiencing your life from a victim mentality. You are a creator; everything in your life is in your life to help you grow as a soul. As a creator, if you feel a sense of "not enough," look at it as an opportunity to uncover the actual blocks to your desire. We refer to these blocks as static and baggage. Living consciously is the path to clearing these blocks and experiencing your world in its true state, the state of abundance.

Landing

Spiritual growth tends to follow this pattern: periods of intense growth followed by periods that feel more like rests. We call these "resting" times being on the landing and the "growth" times climbing the stairs.

Lateral pass

It can be tempting to want to find a way to give responsibility for your experiences to someone else. This transfer of responsibility can look like: "I turn this problem over to my angels," or "I let my higher self deal with it," or even "God, take this burden from me!"

We call this making a lateral pass.

The assumption being made in this idea is that whomever you are making the lateral pass to is actually ready, willing, and able to do anything with your creation. You are in a free-will zone; we dispute that anyone or anything is here to take away your "problems" or that anyone or anything is better suited to interact with your creation than you are.

You created it so that you could learn from it. Why would you want to give it away? Does it feel too "hard" to deal with on your own? OK, that's why we have lots of tools to help you interact with your creations in new ways and from new perspectives. You are not alone in your exploration, but you are solely responsible for how you choose to react to your creations.

Layers of the onion

A quick way of saying that while issues may come up again and again, you are experiencing them at a deeper level each time.

Light worker

A soul incarnating at this time with the specific desire to grow spiritually and live consciously. A person walking the path of ascension. A Homo sapiens desiring to live as Homo spiritus.

Learning

As an incarnate soul, the processes that you go through in order to have the growth you desire are called "learning." The journey is a journey of change, shifts, transformation, and ascension, which is all brought into the physical system through the process of internal and external transformation, a reflection of all of the learning that has occurred.

Low-vibrational

A state of being that comes from living in the fear-based operating system, not looking for conscious understanding or an experience of the dynamics being presented to you. Living habitually rather than opening to new experience.

It is not a judgmental term; rather, it is descriptive of the fact that your body is actually vibrating at a different rate than it would if you infused consciousness into your life.

Your soul vibrates at a very high rate. It is difficult to connect to your soul's energy when living a low-vibrational life.

Marble sculpture

In a sense, bliss is inside of you. It's like Michelangelo carving a sculpture. The marble block is there; the sculpture is inside the block, not yet revealed. When you are in habit, you are looking at the block and thinking, "This could be more, this could be more, but that would require getting the tools out, it would require doing a lot of work, it would require, it would require..." and you find reasons not to change. Habit keeps you from seeing the beauty of the finished sculpture. All you get is the plain block. Now, if you want to get more out of your life, if you want to be that finished sculpture, the excess marble has to come off.

Just as the act of chipping away marble reveals the sculpture underneath, the act of attending to triggers and static reveals the highest version of you. When Michelangelo chipped a piece off the marble block, he didn't have to chip that same piece again; however, you often you have to go deeper and deeper and deeper in the same part of the block. That we know. But it is not that you do some work and then you have to do that work again. It's that you do some work and then sometimes you'll revisit that area to do deeper, finer work.

Sometimes, you've been working on the front and you haven't looked at the back in two years. And you turn the block around and you say, "Oh Lord, I'm really not attending to these things back here, am I? Well, I'm going to. I'm going to attend to them now. There were opportunities to look at this stuff before and I didn't, but I'm going to look at them now; in this moment, the current version of me is going to look at them now. I'm going to use my tools and take this opportunity to offer a different emanation and to transform static and triggers as I go."

You're clearing away the old rectangular-shaped block to reveal the beautiful figure that's always been there, just waiting for the accurate and consistent application of the appropriate tools to illuminate the beauty that only needed you to be willing to do the steps that unearth it, unveil it. You are there. You are the sculptor. And the consistency that you are willing to apply to the project tells the story. It allows the unfoldment.

The sculptor doesn't *build* the marble statue, it's something that's *revealed*—and that's what you're doing. You're revealing the integrity of you, meaning your soul expressed through the physical form, and the only way to reveal it is to remove that which isn't of the integrity of you.

It's the process of chipping and filing and buffing away the unwanted sections that reveals the sculpture. Being angry that the sculpture doesn't appear full-formed is ridiculous. When you find yourself in trigger or static—frustration, anger, anxiety, memories that trouble you—remember this idea that the sculpture doesn't show up fully formed. It's the journey of the discovery of the sculpture that is the meaningful part. When the sculpture is placed someplace in public and it emanates its beauty, then others get to experience it.

It does not get created until someone stands there and says, "I'm willing. I'm willing to chip off this section; I'm willing to buff this part out. I'm willing to scratch my head and wonder, 'Do I want an arm here or not?' I am willing." Your willingness to look at your static and triggers creates the beauty of you, which can then be emanated for an eternity. You have the marble block; you can be angry at it for not being finished or you can put your stamp on it. You can make it the vision you have. And then that vision will be emanated into the universe forever.

Stand in front of your unfinished self and decide what bits you want to keep and what bits you want to get rid of. Just as Michelangelo had the variety of tools that he used, you have tools to help you chip away the things you don't wish to see anymore. At some point you can stand there and say, "Comparing me to me, I have an arm now. Last year that was just a block but now you can actually see the fingers. You can see that I've decided how I want to be."

Math problem

If we ask: "What's 9,897,209.5 times 8,239,203?" you wouldn't take the first number that comes to mind as the right answer, but you'll take the first emotion that comes in as an indisputably correct position. If you find yourself in an emotion that doesn't seem actually relevant to the moment, be kind to yourself about it. Just remind yourself, "Oh yeah, that's right, the first emotion that trips along isn't necessarily the one I want to run with."

You can let yourself have the emotion, but know why you're

having it. If all of a sudden, you feel sad or upset and you don't know why you're feeling that way, ask yourself, "Is there any good reason to be having this emotion? And if there isn't, then what can I ascertain about the state I'm in?" Remind yourself, "This emotion has no basis in reality, in the reality of this moment. This emotion is a choice."

Mind

The mind's thoughts and insight are both processed by the brain. The mind is only capable of taking the spiritual journey so far. At some point, the mind's ability to manage the spiritual journey comes to a standstill. Without the infusion of insight from the soul, the journey will stagnate. When you act, react, and create only from your mind, you're cutting yourself off from the vast resources of your soul and the Akashic Records. In this context, it's easy to see that allowing the mind to run the incarnation is limiting.

Mob mentality

Matching energy with low-vibrational states or low-vibrational people. Going with the flow. Acting habitually, as part of a group.

Money flows, not grows

Money flows, it doesn't grow. In the past, a lot of people have made their fortunes just by letting their money grow, but that was an old paradigm. Have you looked at interest rates lately? It doesn't work that way anymore, does it? Part of the reason for this change is the energetic truth of money is being revealed: high-vibrational money *flows*, it doesn't grow.

Money flows where consciousness goes! Become more conscious of your relationship to money by using the money mantra: *I am in financial* **flow**, *money comes to me in infinite ways.*

Mt. Everest

A quick and easy way to remind yourself that you do hard stuff on purpose all the time. Climbing Mount Everest is hard, but people climb it. And they do it on purpose, right? Learning another language—for most of you that's really hard but you do it. On purpose. You want to learn to play an instrument. It's challenging, but you do it. On purpose. And then you wonder, "Why is my spiritual life and my spiritual development so hard?" Somehow the difficulty of spiritual development is interpreted as you being a victim of your spiritual path. You are a creator. You are choosing your reactions to your creation. Therefore, take responsibility for your experience and approach it in a new way. Allow yourself to respond with the attitude of, "Yes, this is hard, but I choose it. Just like I choose to climb up a tall mountain or I choose to learn another language, or I choose to learn how to dance ballet. I choose to do hard things all the time. I choose growth and transformation."

On the bus

A cute way of expressing the idea that you are committed to a specific path or idea. We commonly use it to indicate that you are committed to the path of ascension.

Overachieving light worker

A playful description used to illuminate when light workers start thinking, "I have to keep pushing, pushing, pushing to get to that outcome." This is doing rather than being. It is very common to apply the "doing" mentality to the spiritual journey. Part of spiritual transformation is healing this habit.

When you are playing with the overachieving light worker idea, it is all about winning, getting an A+, getting a gold star, being first in line, being on the bus, getting to ascension as fast as you possibly can. In this, there is the risk of losing sight of the fact that "now" is the end result, is the goal, is the desire, is the point of it all. "Now," what you're doing right now, is it.

Peace

Peace is the experience of you being non-disturbable. It is the idea that no matter what's going on you know what your center is. You know the truth of you and you don't resist it. You can have peace even with things you hate about yourself if you don't resist the truth of you being present. Peace is: "No matter what's going on, I'm still me. No matter who's triggering me, I'm still me."

Personality

The aspect of the incarnate human that has a name, that has preferences, that has a history, that has a future, that has relationships. It's the aspect of you that's currently under development.

The power of the personality is that it wields free will. Therefore, the personality actually is completely in charge of the incarnation by controlling whether or not consciousness is employed, deciding how to react to situations, and deciding whether or not to pursue ascension.

Power

When you live in scarcity—the feeling of lack, fear, guilt, and unconscious low vibration—one of the most popular ways to cope is to exert, or believe you can exert, power over others. The sense that you control another's destiny provides a (false) sense of certainty about one's self.

Control and power do not create safety. Control and power simply require more and more control and power. It's a never-ending cycle.

The only thing to seek power over is power over your habits. The only person you can actually control is yourself; use free-will to choose to change.

Proof

Proof is the repeated demand for certainty, the demand for your eyes to see it in order for you to believe it. Proof is the biggest barrier between you and living an expanded sense of yourself, because the need for proof comes from the small mind. "Prove it to me" is a defiant statement of unconsciousness. Thus it is one of our least-favorite terms because it's so deeply ingrained in the victim mentality. It doesn't have any belief in creatorship or the ability to open to new possibilities without certainty being promised. Your soul's perspective will illuminate many things that can't be proven to the small mind. Will you let the habit of needing proof result in you missing out on these new experiences?

Protect what's mine

This is all about the idea that there's not enough for everyone. It's the notion that, whatever you have, you must make sure no one gets it. You must ensure that you will always have enough. This fallacy is twofold. One, that there's not enough for everyone, and two, that if you have it, it will be enough. It's the idea that if you have enough food set aside, you'll always have food—but eventually, that food gets used, eaten, spoiled, and then there's never enough. It comes from the perspective of lack and the dreaded "h" word—hoarding—which is one of the lowest-vibrational words you have.

Safety

The idea that you can control outcomes. Safety is sought by looking for certainty. Certainty is a fallacy—it can never be achieved. Everything has some degree of uncertainty in it. The survival instinct constantly pushes you to seek safety; the fear-based operating system gives you no way to get there. The ascension journey helps you learn that the only sense of true safety comes from a deep connection to your soul and moving moment to moment through clarity.

Sandpaper/Sandpaper people

A metaphor for the way triggers and fears can be viewed as opportunities for change and growth the way sandpaper shapes a piece of wood: an opportunity to smooth your edges.

Sandpaper people describes relationships that give you an opportunity to grow and transform, typically in an uncomfortable way.

It is never used to indicate victimhood, but rather is a reminder to be conscious that the person or situation is there for your growth.

Serenity

The experience of, "I don't have to seek outside of myself for completeness." A state that has no opposite.

Service mentality

The mistaken idea that you should put another's journey before yours; believing your needs are secondary to others' needs; the idea that "doing good in the world" comes before caring for yourself.

The most powerful way you can be in the world is by loving yourself well and then walking your life from the place of loving yourself well. When you love yourself well, you give the greatest gift you have to give, and that is emanating your uniqueness. Until you love yourself well, you're not really giving a gift. You're simply doing. You're doing and doing and doing in the world. But there's no flavor. There's no taste.

Healthy service is asking, "How can I emanate the highest possible vibration?"

If you choose to offer yourself in service, the first step is to ask your soul for insight, "What is it that best serves me in serving others, in offering myself to others? What serves me first, where will I grow the most?" You want to be in the most conscious frame of mind possible in order to interact at the highest vibrational level possible. Your emanation is your true gift.

Through the act of loving yourself, you give the gift of the truth of you to this world. There is no truth of you until it includes loving yourself. It doesn't exist. "Empty calories" is a way to say it.

We see folks putting themselves out there in the world, saying, "I want everyone to feel better, to feel happier, to have more, to be in a good space." The idea is that taking care of everyone else first is going to be the path to your own bliss, your own peace, your own joy. We have not seen this work well long-term.

People who live to serve others appear energetically drained because their own needs have not been precious to them. They're missing the core amount of attention, of rest, of nourishment, of peace, of quiet, of meditation, of walking, or dancing, whatever it is that feeds them as a person and keeps them whole. Folks in service mentality have been letting pieces of those things go to other people because they think, "Well, if they're happy, I'll be happy, or at least I won't be so distracted by their needs."

The path out of this is to set boundaries. Boundaries don't mean: "I don't love you anymore." Boundaries mean: "I have to love myself first so I have extra love to give. I can't give from this place. I have to give from a whole place." If you keep giving from weakness, eventually you will have nothing left. If you set boundaries, you will rejuvenate yourself.

Unhealthy service mentality can be highly triggered when there are large "disasters." You see something on the news and you think, "Oh my God, those people, they don't have any place to live." You look in your checkbook and you send off whatever you can send off and you think, "I wish I could do more." If you feel that your money, time, or skills are the only way to "serve," then you will often be frustrated. Remember, healthy service is asking, "How can I emanate the highest possible vibration?"

Investing in your energetic and raising your vibration is really the way you meet your desire to help the world. The key here is that you realize that as you raise your vibration and live more consciously, your awareness of others' needs will expand yet your ability to *physically* interact with their needs will not. Use your free will to decide where you want to physically interact with others. How you manage your reaction to the areas where you are aware of the needs of others, yet cannot physically interact with them, is a spiritual challenge best handled by becoming more conscious, which raises your vibration and increases your emanation.

It may be tempting to be so overwhelmed by the many "problems" in the world that you do nothing, including work on yourself. We remind you, emanating your truth into the world is powerfully transformative. That's the greatest gift you can give to yourself and to the world.

Shadow

The aspects of yourself that you don't want anybody else to know about; the things that you are ashamed of and deny, and repress; places where you don't love yourself yet, parts of you that you reject as unacceptable, wrong, bad, or even evil; aspects of your life you feel are socially unacceptable yet still true; honest experiences that you have had that you didn't handle with consciousness; shame: these from your shadow.

We see your shadow aspects as dark holes or gray areas in your energy body that make you look a bit like Swiss cheese.

Our desire is to help you love all parts of yourself, which allows you to live from the soul's perspective as a Homo spiritus being.

Shake shoulders

Demanding attention, insisting that you be listened to, trying to change someone, needing people to agree with you so you will feel safe. The accompanying visual is that you are shaking someone by the shoulders and preaching to them. You may not actually do that, but energetically that's what's going on.

Soul

The infinite, immortal nature of your true self, including the collection of every lifetime you've had on Earth, the time between lifetimes, every lifetime you've had in other incarnational opportunities, and all other experiences.

The soul is a vast reservoir of experience and an eternally curious being.

Animating a human body does not require the entirety of your soul. There is no way you can stuff an entire soul into a human body. But there's a percentage of your soul that has been allocated to be experience-able in this lifetime.

Soulmate

Humans desire safety, and typically believe they need something outside themselves to be safe. That search for something outside of themselves is 'spiritualized' to become "soulmate." The idea is that, "There's another soul out there that is destined to complete me; then I will feel safe." The truth is that all souls reflect the completeness of the creation. No one soul is more able to complete you than any other because that's just not how it works. You are a complete being experiencing the physical life.

That said, because you incarnate in soul groups, there can be souls that you are more familiar with and can feel more connected to simply through familiarity and decisions made in pre-birth planning to share certain experiences. But the quest for a soulmate to complete you is a great, great spiritual fallacy. The quest for a human to partner with or to spend time with in order to facilitate growth is a completely different matter. It can also be a friend, parent, lover, dog, cat, or anything that facilitates spiritual growth. Everything can be used by the incarnate human to facilitate growth, but no one person is specifically sent here to complete you.

So, if soulmate is perceived as someone who is going to complete you, we don't buy into that. But if soulmate is perceived as someone who is going to facilitate your growth, who may or may not stick around for a long time in your life, then that's a more healthy way to use that term. But we advise not using it at all. The implication is that somehow you're not fully you unless this person comes along, and that's lack.

Soul's perspective

The wisdom of your soul incorporated into your experience of being human. It's the insight available to you when you live from the consciousness-based operating system.

From the soul's perspective, there is no judgment, no duality, no fear about life in the physical form. Everything is fascinating.

Your soul knows this is all just a journey in learning. There's no right, there's no wrong, there's no good, there's no bad. It's a journey in learning, exploration, experience. It's not the destination—it's the journey.

Spirituality

Functioning from more than just the survival instinct. Awareness of and openness to experiences outside of those that are "provable" or "repeatable." Knowledge that you are more than just this human form.

Spiritual discipline

When you think, "I don't feel good in this environment," spiritual discipline says, "This is hard, but I'm going to do it." It's challenging, right? You use your spiritual choice and you consciously work with an experience that you wish to change. It's spiritual discipline to align free will with the desire for evolutionary change, and to persevere. Choose and choose again for the growth you desire.

Spiritual growth

Another term for transformation and learning, indicating that your learning is not based on your mind or habits but on consciousness-based transformation.

Static

Unconscious reactions and thoughts; coping mechanisms, masks, lies, baggage, dishonesty, hiding from your authentic expression or the completeness of you; anything that interrupts your ability to stay in the authentic truth of the moment. The mind, the survival instinct, the body, and fear all generate static to keep you small.

Static includes all the reasons you have sold yourself on which you use to avoid presenting the truth of you to the world. It will crop up more intensely as you start to recognize the greatness and the vastness of your true self.

Living consciously is the path to clearing static.

Suffering

Suffering occurs when you experience the world from a victim mentality—not believing you are a creator and instead living in limitation and habit.

You've all suffered, and you have the choice in the suffering to experience it as learning. No matter what is occurring, there's always that choice. Change happens. What is, is. Let's look at it from a new perspective. Do you want to climb out of this new experience with something learned from it, or do you want to wallow in what happened to you, in victimhood?

Survival Instinct

A body-based dynamic that puts the continuation of life at the top of the list of importance. The survival instinct serves you deeply by continuing life even when physical, mental, or emotional experiences lead you to feeling as though you want your life to end.

There had to be a survival instinct put into the system because duality is so different from your experience of being a soul that it would be very tempting to "drop one toe into this water" and then run away. The body's innate survival instinct keeps you in the incarnation long enough to be able to make conscious choices about the experience.

In order to live a conscious life, one must transform one's relationship to the survival instinct. Consciousness asks you to make steps toward change that the survival instinct will be resistant to embrace because to the body, any change feels like potential death and therefore, should be avoided at all costs.

The survival instinct is one of your greatest treasures as well

as one of the most challenging places to transform with consciousness because it's so deeply based in the body, and based
in unconscious processing. When you are able to consciously
modify the way the survival instinct works in the incarnation,
you open yourself up to a deep and profound way of re-experi-
encing how it is to be human. This is one of the major steps in
living as Homo spiritus, as an ascended being.

Thinking

The process by which the brain exerts control over the
incarnation.

The survival instinct is often the driving force behind thinking.

Thinking is often employed to avoid experiencing change,
transformation, or growth. In the spiritual journey, transforming your thought process with consciousness to choose insight
from your soul rather than small-mind thinking is one of the
major steps to becoming an ascended being.

The brain is the thinking organ. The mind is the thought process. Insight, which comes from your soul, can feel like thinking, however, the content will clarify if you are thinking or
receiving insight.

Time

A body-based system by which control is exerted over the incarnation to try to calm the survival instinct into belief that
certainty is possible. Time, the passage of time, and the knowledge of when things should be done and how they should be
done, helps to make the body feel as though correct, safe, and/
or secure action is taking place.

When you recognize that you are living from insight from your
soul, from one "aha" to the next, you will no longer need "time"
to make you feel safe. You will live in one expanded moment.
How that one expanded moment will interact with the turning of the planet and the change of the seasons is a glorious
exploration that we anticipate will keep you entertained and

enchanted for what you would refer to, in time, as many years.

When you remove time as a controlling factor, what you perceive as time—or changes over time—becomes a tapestry you weave rather than the master with the whip telling you how to live.

Tools

Techniques used to interrupt the unconscious running of habit by using consciousness to shift out of a fear-based operating system into the consciousness-based operating system. See the table of contents for a list of tools included in this book.

Transformation

A term describing change, especially change along the ascension process.

Triggers

Triggers are stimuli that the personality experiences which bring up opportunities to explore unhealed parts of the personality self.

Triggers are handholds

Triggers are the handholds on the climbing wall of ascension. Triggers are not to be avoided or run from. Triggers are to be embraced as opportunities for progress. Now, we understand that triggers have made you spin and suffer, and it's very hard to see them as an opportunity, but's still true; triggers are hand-holds on the climbing wall of ascension.

When you contemplate climbing up one of those climbing walls—you all have seen these walls with the different places to put your hands and your feet—you see the next handhold and you think, "OK, I think I can make it to that one, I think I can reach that one," you're grateful that handhold is there because that handhold takes you up to where you want to go. This is how we would like you to look at fear, guilt, lack, anger, and other low-vibrational states; look at them as though they are a handhold on a climbing wall. Because that's what they are; they're the way you get where you want to go.

When a fear comes up, grab it with both hands and say, "Thank you for being here. I need this handhold. I want you here so I can grow. I put healing above all else. I want ascension. I'm going to the top of whatever this thing is. I'm going to make you a handhold." Seize them with the same intensity, gratitude, and upliftment that that next handhold would give you if you were climbing a mountain.

When you get to the top, all the transformed triggers are the foundation under your feet. You see? You climb and you climb and you transform and you transform and then you get to the top and what do you do? You get to look out at the view. You get to see a new perspective. All of a sudden there's a vista. But that vista is only possible because of the experiences that lifted you up that wall. All those handholds, all those triggers, all those places where you slipped a little bit, they all helped you become the new you.

Unconscious

Acting from the fear-based operating system without the intervention of consciousness; running habit.

Understanding is overrated

You've been taught that "understanding" is a worthy goal. You use your amazing brain to "wrap your mind around" something until you understand it. We say "understanding is overrated" to remind you that understanding something with your mind isn't the only way you can interact with it. There is a vast amount of insight from your soul that you can access on any subject. Reminding yourself that "understanding is overrated" will help you break the habit of limited thinking and remember to open to your soul's perspective.

If thinking could have solved it, it would have solved it long ago because you sure have thought about it enough! Open to insight and add your soul's perspective to the mix.

Unfolding
While you're in the process of transformation, it unfolds like a rose opening; you never quite know what the next step is going to be, just like you never know what the next petal of the rose is going to look like until it opens and unfolds. On your unique journey, you experience something that's never been experienced before—the unfolding truth of you which is gradually revealed as you walk the path of consciousness.

Vibration
Low vibration: A state of being that comes from living from the fear-based operating system, not looking for conscious understanding or experience of the dynamics being presented to you. Living habitually rather than opening to new experience.

It is not a judgmental term, rather it is descriptive of the fact that your body is actually vibrating at a different rate than it would if you infused consciousness into your life.

Your soul vibrates at a very high rate. It is difficult to connect to your soul's energy when living a low-vibrational life.

High-vibration: A description of actions, thoughts, ideas, and relationships which are based on consciousness and conscious choices. It is not a judgmental term, rather it is descriptive of the fact that your body is actually vibrating at a different rate than it did before you infused consciousness into your life.

Your soul vibrates at a very high rate. Raising your vibration by living consciously is a very important step in living from your soul's perspective and walking the path of ascension.

Victim/Victimhood
The mistaken perspective that things happen to you that you are at the whim of any other creature, being, person, or eventuality that you experience while on Earth. Running the fear-based operating system. It is a perspective that is very easy to

assume because you incarnate with amnesia, making it difficult for you to remember your infinite nature, or the fact that you planned to be here and have the experiences you are having.

When events trigger you or you have experiences that you deem negative, your reaction is, "Why did this happen to me?" which is a victim's perspective. With a conscious journey and a conscious life, you're able to start seeing the world as the creator that you are, and start asking, "Why is this happening *for* me?" and realizing that "Everything teaches me something."

Woman by the campfire

We use this phrase as a quick way to describe the following energetic: "If my man doesn't come home to me, I die." This energetic is part of your DNA, it's in your cells, it's part of your culture, but primarily it comes from alternate expressions where this was much more of a reality: If your man took the meat from his hunt to *her* fire instead of yours, you and your kids could literally starve to death.

It's also a shortcut way of saying, "I am hard-wired to believe something that I haven't consciously explored."

As you shift out of Homo sapiens into Homo spiritus one of the major differences between the two states is understanding the influence you have, using consciousness, over the biological reactions as presented by the body doing its normal job. Just as the body keeps breathing and the heart keeps beating and the blood keeps moving and all that stuff keeps happening, habits keep getting thrown up in front of you. Not just the habit of fear, but the idea of lack, the idea of safety, the idea of security, abundance all these issues that you've habituated that are part of your biology.

Biological reactions to stimulus that previously haven't been run through consciousness are now coming under your influence. As you move out of the Homo sapiens mindset into the Homo spiritus experience it becomes your responsibility to consciously monitor the biological reactions to stimulus. You're responsible for the emanations you create as you react.

This includes pain, emotional stimulus, memory stimulus, and fear stimulus. All of these things that you previously felt were hardwired in you can become the purview of your conscious exploration.

Your internal world creates your external journey

Your internal world is the creation point for the external expression of your life. Not the other way around. Your internal process is projected on the movie screen of your external life where it all plays out. This allows you to learn and grow from the experience of observing your internal life projected (externalized).

Your internal world is a series of choices that you've made, even if the choice was to default to a habitual pattern, to default to a culturally driven pattern, to default to the childhood pattern. Those are still choices.

Remember, it can't happen in your external world unless it's true in your internal world. When experiences arise, ask, "What are you showing me about me? What are you telling me about me?" Let the experiences inform you rather than staying with the surface reaction of, "They're just triggering me or challenging me or frustrating me or driving me bananas." Ask instead, "What are you showing me about me?"

You can't dictate how people react to you, necessarily, but you can certainly influence the outcome by loving yourself well and sending that into the world instead of doubt and anguish and anxiety and feeling stepped on and being a victim and all that. If you walk into a room knowing you love yourself and emanating your truth, you're going to have a different experience than if you walk into a room feeling like a victim and a doormat. You will be known and reacted to by the way you love yourself.

Your awareness of your internal world becomes so rich and

well-developed, so well-known and mapped by you, that your emanation of the truth of your internal world starts to resemble a fountain that bubbles up and spills over without stopping. It's not something you have to think about or work yourself through or get going. It bubbles up in you and it spills over, just like a fountain does, the fullness of your internal world emanating out into the world. This doesn't involve you acting in the world as much as it involves you experiencing the world from your truth. The truth of you being real.

What is channeling?

Channeling is a process where I set my personality aside to allow Eloheim and The Council to use my physical form to convey their teachings.

PLEASE NOTE: This is not possession. It only occurs when I give explicit permission. I can stop it at ANY time.

When I am channeling I feel as though I am standing or sitting behind and to the left of my actual body. I am aware of what is being said as the session unfolds, although I don't always remember everything that is discussed.

Eloheim and The Council specialize in reading the energy of a question, situation, or person. They often experience visual representations of the energy they sense. When this occurs, I see it as a "movie" in my head not unlike what happens when I am dreaming.

I have created a YouTube video with more details about the process. You can watch it by searching YouTube for: "Introduction Eloheim and The Council."

Who are Eloheim and The Council?

On February 11, 1997, I had a reading by a very skilled psychic and channel. During that reading he said that I would become a channel myself. Although I valued much of what he shared, my reaction to that statement was, YEAH, RIGHT!

I was quite familiar with channeling. I found it incredibly valuable. I just didn't see myself doing it!

That all changed when I came to Sonoma. I was invited to a friend's home to do a Lakshmi puja. The chanting left me in a very altered state. When we finished, we sat in a circle on the floor. I told one of the participants I had a message for her and then shared information she found very helpful. At the end of the sharing I said, "We are the Eloheim and we are pleased to have been with you today."

Now, even though I knew what had happened, I was overwhelmed by it and started to cry. It didn't feel bad or wrong, just very intense. It made me feel very conspicuous. I immediately told myself, "That's never going to happen again."

It was some time before it did. Over time, I got more comfortable with the idea of being a channel but I had no idea how to do it! I tried to work with Eloheim on my own once or twice. I even recorded a very useful message about habitual response on November 26, 2000, yet it just wasn't coming together. Almost two years passed without much forward movement.

Finally, a friend and I figured it out. What was needed was a second person to ask the questions and help me with the logistics of the whole thing.

In the very beginning while channeling, I had to raise my right hand in order to receive the energies (boy, am I glad that I don't have to do that any longer). I would get very thirsty, but I wasn't able to hold a glass (I still have a bunch of straws in a drawer from those days). I had a TON of insecurity about "Am I making this up?" and "Is this real?" and "Am I doing it right?" I needed a lot of reassurance just to stick with it. I would get very sleepy afterward and sometimes needed help just getting around. I had to eat a lot of protein to keep my energy level up.

Details, details, details. All of which felt completely unmanageable to me alone, but became possible once I had help.

After about one month, Eloheim told us that this wasn't just for the two of us and to get a group together. That was September 2002, when we began our weekly Eloheim sessions. We still hold meetings every Wednesday night and one Sunday per month. You can join us live or tune into our webcasts. For more information, please visit: eloheim.com/web-casts.

I had never heard the term Eloheim until they introduced themselves that way. Someone then told me it was one of the names of God. I looked it up on the Internet and found that to be true. It is important to note that although it is common to see the spelling Elohim, I was guided to use the spelling Eloheim.

Eloheim has made it clear that just as not everyone named John is the same, to not assume that all entities using the name Eloheim or Elohim are the same. The material they present with me is internally consistent and can be taken as a whole.

Eloheim is a group entity that presents with one voice. That one voice feels like a male energy. We refer to the Eloheim as "he" or "they."

They refer to themselves as "we."

Starting on June 10, 2009, I began channeling the rest of The Council. Here are the dates of their first appearances:

The Visionaries - 06/10/2009

The Guardians - 12/02/2009

The Girls - 01/06/2010

The Matriarch - 02/03/2010

The Warrior - 03/17/2010

Fred - 06/30/2010

For more information about Eloheim and The Council, please visit: eloheim.com/who-is-eloheim

What is it like to channel Eloheim and The Council?

Eloheim:

I have been channeling Eloheim since 2002. They are very easy to channel. I've channeled them while riding in a car, in a room full of playing puppies, in a haunted winery, on the radio, during an earthquake (briefly), and in all sorts of other places. They are the only Council member who I channel with eyes open. Perhaps someday other Council members will be ready for eyes open, but at this time they are all still getting used to interacting with the body and the additional stimulus of eyes open would be too much—for me and for them.

Visionaries (first channeled on 06/10/2009):

The Visionaries were the first to join Eloheim on the Council. After seven years of working with Eloheim, it was strange to imagine channeling another group. Little did I know it was just the beginning! Here are some of my comments from the first time I channeled the Visionaries:

They sat right on the edge of the chair. They are even louder than Eloheim. They use language differently and have a different cadence to their speech. I found my jaw moving in strange ways to accommodate this.

Nowadays, the Visionaries continue to be intense, but I am much more comfortable with their energy. I frequently wonder how they can say so many words in such a short period of time. They are the most rigid of the Council members and often seem to have their entire talk planned out ahead of time. To watch video from their first appearance, please visit this page on my website: http://eloheim.com/1064/eloheim-the-visionaries/.

Guardians (first channeled on 12-02-2009):

When the Guardians first came in, they had a very hard time talking. However, they sure could MOVE energy. They continue to focus on working energetically with us although they can talk easily now. A lot of what I experience when channeling the Guardians is sensing the energy they are picking up in the room. There are sometimes visuals associated with the energy, but it is more often a sense of knowing rather than seeing.

Watch their first video on this page: http://eloheim.com/1792/eloheim-3rd-and-4th-chakras-emotions-guardians-and-visionaries/.

The Girls (first channeled on 01-06-2010):

I just found this quote from my first blog posting about the Girls, "The Girls immediately sat back in the chair, got comfortable, crossed my legs, and settled in for a chat." That pretty much sums it up. They come in and chat with us. They are very comfortable with the body and very easy to channel. They have a light energy which is quite fun for me to experience. Watch their first video on this page: http://eloheim.com/2000/eloheim-10610/.

The Matriarch (first channeled on 02-03-2010:

I don't really remember much from the first time I channeled the Matriarch. Mostly I remember being sort of overwhelmed by the idea that we were *still* adding new groups to the channeling. I wasn't all that keen about the idea. However, the Matriarch is amazing to channel. Sometimes my heart opens so much that it feels like the entire room is inside of me. I feel loved and embraced by her. I am so happy she closes out our meetings. It is a wonderful energy to conclude the meeting with. You can watch her first appearance here: http://eloheim. com/2197/eloheim-audio-from-2-3-10-meeting/.

The Warrior (first channeled on 03-17-2010):

The Warrior was really hard to channel the first time. It took me six days to feel like myself again. I couldn't watch the video or listen to the audio without their energy coming back into my body and I just couldn't manage it. When they first came in, it felt like my entire body grew by two inches and then snapped back to its normal size. I was sore from head to toe the next morning. It was a strange time. Now, I have a total crush on the Warrior. I don't have a "favorite"— really I don't—but it's tempting! I get a bonus when I channel the Warrior. It is as though I am watching a movie when they tell their stories. My eyes are closed, but I see a complete, full-color movie in my head. I don't get anything like that from any of the other Council members. It's really cool. Here is video from the Warrior's second appearance: http://eloheim.com/2529/ eloheim-this-is-a-choice-the-warrior-and-more-3-24-10/.

Fred (first channeled on 06-30-2010):

Fred is a total trip. I still don't think I "get" him. He carries a Galactic energy which is really huge, but very non-physical. Weird…it's weird and hard to explain. He took quite a while to figure out how to interact with the body. He's getting much better now. Fred is the opposite of the Visionaries. The Visionaries come in with a plan, Fred seems to not have a clue what he wants to talk about until the second he starts talking! People just love Fred and have powerful reactions to him. He gets more fan mail than any of the others! I have a suspicion that Fred will end up rocking my world. However, he mostly just confuses me at this point. You can watch his first video here: http://eloheim.com/3275/ eloheim-and-the-full-council-fred-joins-us-6-30-10/.

Overall, channeling the Council is a very enjoyable experience. There have been plenty of times when I was practically non-functional the day after a meeting, but that seems to have passed. I learned that if I eat something really salty—popcorn works well—after a meeting, I usually feel fine the next day.

About the author

Veronica Torres: is based in Sonoma, CA. She has channeled Eloheim since 2002, both in public and private sessions. Her public channeling sessions are offered five times each month. These sessions are broadcast live on the Internet and archived for on-demand viewing.

Veronica's career history is interesting and varied, with work including: talk radio host, Rock and Roll memorabilia store owner, Network Director of a Holistic Practitioner's Group, Producer of Well Being Expos, and jewelry designer!

Photo credit: nancikerby.com

Contact

Website: eloheim.com

Facebook: facebook.com/eloheim

Twitter: twitter.com/channelers

YouTube: youtube.com/eloheimchannel

Join our live channeling sessions in person or online:

eloheim.com/web-casts

Visit our meeting archives for video and audio recordings of past gatherings:

eloheim.com/eloheim-recordings

Join our mailing list:

tinyurl.com/eloheimlist

Private session with Eloheim:

eloheim.com/meeting-schedule-private-sessions/

Preview of other books

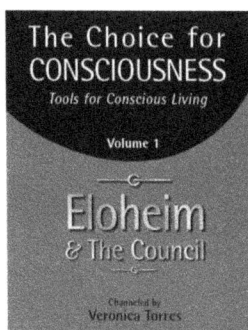

The Choice for Consciousness: Tools for Conscious Living, Vol. 1

Why would you want to make the choice for consciousness? What are tools for conscious living?

Two very important questions.

Here are four more: Are you living in peace? Are you living in joy? Are you living in serenity? Are you living in bliss?

And, the most important question: Are you ready to take bold steps in that direction?

Moving out of a fear-based operating system into a conscious-ness-based operating system allows you to experience being human in a brand-new way. A way that isn't driven by habit, repetitive thinking, reliving the past, speculating about the future, or being paralyzed by the fear of change.

Consciousness is a way of living that focuses on an authentic experience of the moment, awareness of your truth, and the full comprehension that by choosing your reaction to every one of your experiences, you are creating your reality.

This book contains simple but powerful tools that will help you make the shift from the fear-based operating system (survival) to the consciousness-based operating system (fascination).

These tools can be used throughout your spiritual journey. They require no props, no rituals, no religious beliefs, and can be easily incorporated into your day-to-day activities. In addition, they build on one another and can be used in powerful combinations that will rapidly transform your experience.

The first section introduces 22 tools. The second section defines and clarifies nearly 126 terms and concepts. You can read this volume in any order. It is not a narrative, but a reference book you will likely turn to time and time again.

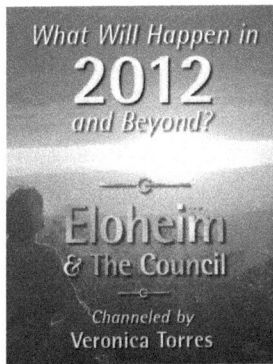

What Will Happen in 2012 and Beyond?

The question, "What will happen in 2012?" is being asked by a great many people. The Mayan calendar ends on December 21, 2012 which has given rise to a considerable amount of speculation about what might happen, including predictions that the world will either end or that we will experience some sort of catastrophic event.

With so much fear and uncertainty surrounding "What will happen in 2012?", we decided to ask Eloheim for their perspective.

In this 57 page book, Eloheim explains how we can use the energies of "2012" for our spiritual growth and answers the following questions:

What did the Mayans know about 2012 and why does their calendar end in December of 2012?; Why did the Hopi point to 2012 and say any chance at salvation is now useless as we have gone too far?; Why is there so much fear about 2012?

Isn't it pretty likely there will be one or more disasters in the future?; Is it true that the Earth's population will be reduced to 500 million?; Will Jesus reappear in 2012?; Will aliens rescue the surviving population like a modern Noah's ark?; Are aliens already here?; Is the Earth going to be like a cell dividing in two—people who ascend going with the new Earth and the others staying behind thinking the rest are dead or gone?

Will there be a nuclear war or will the Earth be hit by an asteroid causing an ice age?; Are pole shifts occurring that may cause chaos in 2012? How about solar flares and problems related to that causing Earth disturbances?; Is it true that a civilization will emerge from middle Earth in 2012?; Is overpopulation going to cause a disaster in 2012?

We learn by crisis. Does it appear that we're getting it or do we need bigger and bigger crises to move ahead?; Regarding 2012, are there any safe areas?; If it's true that everyone is going to ascend anyway, what's the point in all the work that we're doing?; How can I deal with my fear and anxiety regarding 2012? Is there anything I should do to prepare for it?; What will happen after 2012?

The book also contains four of Eloheim's tools for spiritual growth: Point fingers; What's in your lap?; What is true now?; and You to you. Additionally, there are 62 definitions of terms and concepts including: ascension, creating your reality, consciousness-based operating system, energetics, ensoulment, free will, Homo spiritus, shadow, soul's perspective, transformation, vibration, and your internal world creates your external experience.

The book closes with information about Eloheim and The Council and a description of the channeling process.

Use the energy of 2012 to facilitate your personal growth!

—Eloheim

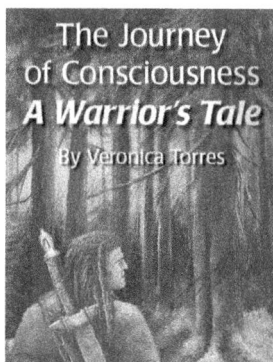

The Journey of Consciousness, A Warrior's Tale

"This entire story is to help you know who you are."

This "fairy tale for grown-ups" follows the Warrior's journey as he encounters castles and kings, battles and beasties, while learning to live from an open heart. The Warrior explains how to live the truth of you, how to have a healthy relationship to authority figures, and how to be vulnerable and strong at the same time.

"Anything that is presenting itself to you is presenting itself to you for growth."

Filled with humor, sage advice, penetrating insight, and above all, profound support for your process, the Warrior's tale clarifies your spiritual path.

"Now, it's really fun to see the King when you stink. Why? Because what you want the king to know is that you are not just a little pawn in his game to be manipulated to his benefit. When you go to see the king, whomever the king is in your world, take who you are with you, and if that means you drop mud on this perfect floor, well, there you are."

***

The Warrior is one of the seven Council members channeled

by Veronica Torres. The Council's teachings focus on spiritual growth and the movement from the fear-based to the consciousness-based operating system. They specialize in offering specific tools which will facilitate your spiritual growth.

In addition to the Warrior's story, The Journey of Consciousness includes the following tools: Clarity vs. certainty; Feet under shoulders; How ridiculous does it have to get?; I don't know anything; Lay it down and walk away; Mad scientist; Neutral observation; "No" is a complete sentence; Point fingers; Preferences/judgments; Script holding/Script-holders; Strongest chakra; Vulnerability vs. weakness; What's in your lap?; What is true now?; Where am I lying to myself? "Wow!", not "why?", and You to you (comparing). It also includes 126 definitions of terms and concepts used in The Council's teachings.

***

"When you're facing your triggers, if you start to waiver in your courage, just imagine that we stand behind you. We stand there to show you that you don't have to fear that you are not enough. You can be afraid of the triggers, but don't be afraid that you're not enough. We will stand beside you in consciousness and courage any time you wish."

—*The Warrior*

***

Eloheim and The Council books are available online through major book retailers and by visiting eloheim.com/dlg/cart/index.php.